Prisoners of Nazis

ALSO BY HARRY SPILLER

*Scars of Vietnam: Personal Accounts
by Veterans and Their Families*
(McFarland, 1994)

*Death Angel: A Vietnam Memoir
of a Bearer of Death Messages to Families*
(McFarland, 1992)

To former prisoners of war and their families

Prisoners of Nazis

Accounts by American POWs in World War II

Edited by HARRY SPILLER

McFarland & Company, Inc., Publishers
Jefferson, North Carolina, and London

Acknowledgments: For their assistance I wish to thank Robin Greenlee, Michael Dann, Gayle Pesavento, Steven Arthur, and the former prisoners of war and their families for inviting me into their homes and telling of their experiences. Between the Parts of this book are excerpts "From a Kriegie's diary"; these are from the diary of Carl W. Remy and are used with his permission.

British Library Cataloguing-in-Publication data are available

Library of Congress Cataloguing-in-Publication Data

Prisoners of Nazis : accounts by American POWs in World War II / edited by Harry Spiller.
    p.   cm.
    Includes index.
    ISBN 0-7864-0348-9 (sewn softcover : 50# alkaline paper)
    1. World War, 1939–1945—Prisoners and prisons, German.
  2. Prisoners of war—United States.   3. Prisoners of war—Germany.
  4. World War, 1939–1945—Personal narratives, American.
  I. Spiller, Harry, 1945–   .
  D805.G3P6985   1998
  940.54'7243'092273—dc21   97-34360
                                                   CIP

Manufactured in the United States of America

McFarland & Company, Inc., Publishers
  Box 611, Jefferson, North Carolina 28640

Contents

v

Introduction

The Nazis called them *Kriegsgefangen*—a term that the prisoners of war shortened to "Kriegie." The lighthearted sound of the nickname belied the reality of daily life for more than seven million POWs—American, British, French, Polish, and Russian—held by the Nazis between 1939 and 1945.

World War II's first American prisoner of war in Europe was navy lieutenant John Dunn, who was captured on April 14, 1942. On September 25, 1942, the first American army land troops were reported as prisoners of war by the Nazis to the Central Agency for Prisoners of War, which had been created by the Geneva Convention. From that point until the end of the war, Hitler's Third Reich captured 76,474 Americans in the European Theater, 20,171 in the Mediterranean Theater, and 1,667 in the North African Theater: a total of 98,312 American prisoners of war.

The Nazis had three principal types of camps: the *Offizier Lager* (officer's camp), the *Stalag-Stamm Lager* (main camp), and the *Durchgangs Lager* (entrance camp). There were seventy-five of these camps scattered throughout Germany and East Prussia, with a few located in Poland, Czechoslovakia, and Austria. In addition, a number of American prisoners of war were in *Kommandos* (work camps) and hospitals.

Most camps had barracks constructed with ten rooms leading from a central hallway, which ran lengthwise through the building. The rooms were supplied with triple-decker bunk beds filled with paper sacks filled with straw or wood shavings as mattresses. Two washrooms and a pit latrine were located near the rear of the barracks. As the war progressed, many men had to sleep on the floor in the rooms, and it became necessary to use the washrooms to house prisoners. For furnishings, there were a small stove, a table, and a few stools.

How the Germans treated prisoners of war is difficult to summarize in short order. If you compare the treatment of American prisoners by the Japanese to their treatment by the Germans the latter would be considered good. If you compared American treatment of German prisoners to German treatment of Americans, the treatment would be considered bad. Regardless of conditions, no one enjoyed being a prisoner of war.

Though the Nazis generally adhered to the Geneva Convention, the treatment of an American prisoner of war by the Third Reich depended largely on where and when a prisoner was captured and what German units

Map showing locations of the camps where this book's 19 interview subjects were imprisoned.

were in charge of the camp (regular German army or SS troops). For example, Stalag Luft III proved to be a well-organized camp of captured air force officers who were given some of the best treatment among the prison camps. Stalag IIB was a camp of captured enlisted ground forces who were given average treatment. Stalag IXB, established for enlisted men captured during the Von Rundstedt offensive of December 1944, was chaotic, with poor treatment of the prisoners.

As the war progressed, the deterioration of the German transportation system resulted in improper grouping of prisoners according to nationalities and the failure to remove prisoners from air raid danger zones. Food, clothing, and medical supplies for the Germans were severely rationed, causing shortages of these supplies for prisoners of war. However, even given these unavoidable conditions, there is no doubt that the Nazis made numerous, willful violations of the Geneva Convention, ranging from technical infractions to full-scale atrocities.

The treatment of prisoners was also determined by the attitudes of the German soldiers. There was a sharp division between the attitude of the German regular army and that of Hitler's SS troops. The regular army willfully violated many rules. They held back Red Cross packages and clothing, claiming that there was a shortage of food and water as a result of bombing raids. They threatened prisoners with beatings and death. They ignored the medical needs of prisoners. Assuredly, there were atrocities by the regular army; prisoners were beaten, killed, terrorized by police dogs, and placed in solitary confinement. On the whole, however, atrocities by the regular army were more the exception than the rule.

The SS troops were a different story. Their attitude toward POWs and toward human life itself was so grossly twisted that even many of the German regular army troops feared them. American prisoners were frequently beaten, tortured, and murdered by SS troops. Some were beaten and murdered upon capture, others while in prison camps, and some after attempted escapes. Records from the Nürnberg trials show that among the victims of some death camps—Flossenbürg and Mauthausen—were American prisoners put to death by SS troops. Fifteen members of an American mission in Slovakia were executed. In addition, over six hundred American prisoners of war were found in the Gestapo concentration camps of Buchenwald and Dachau at the end of the war.

An author could go on and on about the suffering of POWs in Nazi prison camps, but to get a true picture of what life was like as a prisoner of war—being beaten and threatened with death; aching with hunger; watching helplessly as your friends die from tuberculosis, ulcers, gastritis, nephritis, dysentery, and gastrointestinal problems; facing the unknown each day—to understand this reality one needs to hear from the prisoners themselves.

This book contains nineteen personal accounts of men who fought the Nazis, were captured, and carried out their grim existence as POWs. I contacted these soldiers by mail from a list obtained from the national headquarters of American Ex–Prisoners of War located in Arlington, Texas. I included all of the soldiers who agreed to allow me to publish their stories. The information about their experiences came from taped interviews, written questionnaires, official military documents, or documents the interviewees gave me.

Many of the photos in this book were taken by members of the U.S. Army Signal Corps. All of these are post–liberation photos. It is possible that some of the soldiers' personal photos of the camps were taken before the prisoners were liberated, but it seems unlikely given the difficulty of retaining personal possessions in the camps.

The storytellers in this book range from American soldiers captured during the D-Day invasion to B-17 crew members shot down over Germany during bombing raids. They lived in fourteen different stalags, kommandos, and hospitals scattered throughout Europe. Although treatment for some was better than for others, they all suffered from malnutrition (the approximate total weight loss for the group was 608 pounds). Some were liberated by the Russians and fought beside them before returning to American forces, while others returned immediately to Western lines. Some were liberated by the British, others by the Americans; two escaped and made their way back to American lines. These stories are real, they are compelling, and they give a true picture of POW life under Hitler's Third Reich.

Part I

THE INVASION OF ITALY

PLEASE, DEAR GOD

Please, Dear God, please let me soar
O'er green and yellow fields once more
Where there will be no clouds of black,
Bringing forth the cry of Flak!
Where the sight of specks out in the blue
Will not mean—"Watch it! Fighters at Two!"
Where no screaming demons out of the sun,
Make every man jump with flaming gun.
Endeavors to slay another life
To the dogmas which started worldwide strife.
I do not think it much of a boon,
And please, Dear God, make it soon.

—From a Kriegie's diary

Sergeant William C. Bradley

U.S. Army
88th Division, Company F, 351st Infantry
Captured When His Outpost Was Overrun in Italy
Prisoner of War
July 27, 1944–May 1, 1945
Stalag IIIA and Stalag IIIB

In March 1943, the war was going full blast. Bill was raising hell with his parents to let him join the army, because he already had two brothers in the war. Bill was a basketball player in his senior year of high school. His team was expected to win the state championship that year, but those hopes were diminished when they lost the regional tournament. The next day Bill quit school and joined the service.

Over the next couple of days, he went through a physical and was issued uniforms. Then a trainload of new recruits headed for Fort Jackson, South Carolina. They were forming a new unit—the 106th Division. Over the next several weeks, Bill trained, was promoted to corporal, was put in charge of a twelve-man squad, and won several boxing matches in Golden Gloves.

A few weeks into training, his unit was sent to Tennessee for maneuvers. His squad was dropped off in the Tennessee hills and told to find their way back to the unit. They were to use their compass. Bill and his squad were goofing off when Bill realized he had lost his billfold. He had to have it back because it had several pictures of girls that he felt he couldn't do without. The whole squad backtracked looking for the billfold, but they didn't find it. It was the next morning when they found the road leading back to their unit and hitched a ride from a chow truck. They hid behind the pots and pans until they got to their unit; their lieutenant was mad. Bill claimed they got lost and showed the lieutenant a broken compass. Bill had broken it against a rock to use it as an excuse for being late. That night Bill was in a foxhole, thinking he had fooled the lieutenant. It was raining hard. The lieutenant came by about midnight and ordered Bill and his squad to report to the medic's tent. The whole squad was given injections for overseas, and the next day they were on a train for the east coast.

7

They say we all have a double someplace. We were on the train headed for Baltimore, Maryland. A kid was sitting across from me and I looked at him, then he would look at me. It was like looking in a mirror. We just set there looking at each other. Finally, I broke the ice and asked him where he was from. He had a southern drawl. His name was Charles Burrow from Greensboro, North Carolina. He must have gotten killed, because I wrote to him several times after the war and never got a letter from him. I just took it for granted that his folks—if they got the letters—just didn't bother to answer because he was dead. But I never saw him after we left the train.

After four days we arrived at Camp Meade and stayed overnight. The next day we moved to New York City and boarded the aircraft carrier USS *Carr*. It was real nice going over. We had the run of the ship—movies every night. We zigzagged all the way over because we had a German U-boat following us. There were destroyers with us, and the ship tracked the U-boat on radar. But it never did attack.

Several days later we arrived at Casablanca. Meanwhile, my brother Buzz was in Italy. He had already went through the African campaign. The *Stars and Stripes* came out with several stories that there was going to be a big boxing match in Algiers. I read the story, and it said that Bradley was going to

Sergeant William C. Bradley. (Courtesy of William C. Bradley.)

be pulled back from Italy to fight in this tournament. I went to my lieutenant and got on my knees and begged him to let me go to Algiers for a couple of days to watch my brother fight. We were only about a hundred and fifty miles from it. He wouldn't let me. He said that we were on strict orders to be here. He expected us to be called at any time to back up the 35th Division at Anzio. Buzz made it to the championship rounds. He lost to a Frenchman by the judges' split decision.

Buzz went back to the front lines at Anzio. We just knew that's where we would end up because that's where the big push was going on. We were going to movies every night. Had a bunch of trouble with some lieutenants one night. I had been drinking 3.2 beer—the first alcohol I had ever drank— and myself and a bunch of drunk sergeants set right in the middle of some officers at the movies. We were carrying on, and this colonel came down and told this lieutenant to help us back to our tents. We said, "That's okay, we can make it," and left. We didn't have any rank insignias on, and they never did know we were enlisted men.

We used to listen to Berlin Sally almost every night. She played music for us, and we liked to listen to it. She kept us up on the war, and of course she always let us know that we were losing. Then early one morning we loaded aboard British ships. It was about one in the morning. We knew that we would dock where the fighting had finished and move inland from there. We sailed out into the middle of the Mediterranean, sailed around for a couple of hours, and landed right back where we had taken off. We thought, "What in the hell is going on?" They unloaded us and told us to go back to our tents, but not to unpack. We went back to our tents, and the next morning Berlin Sally was on the radio: "Well, boys we had a party for you last night, and you didn't show up. We sure missed you. Did you have a nice ride?"

Finally, we did ship out and landed in Naples. We were there about two weeks. I got to box one more time. Me and a English lieutenant had a match. I beat him.

The next day we moved out. They walked us through the mountains and through these tunnels that go all the way out into the valleys. There we got our first taste of seeing dead people. Just as we came out of this big tunnel, there were bodies every place. Burned, bloody men, women, and children. They hadn't had a chance to clean them up. They were turning black, and we got the first smell of death. We finally realized we could get killed.

We walked all night and finally got close to the front lines. We got our first taste of gunfire when a German plane spotted us and started firing at us. We got off the road and hid in the trees. Then we got hit by 88 millimeters. After the shooting stopped, we gathered up on the road, and they broke us up into companies. I was assigned to Company F. I met the 1st sergeant, and he had us to dig foxholes.

The war at that time was being fought by small groups. Thirteen- or fourteen-man squads were going out on patrol, setting up ambushes, and then returning to the lines. I was on a patrol everyday for three months. I had a lot of them at night also. I had rather go on an ambush patrol than anything because we could lay down and rest and hope we didn't see anything.

At this time, my brother Buzz and I were writing letters to each other. I was getting his, but he wasn't getting mine. I found out that his unit, the 34th, was right beside ours, the 88th. We were in the middle of the 34th and the 45th. I asked my lieutenant if I could get a couple of days off to go find my brother. I told him that he was in the 34th Artillery Division; they were behind us, I said, so he had to be behind the lines. I didn't know it, but Buzz wasn't behind the lines. He was a front observer and was out in a jeep ahead of the company spotting targets. Buzz had gotten one of my letters and asked his colonel to find me and bring me up to him. The day that the colonel talked to my commanding officer was the day I was captured. My lieutenant told the colonel that I was missing in action. At the same time, Buzz had run over a land mine and been seriously wounded. When the colonel returned, he got word to Buzz that I was on a mission and that they couldn't turn me loose. It wasn't until after the war that we learned what had actually took place.

I did find out that Buzz had been wounded, though. We were out on patrols all the time, and I actually began to feel safer on the patrols than I did with the company because the Germans were always throwing artillery at us. The Germans and the Americans were about a mile apart and in between was no-man's-land. The lieutenant called me up for a midnight; we were going out to set up an ambush. I got the boys lined up for the patrol. Anytime we were going out on an ambush, I would take the B.A.R. from this little Mexican and give him my M-1; I would put it in the middle, with the patrol on each side of me with strict orders not to fire until the B.A.R. opened up. We were laying out there that night, and we could hear someone coming through the hedgerows—from the German direction. It was pitch black. We were in some bushes behind a little hill, and they kept coming. Then we could hear them talking. We couldn't understand what they were saying, but they were talking in English. Then when they got almost to us, I was ready to jump up and open up with the B.A.R. About that time one of them fell over a wire and let out with "Son of a Bitch!" That's what saved them because I jumped up and they yelled for us to hold our fire. It was a squad from the 34th Division. They had gotten lost. Buzz was from the 34th, and I asked them if they had ever heard of him. They said they had and that they had got to see him box a couple of times. When they found out that he was my brother, they told me that he had been wounded, but they didn't tell me he was wounded badly. I just took it that he would be all right.

The farmers in the area built beautiful country homes out of stone. We were sent out one day to one of these homes. It was a big, two-story home with a full basement. Big yard around it. The people that owned it had fled to the mountains until the war bypassed them. But our orders were to set up an observation post. We were to report back everything we saw. We were about a half mile from the Germans, and we could see them moving around. That night I guess the Germans saw us because we laid out around that house till almost daylight. Then I passed the word that we were going back into the house. I told the patrol that I would go in first and that if everything was all right I would wave them in. There was a door that I went through into the basement, and there was nothing in there. I waved at the guys, and they came out of their positions one at a time and nothing happened. All thirteen of us got in that house, and all hell broke loose from both sides. The Americans and the Germans were both firing artillery at us. The 88-millimeter rounds were just bouncing off of the stone walls of the house. So we went into the basement to wait out the bombardment from both sides. While we were down there, I found a vat of wine and we started drinking it. Three hours later the bombing stopped, and needless to say we were feeling pretty good. I told the guys that we had better get out of there and back to the company. We had to let them know that we couldn't stay there, not with both sides bombing us. We started out on the opposite side of the house, on the side of the 34th Division. We were on this hillside overlooking another little valley, and we saw a big German tank sitting beside one little building; two Germans were sitting out on the ground, just eating and drinking, and we seen two others shining the tank. And out in front of them I could see seven or eight Americans crawling on the ground in the leaves, sneaking up on them. I said, "Let's just stay here and watch this." We had a ring-side seat. So we laid down about three hundred yards from them and watched. Pretty soon the Americans got up on them. They threw a hand grenade in the tank and blew it up. The Germans come running up this path right at us. So we just laid there, and when they were close I jumped up and told them to put their hands up. They didn't understand English, but they dropped their rifles and put their hands up. I told the guys that we would take these guys back to the company. We did, and when we got back the lieutenant said that we couldn't keep them with us because they didn't speak English. He told me to have someone take them back to the rear so they could be interrogated by an interpreter. This little Mexican that we had jumped up and said, "I'll take them." The lieutenant said, "All right, let him take them." He wasn't gone fifteen minutes when we heard that B.A.R. fire a couple of bursts. He took them over the hill and shot them. Everybody knew what he had done, but he claimed that they had been taken off his hands. There was nothing else said about it, but he didn't escort any more prisoners.

I told the lieutenant that I spotted a house that was right down on the river about forty yards from German lines. I told him that there was about a four-foot ditch with a sandy bottom between us and the house and that on the opposite side between the house and the Germans there was a levee built right up to the windows. I told him that it would be a great place for an outpost. He told me to set it up there.

About seven that night we headed out. We came up the ditch toward the house, and just before we got there we could see a light flickering. So we stopped and waited until about five in the morning. We still didn't know who was there, but I told my guys we were going to bypass and go on. So we did, and we were able to get in the house without being spotted. The next morning we found out that the flickering was coming from an old Italian and his wife who had been camping in the area. They walked right by the house and over to the German side. A couple of days later the old man spotted our telephone lines and told the Germans we were in the house. We had been watching them and reporting back everything we had seen. As a matter of fact the lieutenant had sent an artist out to draw a sketch of the river and the area where the Germans were located. They checked the ditch bottom to see if it would hold a tank.

After a couple of days, we were running low on C rations and I sent one of my men back to the company to get resupplied. I told him that I would walk back a little ways, because about halfway back to the company area there was an orchard. It had some fruit, and I was going to pick some for the squad. I didn't even take my cartridge belt with me—just my rifle and helmet. I walked back with him to the orchard and told him what to tell the lieutenant, and he went on his way. That's the last time I saw him. I found out later that after we had been captured he was assigned as the new squad leader and was killed.

I started back to the house, and there was a shed a little ways from the house. It was stored full of furniture. I had a kid there as a guard, and when I came by he was leaning back against the building in a chair. He was asleep. When I came by him, I didn't bother to wake him up. About fifteen yards to the right of the shed was a haystack, and I had two men there. The Mexican was watching the Germans and reporting back to the company by phone. I was carrying a helmet full of apples. I had my rifle slung over my shoulder, and I wasn't paying attention to anything as I walked toward the house. I got about even with the shed, and all hell broke loose. There was four Germans standing by that haystack, and they opened up with burp guns. I just froze. I didn't even see 'em till the first shots. I threw them apples up and run around the shed. They never touched me, but I could feel the air of the bullets. God was with me because they were only ten yards from me when they opened up and I was right in the open.

After I got around the shed, I could peek out and see that there was a squad of Germans behind the other four. They all hit the ground. They weren't sure when they approached if we were there, but they had followed the phone line up to where they saw us. They had cut the line. I yelled at one of the men in the house and told them to get on the phone to call the company and let them know that we were being hit. He yelled back and said that he had been trying.

One of the boys in the house opened up with the B.A.R. on the Germans, and they scattered. They were on the opposite side of the shed, so I decided to go through the shed to the corner to get a few shots. When I got there, they really opened up on me. I went back the other way and got to the other corner of the shed. I decided that I was going to make a dash for the house. I told the B.A.R. to cover me. I looked around the corner, and not ten feet from me was a German captain and a regular soldier setting up a machine gun. I didn't have any grenades with me or I could have got them; but it was a good thing I didn't, because the German captain kept me from getting killed. I took off for the house, and I heard someone right on my heels. I turned and looked over my shoulder, and it was this German captain chasing me and firing his pistol. When he shot, I would zig, then zag. His gunner was firing a trail on both sides of us all the way to the house. He couldn't shoot me because he was afraid that he would hit the captain. When I got to the door, I turned and fired a couple shots at him from the hip. He fired and hit me in the shoulder before he turned and started running. If I had been aiming I would have hit him, but I was excited and firing from the hip. I made it into the house, and he made it back to the machine gun.

I looked around, and other than the guy on B.A.R. nobody was around. I went down into the basement, and eleven of the guys were asleep. I kicked them and told them to get up. I just knew the Germans were going to blow the place.

We got up to the windows and were firing at the Germans. While this was going on, we would hear someone run up this cobblestone walk in front of the house. He would stop, and then pretty soon he would run back. What was happening was that this German captain was running up the sidewalk and throwing a grenade in the basement. I don't know why he didn't throw one up on the floor where we were, but I told one of the guys that I would fix him. I had thirteen grenades piled under this window. I waited until I heard him run up and stop, and then I would drop a grenade out the window. Nothing would happen. I did that thirteen times, and not once did the grenade go off. The Germans had such a concentration of fire on the house that I knew we were all going to be killed if we didn't surrender. We signaled to them that we wanted to surrender and were introduced to come out of the house one at a time. When I came out the door, I figured out what had happened to the thirteen grenades. There was a cistern right below the window where I was dropping the grenades. I had dropped every one of them in the cistern, and they were below ground when they were going off.

I found out after the war that our company had just been assigned a new captain. He was the reason we had been captured. When the 1st sergeant found out that we were being hit, he wanted to take a platoon and get us out. The new captain said no. He called the battalion commander and told him that the outpost had been wiped out and that he was going to establish a new one. Two hours later we were still fighting.

Anyway, this German captain came running up to me. There was a dead German laying there, and the captain tried to get me to pick him up. I told him I couldn't because I was wounded. A couple of the other guys picked him up, and the Germans took us across a creek into a small village where there were four or five houses. We stayed there for about five hours. They put us in a room right next to a room where all of the German commanders would meet to make out their battle plans. The Germans hadn't checked me very well because I still had a grenade. We had been told that the Germans were not going to take any prisoners because they had heard our division wasn't taking any prisoners. I told one of the guys that if they were going to shoot us we were going to take some of them with us.

They came in and took one of the men into the room where all the commanders were. They started questioning him. He didn't know anything, so they asked him who was in charge. He told them Sergeant Bradley. They came into the room where we were and started asking for Sergeant Bradley. After they called my name several times, I finally stood up. I still had the grenade under my shirt. When they took me into the room, I stood at the end of the table and saluted them; they saluted back. I had already decided that if they started to shoot me I was going to drop the grenade in the middle of the table. They told me to sit down and I did. They started questioning me. They asked me about crossing a railroad that was near our company position. I told them that they knew we had or we would still be on the other side. They asked where my company was located. I told them I didn't know because I hadn't seen them for a week. They kept it up for a while and then finally sent me back to the other guys.

They took our billfolds. Mine had a lot of clippings in it about the boxing tournaments and pictures of my girlfriends, and addresses in it. They kept them and sent them back to the rear echelon, but I didn't know that at the time. Then they started marching us to the rear. We got back there to a little town. There was German activity—tanks and troops moving everywhere. They threw us in a little town jail. They took one of the guys out to question him. He told them that I was in charge, and they came and got me immediately. I went into these officers' quarters, and there was a big fat German officer setting there. He got real friendly, offered me coffee and cake. I took them because I was getting real hungry. Then he started asking about that railroad and the location of the company. I told him I didn't know where they were at. He said, "I see you did a lot of fighting. How would you like to fight Max Schmeling [the German world heavyweight champion]? I told him that you were quite a fighter down in Fort Jackson." I thought how in the hell did he know that. Then it dawned on me that he had my billfold. I said, "How about I get Joe Louis to fight you?" He got a big laugh out of it. He finally gave me back my billfold. He told me he could have me shot. I told him that I knew it, but there wasn't much I could do about it. He sent me back to the little jail. We had the best meal we would have that night. They brought us in some beef stew and gave us a loaf of black bread. I couldn't stand the smell. I took one bite out of it and threw it over in the corner of the cell. A German soldier told me I had better save it because I would think it was cake in a couple of days. So we wrapped it up and kept it. The German guard was right, because we didn't get anything to eat for four days.

They took us down to the train depot. There were prisoners of war sitting all over the place. The first guy I saw was my old squad leader from Fort Jackson, John Hally. I was lucky I knew him because we shared everything in the prison camp. His folks would send a parcel every week, and we lived on it. What was his was mine, and the same with me. The Germans usually took half of the goods, but they didn't bother his. On the other hand, my folks sent a parcel every week, but I never got one of them. Between that and the parcels that the Red Cross sent we made it.

German guards would come in about once a week and shake us down. They would bring in these metal detectors and check the area. They found a few rusty nails, but that was about all. We had this interpreter by the name of Ralph Hill. He was from South Carolina. He was a staff sergeant and had been a prisoner for three years. Every day they would come in and take a few of us from each barrack outside to cut wood. Most of us didn't have much clothing, and it was really getting cold. We came back in off of this work detail one day and we had received field jackets from the Red Cross. This German SS officer came into the camp and was going to take all of these field jackets back to the front for the German soldiers. They were really hurting. It was the coldest winter they had had since 1888. It got to be thirty and forty below zero. Our building didn't have any heat. The wind would blow through it like it didn't have walls. We would huddle together and sleep in the straw, trying to keep from freezing to death. There was ninety-eight of us in the building, so we did pretty good. We had to take turns. One time your butt would be against the wind, next time it was someone else's turn.

They had just come into our barrack and lined us up against the walls. This German officer would come around and point his finger right in your face: "Are you the one that got that food? Were you the one outside?" "No sir," we would answer. It was just a game with them. Well, the word got out that the SS was going to get the field jackets. The sergeants in each barrack sent orders for us to tear up the field jackets. This SS officer went to all eighteen barracks and lined the men up, trying to find out who tore up the jackets. There was only one jacket left, and this sergeant was wearing it. He had just come in from the field, and he didn't know what was going on. He walked in, and this SS officer told him to take it off. He looked around and saw the pile, then he looked at the SS officer and said, "No sir." The SS officer ordered one of his men to shoot him if he didn't take it off. A German soldier stepped up and stuck the rifle in his belly. The sergeant stood there for a minute and then took it off. He ripped it up standing there with the German soldier aiming at him. The SS officer started yelling and cussing and walked out. He never did do anything to the sergeant.

We had a new sergeant from the 106th Division brought into our camp. We had been saving all of our cigarettes for Christmas. We were going to have a fire all day. We were going to set around it and sing Christmas carols all day. We had saved twenty-eight packs of cigarettes to buy coal from the German guards. We woke up about two days before Christmas, and all of the cigarettes had disappeared. When we went out for formation, one of the guys told the 1st sergeant that our cigarettes were missing. He went to the German guard and asked him to hold the men outside while he went inside to do a search. The guard agreed, and the 1st sergeant, myself, and a couple of other guys went in and found all twenty-eight packs in this new sergeant's blankets. We had what you called a kangaroo court. This is one thing that you didn't do—you could steal from the Germans, but not from your buddies. We all got together and decided that we were going to beat the shit out of the sergeant and throw him out into the snow. They also decided that I was to fight him. They got some tape for my hands and a pair of leather gloves from the Germans. When we started, this guy came at me like a madman. He was swinging, and it was obvious that he didn't know how to fight. I bent down under and came up with a couple of uppercuts. I knocked two of his front teeth out with the first punch. He had guts, though, because he just kept coming. I knocked him down four times, and he would just keep getting up. Finally I said, "That's it. I quit." One of the guys threw a bucket of water on him, and they put a sign around his neck that read, "I am a thief. I stole from my buddies." Then two of the prisoners got him by each arm and marched him through all 2,800 men in the prison camp. After that, none of the prisoners would let him come into their barracks.

That night it started snowing. We always went outside at night to watch them bomb Berlin. We were only fifty miles from it, and it would always light up like a Christmas tree. We went out, and this sergeant was leaning up against this barrack. He was shaking so bad the snow was shaking off of him. I told one of the guys that he was going to freeze to death if we didn't bring him in. So we took a vote, went out, and got him, and threw him in a bunk. Everybody threw blankets on him until he warmed up, and then we left him with his own blankets. After that we all forgot about it.

There was a little German sergeant that was recuperating from a wound he received while on the Russian front. He loved to play poker. The Germans had American cigarettes that they had taken from the Red Cross packages.

This German sergeant would come in each day with a carton of cigarettes, and we would play with him. Let him win a few hands and then take him for the big pot. He always came with a carton of cigarettes, but he never left with any. He would get up and say, "See you tomorrow." We were about to get kicked out of this place, because you could hear the Russians in the distance; but just before we did, he came in and wanted to play. He was playing poker and got to bragging about how great of a soldier he was and how many Russians he had killed before he got wounded. He said, "You know, when I go back to the front I want to go to the American lines. I want to kill some Americans." When he said that I grabbed his pistol out of his holster, pulled the clip out of it, and threw it out in the snow. He looked at me, his face was red, and he started calling me all kinds of names in German. He stormed out of the barrack and was on his hands and knees in the snow looking for his pistol. We were all at the windows laughing at him. He found it, slammed it in his holster, and took off out the front gate. Two days later that little fart was back again with another carton of cigarettes, ready to play poker. Everybody was quiet when he walked in because we didn't know what he would do. He stopped and looked at us and said, "Ha, you guys thought I couldn't take a joke. Come on, let's play poker." Two hours later he left without any cigarettes.

Most of the guys had pictures of their wives and girlfriends tacked up on their bunks. After the Battle of the Bulge, a kid from 106th Division was given a bunk, and after two or three days he tacked a picture of his girl up on this bunk. Two bunks over, there was an identical picture. Both of them had dated the same girl before they left New York. When we got back, we found out that there was a whole pack of these women that were marrying GIs before they went overseas to collect insurance money when the GIs were killed. It was a game.

We could get the German guards to do anything for American cigarettes. You could have gotten a free trip across Berlin if you'd wanted it. But I traded cigarettes with them and they would turn their heads long enough for me to sneak out of the compound and over to an Italian camp, where I could get food. The Italians liked the chocolate bars from the Red Cross packages, and I would trade them for potatoes and other vegetables. Then I would bring them back for us to eat. I got caught several times. Each time you got caught, you were supposed to do five days in the hole. It was a little outhouse-like building made out of blocks. It had a little stool in it. You couldn't lay down and stretch out. You could set down and stretch a little, but you had five days in there with one piece of bread and a glass of water a day. I had twenty-five days coming. They never did get any food from me because every time they would catch me I would throw the food over as I lifted my hands. One of the other guys would get it and take it into the barrack for the other guys. It was a standing rule in the camp that the food always got back into the original hands that it had come from. But I hadn't done any time yet.

Then Phil Weatherall got caught and had five days to do. When I had signed the little black book, I had signed right under Phil's name, so I knew when they took him for his five days that I was next. For the next five days, I saved a little food to take with me. They brought Phil back, and I knew I was going the next day. I rolled my blankets up and hoped that I could bribe the guard with cigarettes to let me have them. You could easily freeze in this weather. The next morning this German sergeant came in, and I was sure he was after me. By now we could really hear the big guns of the Russians. They were really close. When he walked in, I started walking toward him with my cigarettes, but he stood there looking at me. Then he said, "I have orders for you men to pack up anything that you want to take with you. We are leaving in an hour."

About an hour later we started on a march. I never saw so many prisoners of war in my life. We were all congregating and heading toward Berlin, to Stalag IIIA. The Germans would let us stop on the side of the road every four or five hours and catnap for five or ten minutes. The guards were getting a ride in between us every hour; they were the old guards. One man was placed about every five hundred yards. We could have easily killed them, but there was no place to go. The snow was several feet high. I tried to run through it one day to chase a jackrabbit I saw, but I couldn't get through the snow. So we walked and walked. The sergeant that had stolen from us passed me on the march. I will never forget the look on his face. He didn't even know who I was. He walked as if he was in a complete daze.

The worst thing that I saw on this trip was done by some SS troops that were moving as we were. They were moving some young Jewish boys—all thirteen, fourteen, or fifteen years old. We were laying over in this ditch one day, and these German officers come riding through on Clydesdale horses. They were running these fifteen Jewish kids. All of the kids were dressed in striped uniforms. These kids were run out. The Germans pushed them over to the side of the road and just came along and shot each one in the back of the head. It's the worst thing I ever saw. We couldn't believe this went on.

We went on through this little town. There were bodies along this road where the Germans had shot kids and Jewish prisoners. They didn't fool with the Russian prisoners either. I saw a lot of Russian prisoners alive, but all of them had an arm cut off. The Germans had maimed them on purpose, so they couldn't hold a rifle again. But some of them did hold one again and escaped. I saw a lot of Russian soldiers murdered by the Germans.

The Germans also had the gas chambers. I went through one of them, took a shower, and then stood outside getting dressed and saw them run fifteen Jewish kids in there and gas them. Right after that the Germans ran about ten Russian soldiers in and gassed them too. There are a lot of people

Top: A post-liberation photo of the soup cauldrons in the kitchen of Stalag IIIA near Luckenwalde, Germany, where William Bradley was imprisoned. *Bottom:* After liberation, prisoners celebrate inside a barrack at Stalag IIIA U.S. Army Signal Corps photos by TEC/4 John E. Feeney. (Courtesy of the National Archives, Washington, D.C.)

Top and bottom: Exterior and interior shots of the tent quarters at Stalag IIIA, post-liberation. U.S. Army Signal Corps photos by TEC/4 John E. Feeney. (Courtesy of the National Archives.)

Facilities at Stalag IIIA included this athletic field for the prisoners, as well as air raid trenches. U.S. Army Signal Corps photo by John E. Feeney. (Courtesy of the National Archives.)

who say this type of thing didn't happen. But I saw it. And what little I saw was nothing compared to everything that went on.

We marched right through one beautiful town that hadn't been touched by the war. It was a very clean town. One of the prisoners commented on it. We just couldn't believe that it was that clean in the middle of a war. We spent four hours in the town resting, and one of the guards ordered us to get in this garage and rest. We went in and laid down. We could see him out front marching. About midnight we heard the door squeak, and someone came in. We thought it was the guard, but it was an old German lady. She had a couple loaves of bread. It was probably the only food she had in the house, and she shared it with us.

We left the next morning and walked by a big garrison where the SS troops took their training. It hadn't been hit by the bombing yet either. Finally, after seven days of marching, we arrived at Stalag IIIA. There were prisoners everywhere, and they didn't have anymore room. So they put us out in a great big field with one strand of fence around it. We could walk right through it; you would see a guard every so often—but we weren't going anyplace, we were so beaten down.

Liberated soldiers in Stalag IIIA cooking rations drawn from the camp kitchen, just as they did while prisoners. U.S. Army Signal Corps photo by John E. Feeney. (Courtesy of the National Archives.)

In spite of our situation, every night while we were there we had a dice game. The old German guards loved it. They would bring in cigarettes and roll the dice. Some of them would even bring in blankets at night and shine lights on them so we could play.

After a couple of days, we were staying in big tents. They had four or five of them put up, but it still wouldn't hold all of us. I was lucky enough to get to stay inside the tent. They had straw on the ground for us to sleep on.

After a few days we could hear the guns getting really close. I had my talk with the former world champion Max Schmeling. He said that he would like to come back to America. He had come to the camp in a new suit that he had bought while he was in New York. He said that he had been in the German paratroopers and was wounded in Poland. They discharged him after that. I found out later that they had sent him there to see if he could find out any additional information. The Germans wouldn't give up. They were trying to find out if we had any secret weapons, and the war was only a few days from being over. They just wouldn't admit it or accept it.

The next morning, about 4 A.M., it got just quiet as could be. It was still. There wasn't a gun firing anywhere. During the night the German guards had all taken off. We didn't even know it. There was a great big woods over from the camp, and four or five of the old German guards had run over there and hid. Right at sunup we could hear the tanks coming. We thought it was Americans, but it was the Russians. They come swarming in. They had their women and children with them. The first thing we saw was a big Sherman tank bust through the front gate, come rolling up there and stopped. There was a Russian woman jumped down off of the tank. She had to have cleaned up before they came in because she was so white. Nobody could have rode a tank and stayed that white. She had shoulder-length black hair. It glistened in the sun. She was dressed in white and had a .45 pistol on each hip—just like Patton. She looked us over, jumped back on the tank, and waved them on. Right behind them come the ragtag army—Russian soldiers, children pushing wheelbarrows full of kitchen utensils. They pitched their tents right by the camp and went to cooking. We really had a meal.

Myself and some of the other guys took off up to Hitler's mansion, because we knew there would be food there. I took a couple of P-38 pistols off the wall. They were special-made with pearl handles. They were stolen later when I was returning home.

For a couple of days, we were in the camp, and one day a Russian lieutenant came up and asked us if we were hungry. We told him we were, because we couldn't get filled up. He took us up to this beautiful home owned by a German aristocrat. There was an old man and woman in the house. They even had a servant. This young Russian guy didn't even knock, he just walked in and motioned for us to come in. The old man and woman was just sitting down to a great big meal. You could have fed twenty people with what was on the table, and there was just two of them. The Russian officer told us to set down and eat—we had all day. We started to set down, and this old German man jumps up, "nichts, nichts, get out." This Russian lieutenant jumps up and walks over to this old man, points his finger in the old man's face and tells him to set down. We ate like kids. The Germans hadn't eaten while we were there, but there was plenty of food left. I stood up when we were finished and told the Russian we were ready to go. He walked over and picked up a turkey leg and started eating on it. This German came at him again. The Russian pushed him back into his chair this time. Then he walked over, took hold of this table, and turned it upside down. Then we left.

A couple of us took off the next day because we weren't going to sleep in that prison camp anymore. We knew there was a motel in a nearby town because we had been by it a few times. There was a great big arms factory that made ammunition at the edge of this town, and we heard that the Russians had been moving prisoners in there. There was an estimated 40 to 50 thousand of them that had been put in there in the last week or so. We walked over to this motel. We were the first Americans to come into this town. I guess most of the Americans were afraid to leave the prison camp because of

Liberated British and American prisoners at Stalag IIIA being removed to American lines by the 83d Division of the United States 9th Army. U.S. Army Signal Corps photo by TEC/4 John E. Feeney. (Courtesy of the National Archives.)

the Russians, but we were at the point that we didn't care. This old man came out, and he begged us to stay there. He told us they would put us up. We didn't know it at the time, but if you were there first it was yours. The Russians wouldn't come in.

We stayed, and that night we were sound asleep when about one in the morning someone was beating on the door. I went to the door, and there were two Russian soldiers at the door. They had come to see what they could find. Both of them were drunk. One had a bottle of vodka in his hand. He would take a drink and then hand the bottle to the other soldier. One said, "Ah, American. Have a drink." I took the bottle, stuck my tongue down into the bottle, and acted like I took a big drink. "Thank you comrade," I said and handed the bottle back to him. They just walked off and never bothered us again.

The next morning we were sitting outside, and we could see down in the valley where this big factory was located. We could see the German prisoners standing around the building and in the yard. The Russian guards were out in the yard walking around. Then all of a sudden every building blew. Gas, flames, and black smoke came gushing out. The German prisoners came running out with their clothes on fire. Many of them ran to the fences and tried to climb over, but the Russians shot them. We found out later that there was at least 35,000 Germans killed. The Russians had set the place on fire. It was payback time.

A couple of days later, we found out that the trucks was coming to get us. We caught the last truck out. After a three- or four-hour drive we stopped at a big airbase that the army had set up in Hildberghausen. We stayed there for a day, and then they flew us to France in a C-47. We landed in Paris, and I rode under the Arc de Triomphe and out into the country to Camp Lucky Strike. At Lucky Strike they fed us boiled chicken every day. We got new clothes. We seen movies every night. That lasted for about a month.

Then we were loaded aboard a ship. My shoulder had completely healed, and I decided to box one of the heavyweights on the ship. I had the intention of being a professional boxer. During the match I tore the shoulder up again, and the healing had to start all over.

When we landed in New York, I was sore. I couldn't hardly move my shoulder. I got home and went to the old house where we had lived. My parents had moved. It just so happened that the mailman lived next door to the old house, so I went to the post office. The mailman was there picking up his mail. It was four a.m. I said, "Do you know where my parents live?" He knew me right away and said, "Yeah, get in the truck. I'll take you home." He pulled up in front of the house and told me I lived here. I said, "I guess I do." My old dog was laying on the front porch. He was fifteen years old, and he died the day after I got home. The first person I saw when I came into the house was a little fat guy laying on the bed. I thought, "Who in the hell is that?" It was Buzz. Mom and Dad heard me open the door and came running out. All my brothers and sisters came in, and we had a good homecoming.

I got to stay home ninety days. After my ninety days were up, I went to San Antonio. There was a prisoner of war camp there, holding German soldiers. They made the mistake of putting a bunch of us ex–prisoners of war in charge of them. They told us we only had to guard them a couple hours at a time. We started pulling guard duty. They told me to go down and get three or four of them to go empty the garbage cans. I asked where I was supposed to check out a gun. They said that I didn't need a gun. "I do if I am guarding prisoners." They sent me down to ordnance, and I was issued a sawed-off pump shotgun and a .45 pistol. The Germans had gotten the word that we were there to guard them, and they were on their best behavior. When I went to get them, I told them not to utter a word, I would be right behind them. I walked them in the alleyways for four hours, and they didn't say a word.

The next day the Germans were complaining that the steak they had been given was too tough. They had put a kid on the machine gun corner who had had a rough time in the Nazi camps. The Germans had beaten him and almost killed him once. These German prisoners came out and started raking their tin cups on the fence in protest of the steak. "We want better food. We want better food." This kid told them once to get back into the barrack. The Germans started throwing their tin cups at him. He opened up on them with the machine gun and killed six of them. The next day all the ex–POWs were moved. That never even got in the papers. It was hushed up.

They transferred us to California. While I was there, I boxed a few times. Met a girl there and dated her for awhile. Then they transferred us to San Francisco to guard the dock gates of Alcatraz. After a month I was discharged.

I came home, and me and my brothers all went to McCarthey College. We all became high school teachers and coaches.

Corporal Harold W. Gattung

U.S. Army
Company D, 361st Infantry
Captured In An Ambush Near
The Arno River In Florence, Italy
Prisoner of War
July 28, 1944–April 28, 1945
Stalag VIIA and Stalag IIB

Harold was inducted into the army on September 28, 1943, after working as a truck driver for the Civilian Conservation Corps. He took his training at Fort McClellan in Alabama. He was assigned as an anti-tank gunner. Shortly after training, he was shipped overseas. He trained through March 1944 near Naples, Italy, before moving to the front lines on his birthday, June 25, 1944.

On July 28, 1944, at about two in the morning, seven of us were on a patrol near the Arno River, which runs next to Florence, Italy. The moon was bright, and I remember seeing the Leaning Tower of Pisa in the distance. Suddenly, all hell broke loose. We were in the middle of a German ambush. The point man, our sergeant, and the last man in the column were killed immediately. I was the second man in the column and I dove for a ditch at the side of the road. I was pinned down for what seemed like hours. The four of us that were left finally had to surrender. As we stepped out of the ditch with our hands up, I looked down and saw I had three bullet holes in the front of my field jacket. To this day I still don't know how I kept from being hit. The Germans made us wade across the river with our hands over our heads. The water was up to our chins, and we struggled to keep from drowning.

We walked at gunpoint to the nearby town of Pisto. We were lined up against the wall to be shot. The German sergeant stopped short of letting his men fire. They came up to us and took all our valuables, watches, rings, knives, and food. After that, they marched us through town to the town jail. The Italian people were friendly to whoever was in power. They acted with approval toward the Germans.

That night one of the German guards got drunk and tried to shoot us with a machine gun. He opened up on the jail, but we were able to hug the

Corporal Harold W. Gattung. (Courtesy of Harold W. Gattung.)

floor without being hit until some of the other soldiers stopped him.

The next day we started on a march north toward Germany. We walked for several days with no food and very little water. To add to our misery, we were constantly strafed by our own airplanes. We finally arrived at a prison camp in Mantova, Italy. The prison camp was a gathering point for all prisoners captured in Italy. Most were English. One of the first things the Germans did was look for Americans of Jewish descent. They found three, and they were taken away. I never saw them again. We had been there for about a week when we got a visit by Max Schmeling, the former German heavyweight boxing champion, who tried to tell us the Germans were doing the right thing.

We were desperate for food. All we got was soup with a little bit of potato in it. We killed a small dog that came through the camp and used the meat in our soup.

We started digging a tunnel to escape. When we finally got the tunnel far enough out to be past the fence, we quickly found out that the tunnel was too close to the surface. One of the German guards walking outside the fence fell in. That ended our tunnel digging and sure caused us problems. They cut our food supply, beat some of the prisoners, and generally gave us a hard way to go.

After several weeks in the Mantova Camp, we were loaded into boxcars for a trip to Germany. We traveled for four days and three nights with no food and little water. We went through the Brenner Pass, high in the mountains. The first stop after four days was in Austria. The German Red Cross gave us some soup and wanted us to eat slowly. Most of us got sick, and since each boxcar had only a wooden box for a toilet things got pretty bad.

A couple of days later, we arrived at Stalag VIIA Moosburg, Germany, near the city of Munich. Conditions were a little better during my time at this camp. We received Red Cross parcels, which had cigarettes, food, and candy. It was a wonderful gift to us. The Germans also issued us some clothes.

We slept on mattresses filled with straw. The mattresses were infested with lice. We all got them, and a good friend Randy Balasko got infected so bad that he was sent to a hospital. The next time I saw him was on a street in Miami Beach, Florida. We were there after the war, waiting on reassignment.

The entire time that I was at this camp, our bombers were bombing Munich. The Germans made us work in the city clearing streets. The hard labor and the lack of food made it very hard on all of us.

After several weeks at Stalag VIIA, we were crowded into boxcars and taken to Stalag IIB near Hammerstein. This is close to the Elbe River in northeast Germany, near the Polish border. I stayed in this camp for two weeks and was then moved again.

This time I was moved to a kommando [a work camp], a large farm near the town of Kessburg, on August 23, 1944. We worked from daylight to dark picking potatoes in the fields. If we picked our quota, they would give us more potatoes to pick the next day. If we didn't finish, we worked in the dark. It was a no-win situation. We decided to pull a work strike at this place, when I tried to negotiate with the head guard, I got a rifle butt in my back. It has

View of Stalag VIIA near Moosburg, Germany, following liberation of prisoners by the 14th Armored Division, 3rd U.S. Army, on April 29, 1945. The camp, which contained the largest number of Allied prisoners liberated at one time, had 29,284 prisoners, 14,981 of whom were Americans. More than half of the American prisoners were officers, mostly from the Army Air Forces. U.S. Army Signal Corps photo by PFC Joseph W. Lapine. (Courtesy of the National Archives.)

hurt every day since, and I take Motrin even today for the pain in my back. Food was scarce. We got imitation coffee and one slice of brown bread with marmalade in the morning. At night we got some soup made with potatoes and greens. We stole potatoes when we could and ate them at night. As the weather got worse with winter coming on, we did all kinds of farmwork.

At different times while we were at this camp, we were abused by Hitler's youth gangs. They shot at us, threw rocks, and spit on us at every opportunity. Those kids had been completely brainwashed by Hitler's policies.

I was moved again on January 3, 1945, to another kommando, a large farm in Melgast, Poland. They crowded twenty of us into a room in the barn. The work, the food, and the guards were worse than before. Two of us managed to escape for three days. We didn't get far enough away before they caught us, and we were sent back to the same farm. They beat us and kicked us severely for the escape. They cut our rations of food and water. Then at night they would take our shoes and pants when they locked us up. We almost froze to death because of it.

On January 26, the Russian army was pushing our way. They were approximately twelve kilometers from the farm. The Germans decided to evacuate. We started down the road with two oxen pulling a cart in a snow storm. When we reached a town, more prisoners would join us and we would continue on our way. In a few days we had a large group of men. I had saved some food from the few Red Cross parcels. It was mostly prunes. We spent forty days on the road in very bad weather. Any prisoner that could not keep up was shot. We were in such need of food that we killed one oxen and later the other. Water was no problem because of the snow.

On March 5 we arrived at another kommando, near Freidland, Germany. We had forty men left. We were going to be here temporarily while arrangements were made to march us to Rostock, Germany, and then to cross the Baltic Sea to Denmark. In the meantime we were put to work killing cows with hoof-and-mouth disease. First, we would dig a hole, lead the cow next to it, kill the cow, and put the insides in the hole; then we would load the carcass onto a wagon for shipment to the German army. For this work we got the liver from the animal. We spent part of our nights cooking liver on homemade stoves. I have never eaten liver since.

While we were at this place, President Roosevelt died. The Germans told us, then laughed about it. That afternoon a formation of our big bombers flew low over us. This really lifted our spirits, and we jumped up and down yelling and waving as they passed. The Germans never said anything else to us after that.

A few days later we were working, and we saw a strange plane overhead. It was black and fast. I found out later that I was looking at the first jet fighter plane.

The small building that we were living in was setting alone on a large flat field. At night we would look out and see gun flashes from both the east and the west sides. We knew something was going to happen. Each night the flashes appeared closer and closer. We tried to tell the Germans that we were about to get caught in the middle, but they wouldn't listen. Early one morning they came running in, wanting to leave. We told them that it was too late and that it would be safer staying where we were at. When they fixed bayonets, we decided we had better do what they said.

There was a narrow-gauge railroad track nearby, so we started along this track pushing a small railcar. After a few miles Russian fighter planes started strafing us. We scattered away from the track, but not before some of the guys were wounded. None were seriously wounded, so we could continue on.

We finally made it to a town and to another kommando. We were locked inside a building. As soon as the Germans left us, we found a shovel and immediately tore up the wooden floor of the building and started digging. While we were under the building digging, shells started falling in the area. The Germans screamed for everybody to run across the field. By the time we came out, everyone else was ahead of us. This field that we ran into had hedgerows running across it. About the second or third one, we decided we had run far enough so we stopped and all started digging. By the time we got the holes deep enough and big enough for two to sit with knees under chins, the battle for the town was getting fierce. We sat in those holes fourteen hours while the Russians and Germans fought. One of the guys was carrying food in an extra pair of pants. He had laid the pants at the edge of hole. A bullet hit a can of pork and beans, and the juice ran down his shoulder and arm. He thought he was hit and moaned and groaned all night.

The next morning when the firing died down, we raised ourselves up and looked around. There were bodies and German uniforms laying all over the field. We started walking toward the town with our hands up. I think we would have been shot if we hadn't. Two Russian soldiers ran to us. As they approached, we started shouting "Roosevelt" over and over. I think it is the only thing that saved us from being shot.

The soldiers took us to their commander, who could speak German, and by showing him our shoes, which had the letters U.S. on them, we convinced him we were Americans.

He told us we could fight with them or he would send us to the rear. At that time we thought we should fight. We were put with a tank-destroyer crew. Our daily food ration was a hunk of black bread, some sugar, and either horse or cow meat. Their way of issuing the meat was to kill a horse or a cow, slice off a chunk of meat for each man in line, and give it to him. It was up to each of us to skin and cook our own meat.

We fought with them for several days. Their way was to capture a town and stay awhile. The next unit passed through to take the next town. These Russians did a lot of horrible things. The roads were crowded with Germans fleeing their towns. The Russians ran over and shot as many of them as they could. When they stopped in a town, they would search the houses. The people were forced out of their houses, and then the Russians would burn the houses to the ground. They would shoot the men. Then they would rape the women. Most of the time, it would be a group of soldiers raping one woman. Sometimes more than one at a time. After they finished they would cut their stomachs open and leave them in the streets to die. I was constantly sick and vomiting at the scenes of these atrocities; the Russians told us that they were paying back the Germans for the way the Germans had treated them. We told them that we didn't approve of this way of fighting and asked to be sent to the rear.

We were sent to a prison camp, where there were several hundred American ex-prisoners of war. We had no food and no water; and the gate was locked, with Russian soldiers patrolling the fence. One of the officers tried to organize us into platoons and companies like we had had in the States.

About the third day, we were told that we would be taken to Moscow and then put on a plane that would take us to New York. That didn't set right with me, I just didn't believe them. That night me and another guy climbed over the fence and started running. The Russian guards opened up on us. Luck being with us, we weren't hit. I had a German compass, and we worked our way west. We walked and ran all night to place as much distance between us and the Russians as we possibly could.

The next morning we took a buggy and a team of horses from a German farmer and took off down the road. A few hours later we came upon a Russian roadblock. We ditched the buggy and horses and found two bicycles. We kept the bicycles for several days, and we were able to avoid several Russian roadblocks. Finally we were stopped at a roadblock and had to trade our bicycles for food. Later the Russians took our German P-38 pistols, which we had taken from some dead German soldiers. They let us go after that.

We continued walking west, and when we got to a town we would hole up in an empty house and live off whatever food we could get. By now the German civilians were on our side, and they would let us know when the Russians were getting suspicious. Then we would move on.

We continued to move this way for over a week after the war ended. We made it to the last Russian checkpoint of the territory the Russian army controlled. They placed us under house arrest. We were interrogated for a week, left isolated, and given very little food or water. Finally, they decided we were good guys and gave us a big party. We had a lot of food, a lot of drinking, and a lot of dancing. The Russian women partied with us. They told us when we got back to America to be sure and tell everyone how good we were treated.

The next day was the day that we had been praying for. The Russians turned us over to the British army. They moved us fast by truck to Hamburg and then put us on a plane to England.

We flew over the Netherlands, and I could see the windmills and a lot of water. Then we started over the English Channel. This old two-engine C-47 started shaking, rattling, and stuttering. There was a pile of parachutes in the back of the plane, and I grabbed one, put it on, and was ready to jump. I had decided that I had made it through the war and this far, and I wasn't going to crash in some damned old plane that couldn't make it across the English Channel. We shook and shuddered all the way across and finally landed at good old Southampton, England. We sure were happy.

When we landed, the first stop was the hospital. Our clothes were taken and burned, and we were deloused and given hot showers and haircuts and some good hot food. After that we got physical exams and then some long-needed rest.

We thought the army would debrief us, but they never did. The Red Cross gave each of us $80.00 in English money, and we got to spent some time in London. After a couple of weeks, they put us aboard trains to Glasgow, Scotland.

Lucky us—the ship we boarded for home was the *Queen Mary*. We were treated like VIPs. The ship was so large that I never did get to see all of it. It seemed no time at all until we were approaching New York. It was very emotional to see the Statue of Liberty. The harbor was filled with boats, whistles blowing, and firehoses spraying water in the air. Boy, it was a wonderful feeling to be back in the United States. I really never thought I would see it again. I was luckier than many.

I was shipped to Camp Kilmer, New Jersey. We stayed there for a few days, and then I boarded a train for Chicago. It took several days, but I finally arrived at Fort Sheridan, in Chicago.

Several days later I arrived home. It was on June 25, 1945. It will always be in my memory because it was the greatest day in my life. It was also my birthday.

Private First Class
John McLaughlin
U.S. Army
Company E, 325th Glider Infantry
Captured in Italy
Prisoner of War
September 1943–February 1945
Stalag IIB,-Stalag VIIA, and Luft III

John was inducted into the army on December 18, 1942. He completed three months of training at Fort Bragg, North Carolina, as a glider pilot with the Glider Infantry Training Regiment. On April 9, 1943, shortly after his training, the unit was shipped to Casablanca, in North Africa. They were there for a few weeks before the unit was moved to the middle of the desert. There was no other way to get to the location but by glider, because there were no trains and it was too far to be trucked. So they flew in the gliders. During their training they had flown only short distances for thirty minutes at a time. This trip was for hours, with the gliders going up and down with the turbulence. All of the pilots got deathly sick. They landed once, only to find out that they were in the wrong place. They resumed their flight and finally landed at the destination: group of squad tents lined up under olive trees in the middle of the desert. They stayed there until September 1943.

They sent us to Bizerte, North Africa, which is a seaport. That's where we saw our first action. The Germans hit us with an air raid. They bombed for hours. We never had any casualties, but the Germans did. They lost a lot of planes.

We stayed at the seaport for a couple of weeks and trained every day. We knew we were getting ready for an invasion. We finally learned that we were going to invade Sicily. The paratroopers always went in before us to clear the way for the gliders, otherwise we would be in trouble when we landed. One day the paratroopers took off, and the next morning we were supposed to go in. The next morning, right before we were to leave, they canceled the

34

invasion. I found out later that the air force had messed up. They had had a certain flight pattern they were supposed to take, but instead they flew right over the navy, who was bombarding the shores of Sicily. The navy had orders to fire on any aircraft in the area, and they shot down most of our own planes, killing most of the paratroopers.

A couple of days later we landed in LCIs [landing craft]. The Germans had already pulled out from Sicily and were setting up a front in Italy. We were on Sicily for about two weeks, and then we got the word that we were going to invade Italy.

There were invasions on the east side and at Anzio beach. We

Private First Class John McLaughlin. (Courtesy of John McLaughlin.)

boarded LCIs and landed at a beach that had already been taken by the Americans. We were at the wrong place, so we got back on the boats and finally landed with the main invasion. The beachhead was pretty much taken. The Germans had pulled back into the mountains. We had this real tall mountain, and we had to climb it. The Germans had their front line set on the top of this mountain. It seemed like it took us two days to get to the top. We had all this equipment to move, and we were carrying a lot of individual equipment, too—rifle, pack, ammunition. By the time we got to the top, we were totally exhausted. Our outfit was in chaos. Part of the men got separated. We lost our lieutenant. When we got sent to the front line, our platoon sergeant took charge.

We moved to the top of the mountain to relieve the rangers. They had been there for a while. They were trying to dislodge the Germans so we could move past the mountain, but they couldn't move them. The Germans had their top SS troops on the front. They were tough.

We took the rangers' positions late in the afternoon, and the rangers pulled back. I was in the first platoon, the first squad. All the time that we had been in training, our squad had been on the point, so I knew that's where we were going to be. There were seven of us on point. Four of us were in one foxhole, three in another. I was in the back one from the sergeant's place. That afternoon the sergeant told us that there was going to be an artillery barrage by the Germans. We were to cover over our foxholes the best we could. We crawled around and got as much wood and stuff to cover us as possible. The next morning they opened up with all they had. They really plastered us. The third platoon, I heard later, was almost wiped out.

The Germans had moved up on us while the artillery barrage was going on. They pinned us down. We ran out of water and food, and our company couldn't get any water or food up to us. We were there for three days, pinned down. On the fourth morning the news came for us to withdraw. We had been the first in, and we knew we would be the last out. When the other units withdrew, we were supposed to receive cover fire so that we could withdraw. We waited all day and realized that the unit had pulled back without us. We were pinned in the holes the rest of the day and that night. On the fifth morning the sergeant decided that we should surrender. The sergeant had a white handkerchief, and he waved it. I watched until he crawled out of the hole, and I crawled out of mine. For years after we surrendered I wondered if we did the right thing, but I guess I wouldn't be here right now telling this if we hadn't. Who knows?

The Germans took us down the mountain to a village that they had occupied. The whole village was in shambles. Artillery was still coming in, and our planes were strafing. We were in as much danger as we had been when we were up on the hill. We had to take cover in ditches and under bridges with the German guards. We were under fire the whole time we were there.

They made us clean up a sugar refinery. We were scooping up brown sugar and putting it in sacks. We found out what it was, and we started loading up our pockets with sugar. We hadn't had anything to eat, and it was good. From the time we were captured, food became a problem, and it remained a problem the whole time we were prisoners. We didn't get much to eat.

After about three days they started marching us. They finally got us to a railroad yard, and that's when the punishment started for me. They loaded us on boxcars like cattle. There were at least a hundred men in each boxcar. They had two partitions with a door in the middle and barbed wire on each side of the petition. The prisoners were on each end of the car, with the guards in the middle. We must have been on that train for two weeks. We went the whole length of Italy and Germany. They give us a loaf of bread and some water a couple of times while we were on the train and one can of dog meat. That's what it looked like, but I don't know what it was. How we survived that I don't know. We were stacked in there like hogs. They stopped the train a lot, but they only let us off one or two times. If you had to pee, you did it in the floor. If you had a bowel movement, you were in trouble. It really got to smelling by the time we got to where we were going.

I remember one time when they stopped the train and let us out to use the bathroom. I ran into one of the guys that had been in my foxhole, his name was Browning. We were squatted down taking a dump. It was dark. All at once I heard him whisper, "Mack, I think I found potatoes." He had been digging around and had sure enough found some potatoes almost matured. We dug up the potatoes and ate them, dirt and all. We stuck as many as we could in our pockets.

When we were almost to Germany, we started getting hit by our planes again. They bombed every night and every day. We were in a railroad yard. They hit us with B-17s. I have never felt so helpless as I did then. The Germans would stop the train and take cover, but they wouldn't let us out of the boxcars. I felt like a trapped animal. These attacks happened several times, but lucky for us we were never hit.

We finally arrived at Stalag VIIA. It seemed that this camp was a holding place for all prisoners. There were French, British, Russians, and Americans. I spent four days in a little room about six by six feet with nothing but water, waiting to be interrogated; but they never asked me much. I didn't know anything anyway. Then I was put in the camp with everyone else. I met Henry Leg. He had been shot down in 1942. I had been walking around for about two days. Nothing to eat, nothing to smoke. All at once I spotted this guy. I thought I knew him. I followed him into the latrine, and finally I said, "Aren't you Henry Leg?" He turned and looked at me. We couldn't believe it. We were from the same hometown and had run around together when we were home. It was a real morale booster.

We buddied around together the whole time we were prisoners. He took me to his barrack and gave me some of his cigarettes. Boy, I would take two or three drags off of them cigarettes and they were gone.

We stayed there two or three weeks, and then they started separating the guys. They took all of us that was airborne troops and sent us to an officers' camp, Stalag Lufts III. Why, I don't know, but we were really lucky because it was one of the best camps in Germany. That's where I got my first Red Cross box. We ate most of what we got, but we would save back some food so we could pitch in when we got new prisoners.

We had all kinds of technicians in the camp, and they put radios together by bribing guards with cigarettes and D-ration bars for radio parts in return. We had radios and got the news all the time about where the front was. We would meet about every three days in one of the barracks and one of the guys would watch for the German guard. If he seen them coming, he would yell, "Tally Ho!"

We also had an escape at this camp. Some men started a tunnel under a bunk bed in the barrack next to the fence. The beds were three bunks high. They would take the bed boards and the straw out of the bottom bunk and start digging. The dirt was carried out in their trousers. They would tie their pant legs some way so that when they got outside they could let the dirt fall while they walked around. It was sandy, and they could get rid of a lot of dirt like that. They finally got the tunnel dug out and a bunch of them escaped. The Germans came in one morning and lined us up and started the count.

This German officer told us that there had been an escape, but that they had caught or killed all the prisoners. We didn't believe the Germans, but we never saw any of them again.*

After that the Germans found three or four more tunnels. They ran water in them and caved them in. After that they started sabotaging our Red Cross packages. They would punch holes in every can of meat we would get which caused the meat to spoil. They told us that it was to keep us from saving up the meat for escape, but I believe that they did it for revenge. It made it a lot worse for our food supply because we couldn't ration it out and make it last for a month until we got another package.

Some time in the fall of 1944, they took all the enlisted men except for the sergeants and moved us to Stalag IIB. We went out on work details in this camp.

During the winter they took thirteen of us and loaded us on a train again. This time the ride wasn't as bad because we weren't as crowded. They took us to an evergreen forest to cut trees. We cut the trees down and trimmed them into six-foot logs for mine props. It was really bad by then. It was really cold and snowed all the time. It was rough working out in that kind of conditions. All thirteen of us stayed in a little building about fourteen by fourteen feet. We had a little stove that we could use to heat water, and that was about it. We still got our Red Cross boxes once a month. The Germans gave us potatoes, turnips, and a ration of barley bread.

We were there for a few months, and then in the distance we begin to hear the artillery fire on the front lines getting closer. We could tell by the way the Germans were talking that the Russians were moving fast. I found out later that when the Germans would stop the American push, the Russians would advance. When they stopped the Russians, the Americans would advance. But, now the Russians were moving fast.

The Germans started marching us back to Stalag IIB late one afternoon. I don't know how far we walked, but it started snowing hard. It got knee-deep. Some of the guys took off out of the column and got away. Most of us decided not to run because we knew the Russians would be there soon, and we didn't want to take a chance on getting shot.

We finally got to this big house. The Germans were all old, and they were about played out. They said that we could stay there that night. We had loaded all of our food when we started out, and we still had some of the Red Cross packages left. We had coffee, too. We told the women in the house to

---

*This was the "Great Escape." The prisoners started three tunnels, code-named Tom, Dick, and Harry. Each tunnel was thirty feet below ground to foil the sound detectors. Harry was 336 feet long and was the tunnel used for the escape. On March 25, 1944, seventy-six men escaped. Hitler was so infuriated by the mass escape that he ordered approximately 5,000 Germans to search for the prisoners. All were caught within two weeks, except for three men who made their way back to Allied units. The Gestapo took fifty of the prisoners into the countryside and mowed them down with machine guns. They also shot the three German civilians from whom the prisoners stole electrical wire to light up the tunnel.

Slave laborers, freed when troops of the 1st Army captured Stalag IIIB near Furstenburg, Germany, line up for chow from a division mess hall in town. U.S. Army Signal Corps photo. (Courtesy of the National Archives.)

heat us up some water, and we dumped a can of coffee in there. They liked to went nuts. They hadn't tasted coffee in years. They really enjoyed it.

After a while, German soldiers started straggling in, wounded and shot up. There were about six of them. They were young, and they got to talking with our old guards. They decided that they would be better off if they surrendered to us. They came in and told us that they were going to surrender to us, and they gave us their guns. For some reason they thought that we could keep them from the Russians; but there was no way we could do it. We couldn't take them anywhere because our front was hundreds of miles away. So what we did was put them in a room by themselves.

The next day we made contact with the Russians. We had met this young Polish civilian who could speak German and English. We found some paint and painted American flags on the back of our field jackets, and then we walked out to the front to meet the Russians. The Polish guy translated for us and told them that we had these German soldiers as prisoners in the house. The Russians went into the house and got the Germans, and that was the last that we saw of them.

By now there was only six of us left. We were in bad shape again. The

Russians were our allies, but you wouldn't know it by the way they treated us. They took everything we had except for a little bit of food we had left from the Red Cross packages. They never gave us any food or transportation back, but they did assign a soldier to go with us. I don't know what rank he was, but he carried a submachine gun with him and he couldn't speak English. The farm where we were at had some horses and a two-seated buggy. So the six of us and the Russian started out in this buggy toward Poland. We stopped at several houses on the way and got something to eat. I don't know how many days we traveled, but we wanted to get to a Russian officer so we could get some help. Someone who could speak English. All this Russian with us wanted to do was to find something to drink and get drunk. Finally, we reached Schwabach, Germany, and found a headquarters with a Russian officer. He got us a truck and got us on our way.

We started out across Poland toward Russia. We rode for days. We didn't get any food and had to stop along the way and get food from civilians where we could. We went through Warsaw, and I will never forget the look of that city. It had had a population of one million, and there wasn't one building standing. The Germans had come in and took it from Poland. The Polish counterattacked and took it back. Then the Germans took it again, then the Russians came in and took it from the Germans. There were no bridges across the river. Nothing was standing.

In one town I saw hundreds and hundreds of Jews who had been liberated from concentration camps. They were in the striped uniforms. You could see the terror on their faces from the atrocities they had experienced. The only others that I ever saw with that look were Americans brought in after the Battle of the Bulge. They were the most pitiful-looking human beings that I had seen. There were pictures that I saw on television of people in the Holocaust being thrown in the graves, and these guys looked almost that bad. You could see every bone in their bodies. We all got together and got them some food.

The Germans were smart, and knew that the 106th Infantry Division was new. There was one guy that was in a foxhole about froze to death. All at once the Germans were all over him. He had the same feelings that I had. Did he do the right thing by giving up? We told him not to ever say or feel that way again. He had no choice if he wanted to live.

We crossed Poland and went into Russia. We got to the seaport Odessa. I never really felt secure or liberated until I started seeing the big white stars on the American trucks. We found the Americans, and an officer talked with us for a while. Then they fed us, and we were issued new clothing. I had on the same shoes that I had on when I was captured—that is, what was left of them.

A few days later they put us on a boat, and we crossed the Black Sea and went to Naples, Italy. We stayed there for a while and got medical attention.

A couple of months later, they put us on a boat, and we landed in Massachusetts. The whole time I was a prisoner I was hungry. I dreamed of food all the time. The one thing I dreamed of most was fried eggs. When I got to my hometown, there was probably a shortage of eggs because that's what I ate for days. They sure were good.

Part II

THE INVASION
OF FRANCE

THE BEST JOKES

Old Jim Bailey had played poker Saturday night until the wee hours, and the next morning he was in church, dozing as was his usual habit. The preacher was getting pretty tired of Old Jim's sleeping through the sermon Sunday after Sunday. So the preacher thought of a way to embarrass the man. In the middle of the sermon, he said, "We will now have a prayer. Brother Bailey will lead us." When Old Jim heard his name his head jerked up, eyes popped open, and he cried, "Lead? Why, hell, I just dealt!"

A wealthy girl out of an Eastern College for the summer vacation went abroad for a few months. In Italy, she met a handsome young Hindu named Yogi. Until this time she was a virgin, but she decided she might as well have a little fun, so she slept with him. By and by, she had to return to school and she was heartbroken at leaving the Yogi, but he soothed her by instructing her that when she became lonely for him, all she had to do was lie down on the bed in her room and say, "Yogi, Yogi, my body!" and with those words spoken she would be able to enjoy his presence. So she went back to school in the States that winter and lo and behold became lonely for Yogi. And when her roommate went out of the room, she went to bed and said, "Yogi, Yogi, my body!", and sure enough it happened. But about that time her roommate returned and said, "Why, what in the world are you doing?"

—*From a Kriegie's diary*

Private First Class
Adam L. Canupp

U.S. Army
101st Airborne, 501st Paratrooper Infantry
Captured in France During the D-Day Invasion
Prisoner of War
June 8, 1944–April 23, 1945
Stalag IVB and Stalag XIIA

Adam was inducted into the U.S. Army in March 1943. He took his basic training at Camp Roberts in California. He volunteered for the paratroopers and after a rigorous physical examination was sent to Fort Benning, Georgia, for paratrooper training. He joined the 501st Paratrooper Infantry in North Carolina. In January 1944 the unit went overseas, where they joined the 101st Airborne Division. He jumped about midnight on June 5, 1944, in the D-Day invasion.

It was like a hailstorm hitting the side of a tin building, the flak was so thick. There were planes going down all around us, but we managed to gain altitude and made it to the drop zone. The plane dropped altitude for us to jump, and when we got the signal to go, my parachute no more than opened and I was on the ground. I disconnected the chute and got myself collected. How the Germans missed me I don't know, because the machine-gun and rifle fire was fierce. I was able to join one other paratrooper, but that was all. Many of the men in the unit were dead or lost.

We made our way into a wooded area and stayed there until the next morning. Then we stayed hidden as much as possible because there were Germans all around us. A Frenchman spotted us and turned us in to the Germans. We were in a ditch, and I had fallen asleep. Something woke me up, and I looked up. My buddy was standing there with his hands up. We were captured by German paratroopers. That was on June 8th.

The Germans kept us on the move. We stayed in empty buildings, barns, sheds, and a couple of time in ditches along the road as we moved north toward Germany. We were constantly being strafed by our planes. We stayed a few days in one of the towns and filled bomb craters there.

45

CLASS OF SERVICE			SYMBOLS

WESTERN
UNION

AA7 2
JA493 42 GOVT=WUX WASHINGTON DC 28. 413P
MRS LILLY MARCH=
     160 NORTH COMMERCIAL ST CENTRALIA ILL=

THE SECRETARY OF WAR DESIRES ME TO EXPRESS HIS DEEP REGRET
THAT YOUR SON PRIVATE ADAM L CANUPP HAS BEEN REPORTED
MISSING IN ACTION SINCE SIX JUNE IN FRANCE IIF FURTHER
DETAILS OR OTHER INFORMATION ARE RECEIVED YOU WILL BE
PROMPTLY NOTIFIED=
     :ULTO THE ADJUTANT GENERAL;

THE COMPANY WILL APPRECIATE SUGGESTIONS FROM ITS PATRONS CONCERNING ITS SERVICE

Telegram to the mother of Adam Canupp. (Courtesy of Adam L. Canupp.)

They finally loaded us on trucks and told us that if any of us tried to jump off we would be shot. They wouldn't even let us off when we were strafed by our bombers. We went to Paris by truck. The German news media was there taking pictures of us. The Germans were holding back some of the French citizens who wanted to beat us. One woman broke through the German guards and started hitting one of the prisoners, and the Germans were taking pictures of all this for propaganda. We thought that it was probably a planned thing by the Germans because the French sure didn't like the Nazis.

They loaded us aboard trains, about eighty men per boxcar. We got one loaf of bread for all of us to share, and it had to last us for three days. It was so crowded we had to lay on our sides with our heads toward the wall of the boxcar and our legs pointing toward the center of the car. Our legs overlapped each other up to our knees, it was so crowded. There was no place to use the bathroom, so you went on the floor or in your pants. I was lucky because my head was by the door. There was a crack in the door, and I got fresh air, which helped me deal with the smell that was getting worse as the days went on. We stopped at Stalag XIIA and stayed there for a couple of weeks, and then I was moved to Stalag IVB about August 1.

I had been there about a month and was assigned to a detail to work in a sugar factory. There was about eighty of us. We were housed on the third floor of a building by the factory. We were fed pretty good there. We got a big bowl of soup every day for dinner. It was better than when we were in the stalag because we were getting about 900 calories a day there.

Private First Class Adam L. Canupp. (Courtesy of Adam L. Canupp.)

The first days we picked potatoes in the field. Then we started picking beets. The weather was getting cold, and we didn't have enough clothing. We complained, but it didn't do any good, so we decided to go on strike. The next day we just sat down and refused to work until we got more clothing. It worked because they got more clothes for us.

After the fields were harvested, they put us to work in the sugar factory. We worked from six in the morning until six in the evening. Six days a week. We worked with German civilians. They were kind to us. Once when I got the flu, they had sent me and several other prisoners who were sick to Holly, Germany, by train. There was a hospital there. The draft age in Germany was for sixteen to sixty-five. We had a sixty-five-year-old guard who was with us. I was there for about a week, and during that time this old guard would come in and show us photos of his grandchildren. He was really proud of them. He wanted the war to be over, and I think that most of the other Germans did too.

Overall I was treated pretty well. I can remember being assigned to unload bags of beets. I couldn't do the job because I was so weak I couldn't lift the bags. The German civilians did the job for me, and I was assigned to do another job.

On Sundays we could do pretty much what we wanted. Lots of times I would sit and talk to the German guards. There was one young guard and I was talking to him one Sunday, and I told him that I had a car when I got home. He said that Hitler had promised everyone a car when the war was over. I would ask him who was winning the war, and he would always say that they were. We never got any news at the sugar factory. When we were in the stalag, we had gotten news; but away from the main camp we weren't getting any at all, so I assumed we were losing the war.

The one thing that I can remember the most is that there was a constant, annoying hunger in my stomach. It never ceased. The last of November we boarded a train and were shipped back to Stalag IVB. There were forty

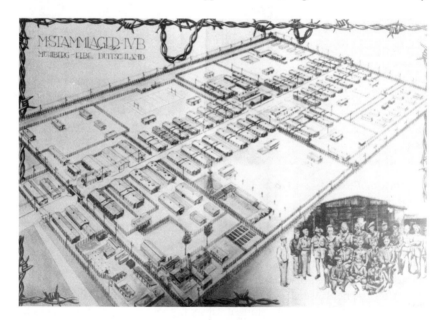

Drawing of Stalag IVB near Muhlberg, Germany. (Courtesy of Adam L. Canupp.)

of us in each car. Our two guards had managed to get a stove somewhere. We had picked up some wood and a few pieces of coal and stayed pretty warm. We could hear the men in the other boxcar stomping their feet to try and stay warm.

We returned to the stalag the next day. It was a very cold winter. I had accumulated seven different pieces of clothing, and I wore all of them, but I was still cold to the bone. I got a bed partner, and we had four or five blankets between us. There was no heat in the buildings, so we used our blankets and slept together to keep warm.

It wasn't long before the body lice took over. It was miserable. I never knew that a little bug could cause you so much misery. We were freezing to death; constantly hungry; and then the lice added to the misery.

My birthday is on April 20, the same day as Hitler's. We only missed being liberated on my birthday by three days. The Russians liberated us on April 23, 1945. They separated us, took us to a camp about twenty miles from the stalag, and gave us physicals. They kept us from April 23 through May 8. The war was over, but they still hadn't let us go. They had armed guards at the gates, and we felt they were keeping us for some reason. So early in the morning a few of us at a time started climbing over the fences and leaving the camp. They never did come after us.

I took a bicycle and rode for a couple of hours until I ran into the American lines. A truck picked us up and took us to the lines. We were loaded aboard C-47s and flew to Camp Lucky Strike.

They gave us physicals, showers, new clothes, and all we could eat. A couple of days after I got there, we were standing in line and General Eisenhower came up to a couple of guys in front of me and asked if they were getting enough to eat. I was real surprised to see him.

I got home about July 1945 and was discharged. I was sure glad to be home.

Private Lawrence E. Roberts

U.S. Army
Company M, 109th Infantry Division
Captured in Northern France
Prisoner of War
July 1, 1944–April 20, 1945
Stalag VIIB

Lawrence worked as a farmhand until he was inducted into the army on April 25, 1941. He was twenty-three years old. He completed his basic training at Camp Croft, Louisiana. Lawrence received further training in the military police before being shipped to Europe. His unit was shipped overseas on October 8, 1943, and he arrived in England on October 18, 1943. Lawrence won three Bronze Stars during combat at Normandy and in Northern France before he was captured.

We were on an outpost in northern France. We couldn't move the Germans at all. The fighting was fierce, and they were really bombarding us with artillery. The gunfire was so heavy that all we could do was hold our rifles above the foxhole and fire in the direction of the Germans, because we knew that if we raised up we would be hit.

This went on for a day or two, and then we got word from our sergeant that the Germans had moved around us and we were surrounded. The only thing we could do was to surrender. The sergeant rigged up a white cloth of some kind and waved it so the Germans would know we were surrendering. We stepped out of the foxholes with our hands up. I was really scared because we had heard stories that the Germans didn't take prisoners some of the time and I thought they would just shoot us.

We were lucky in that respect, because they took all of us prisoner. They took our guns, ammunition, and what supplies of food we had. There were fourteen of us, and they took us to the rear echelon of their unit.

They started marching us at night. We weren't sure exactly where we were going, but we knew we were headed toward Germany. They would march us at night so that we could hide from the strafing by the Allied planes. We stayed in barns, schoolhouses, empty buildings, and one night we slept in a ditch. They never gave us any food or water the entire time we were on the march. One night it was real dark, and two of the men broke out of the column as we passed through a village and hid behind some houses. They escaped because the Germans never realized that they were gone until we stopped the next morning. The guards were real mad and threatened to shoot us if any of the rest of us tried to get away.

We walked for five days and finally reached Stalag VIIB, near Memmingen, Germany. Conditions were terrible. We were assigned to a barrack and had beds of straw to sleep on. The straw was infested with lice, and everybody had them.

We only got a little food each day. For breakfast we got coffee made out of some grain. It didn't have much of a taste, and by the time we stood in line for it, it was usually cold. We usually got a piece of black barley bread to go with the coffee.

For lunch we got a small boiled potato and some water. For dinner, soup or bread if we were lucky. On many occasions we didn't get anything. As the days went by, the agony of constant hunger in our stomachs was just another thing to remind us that we were prisoners of war.

The Nazi guards got Red Cross parcels that were supposed to be given to us to help supplement our diet. They gave us part of the packages, but we learned after the war that they were holding a lot of the parcels from us. The packages helped. They had a D-bar (chocolate bar), cheese, coffee, cigarettes, some meat, vegetables, and cocoa in them. We were supposed to each get a package, but instead the Germans made two and three men share a box.

What really helped was the cigarettes. We could bribe the Nazi guards with the cigarettes and D-bars and in return the guards would bring us bread and potatoes or whatever they could get from the nearby town. We would divide the supplies among all of us. But the increase of prisoners and the fact that some of the guards were caught bringing in food reduced what each of us could get.

Life was the same each day. We got up early and had roll call. If anybody was missing, we had to stay until the Germans found the prisoner. We spent the rest of the time in line for food or water.

I was assigned to a work detail in the village. Myself and several other prisoners had to fill in bomb craters. We also had to clear the streets of rubble from the Allied bombings. It became more and more difficult as each day went by. The heat, the lack of food, the sunburn, and the blisters from working without any gloves began to affect the prisoners. We were getting weak, and we had no medicine for the blisters and sunburn. Often the Germans would only give us a little water, claiming there was a shortage because the bombing had damaged the water lines. We knew the guards were lying to us and just getting revenge for the bombing.

In October, about three months after I had been captured, the Germans let me write home. I was glad to be able to write, because at least my family would know that I was alive. At this point I didn't know if they even knew what had happened to me. When we wrote, though, we were told to tell our families that we were doing okay and that we were being treated very good, otherwise the letters would not be sent. I had to lie when I wrote, but at least if they sent the letter the folks back home would know I was alive.

We had a lot of intelligence guys in the camp. They bribed the guards with cigarettes and D-bars in return for radio parts. They made a radio and

Postcard from Private Lawrence E. Roberts to his family.

kept it hidden in the floor of one of the barracks. One of the guys would watch for the guards while the others got the radio out and listened to the war news. We had meetings every few days to keep up on the war. The Nazi guards were always telling us that we were losing the war, but we knew we were winning.

It really started getting cold. I found out at a later time that it was one of the worst winters in years in Germany. It was below-zero weather all the time, and it constantly snowed. The guards gave us two blankets to sleep with, but it wasn't enough. We didn't have heat in the barrack, and we were cold all the time. At night we slept together to keep warm. There were a lot of prisoners that got frostbite on their hands and feet. The skin would turn black and pop open like burnt meat.

Around Christmas we started getting prisoners in from the Battle of the Bulge. They looked worse than any of the men that I had seen brought in before. Many of them were nothing but skin and bone, and a lot of them were almost starved to death. They had severe frostbite, and some had all but given up hope of living. The Nazi guards bragged about the battle because Hitler had told them that this was the turning point of the war. We were depressed at that point. We knew the battle had gone their way, although we didn't believe they would win the war, we sure did believe we might be in the prison camps longer than we expected. Just another to add to the list of hunger and cold.

We took care of the new prisoners the best that we could. We shared our Red Cross parcels with them, cleaned them up, and took care of their wounds as best we could. The lice, the cold, and the bad diets had taken their toll on us. Many of the guys had dysentery, diarrhea, gastritis, and ulcers. Many of the guys would run for the toilet, but the diarrhea had gotten so bad that they would go on themselves, on the floor, and even on the wall at times. They tried to clean it up as best they could, but it almost became impossible to stay ahead of the problem because so many of the prisoners had it. For some it got so bad that they had to throw away their clothes and use blankets because they had messed on themselves so much and there was no place to wash the clothes. It was a depressing time, but the one thing that helped our spirits was the radio news of the war. The Battle of the Bulge had seemed to be a setback, but not for long. The Americans and Russians were moving fast on both fronts.

The bombing raids were increasing over Germany, and we also began to hear artillery fire in the distance. Night after night the artillery got closer. By late March we could see the flashes from artillery explosions in the distance. We knew that it wouldn't be long before we were liberated. The German guards were getting nervous too.

Then, early one morning in late April 1945, we woke up and everything was quiet. It seemed so still that it scared us because we hadn't been used to that the whole time we had been in the camp. We went outside, and the Nazi guards were gone. We heard tanks in the distance, and just about the time the sun came up a Sherman tank came crashing through the front gate. It was great to see our men.

We were sent to an aid station, where they deloused us, gave us showers, new clothes, and physical exams. Then we were fed five times a day. I just couldn't get enough to eat. Words just can't describe how good the food tasted. After about a month there, I gained some of my weight back.

On May 21, 1945, I caught a ship for the U.S. It took us fifteen days to get home. We arrived on June 5, 1945. I can remember pulling into New York and passing the Statue of Liberty. All of us were quiet as we passed by her. Some men were crying, others were praying, I was doing both. It was the happiest day of my life. I will never forget that day—never.

Private First Class Johnnie C. Womble

U.S. Army,
Company L, 2nd Battalion,
134th Regiment, 35th Infantry
Captured at Moselle River During
Invasion of Nancy, France
Prisoner of War
September 11, 1944–May 3, 1945
Stalag XIIA, Stalag VIIA, and
Kommando Camp Near Limburg

Johnnie Womble entered the U.S. Army on August 1, 1942, and took his basic training at Camp Walters, Texas. On Christmas Day 1942 he was shipped to California, where he joined the 35th Infantry Division. The unit trained in combat maneuvers for approximately one year, moved to a camp in Alabama for a short period of time, and then went on maneuvers in Tennessee. In May 1944 his unit was sent to Saint Ives, England.

On June 9, 1944, our unit hit Omaha Beach. The fighting was fierce, and we lost a lot of men. After several days of fighting, we had a good hold on the beach and began to move inland. That's where we started fighting in the hedgerows. Hedgerows were areas of trees and bushes that were about eight feet deep. They were used by the farmers to keep their cattle in the fields. Once in a while, there was an opening for wagons and cattle to pass through—but these were the only openings. We fought for one hedgerow at a time, and if we were lucky, we would take one or two a day. We fought like that for weeks, finally hit open country, and had the Germans on the run.

In September we were going to cross the Moselle river and invade Nancy, France. We had two companies abreast of each other that crossed the bridge. I was one of the lucky ones that got across. Most of the men didn't make it through the Nazis' cross fire. As soon as those of us that made it got on the other side, the Germans blew the bridge and surrounded us with our backs to the river. We were trapped. We fought all night.

The next morning the Nazis brought in Panzer tanks and aimed them at us. I always said that I would never surrender, but you sure don't want to die. We finally had to either die or surrender, and our commander decided that we should give up. We waved a white flag and stepped out into the open with our hands up. The Germans took our guns and made us throw our helmets on the ground. There were about 150 of us, and the Nazis marched us into the town of Nancy, France. They lined us up against a building, and I thought they were going to kill us all; but they just took all of our valuables and personal things. Then they marched us up and down the streets of the town. As they did, one of their photographers was taking pictures of us for the German newspapers. They would take us down one street and take pictures. Then a different street and take pictures. We didn't know what they were doing until we saw the German newspapers later. They had written a propaganda story and said that they had captured five thousand Americans.

They put us in an empty warehouse overnight, and the next day they loaded us on a train. The cars were "forty and eights." There was horse manure and straw a good six inches deep on the floor of the cars from horses that the Germans had transported by train. We were so crowded in the car that we couldn't clear a spot to sleep, so we just had to lay in the manure. Some of the guys tried to punch holes in the bottom of the car to get rid of some of it, but they weren't able to. The trip took us four days and nights. There were no toilets, so if you had to relieve yourself you just had to go on the floor. Between the horse manure and ourselves, things got pretty bad.

We had no food or water until the fourth and last day. We stopped in a little town just before we got to Limburg, and the Nazis gave us some noodles. We were all so hungry we ate like hogs. I grabbed my food and took a mouthful not realizing that it was red hot. I burnt my mouth so bad I couldn't eat for several days.

We were bombed and strafed every day by our own planes because they didn't know we were a POW train. The Germans locked us in the cars while they stopped the train and took cover. They never once let us off the train during those four days.

While we were going through Frankfurt, the train was attacked by Allied planes, and a bunch of British prisoners were killed when a couple of the cars were directly hit by bombs. The Germans just kept on going.

On the fourth day we arrived in Limburg. I was put in a kommando, where I stayed for about forty-five days. Conditions were miserable. We got very little food and had to work every day. They gave us colored water, usually cold, that they called coffee. I don't know what it was made out of, but it wasn't coffee. A piece of barley bread went with the coffee. We got soup in the evenings. Everyone was constantly thinking about food.

They took us to the town of Limburg and made us clean the streets and fill in bomb craters. We worked from daylight till dark.

Then, after about a month and a half, they moved me to Stalag XIIA. I thought things might be better, but I was wrong. They did have barracks to live in, but with straw floors. You could see the body lice moving in the straw, and every one of the prisoners including myself ended up with them.

The food wasn't much better at this camp than at the other, but we did get a Red Cross parcel on occasion. We were supposed to each get one, but the Nazis made four of us share one parcel. It had coffee, chocolate, and other items that helped us, but even so, we were all still starving.

To make things worse, most of the prisoners had diarrhea and dysentery. It was so bad that the

Private First Class Johnnie C. Womble. (Courtesy of Johnnie C. Womble.)

guards would put buckets in the barrack for us at night. Sometimes we made it and sometimes we didn't.

The German guards never really gave us much of a hard time, except when the SS troops came around for inspection. Then they would usually just yell at us. The regular German soldiers were afraid of the SS troops just like us. The SS troops would do more than just yell. They would beat prisoners with clubs and belts. I never saw them kill any prisoners, but I heard they did.

After a couple of weeks, they moved me again, this time to Stalag VIIA. When we were climbing into the boxcars, I was pulling myself up and I accidentally ran into a German guard who was close to the doorway. Before I could apologize to him he turned and slashed the back of my hand with his bayonet. It bled the whole time I was on the train.

We made it to Stalag VIIA in one day. At this camp they took my picture and assigned me a prison number: 87600. The conditions in this camp was the same as in the others. We had barracks and shared them with the bedbugs. It was getting close to winter, and the weather was getting colder. There was no heat in the barrack and too little clothing to keep warm, which only added to the problems for the prisoners who were already suffering from malnutrition, dysentery, diarrhea, and pneumonia, as well as many other diseases.

I was assigned to a labor unit for about a week. We would get up at three each morning and ride to Munich. We would work all day, then board the trains at dark, and get back to camp about midnight. Then we were up at three in the morning again.

In late October a Nazi guard came in one day and took me and twenty others to a kommando farm in the country near Limburg. We got there on November 1, 1944. They kept us in a small jail at the farm. Since we were out from the camp a ways and in the country, we had escape on our minds. The Nazis had us figured out, though, and to prevent us from escaping they took our clothes at night, so that we had to sleep naked. It was cold at night. We were really miserable.

We had to work every day, rain or shine. For a while I raked hay. Then when winter set in, it snowed every day. They put us to cutting wood for paper. The cold was starting to get to us. By now, my clothes were starting to rot off of me. I had never been allowed to take a bath or wash my clothes. My shoes came loose at the soles, and they would flop when I walked. The Nazis didn't care. I still had to work in the snow every day. My feet froze. They swelled and turned black. They were numb, and I had to continue to walk and work. I never once got any medical treatment for them.

At this camp they made some bread, and they would put it in one big bowl for all of us to eat out of. We got some coffee-water and every so often a bowl of soup. By now, I had lost sixty pounds. What clothes hadn't rotted off of me were falling off.

In April we heard that the our troops were getting close. The war was almost over, and we could tell by the way the Germans were acting that it wouldn't be long. They gathered up about five hundred of us and put us in two big barns. The Germans said they wanted to protect us from the SS troops, because they wanted to kill all the prisoners.

The guards started acting a lot friendlier toward us. They kept us in the barns for two weeks. Each day the guards brought us boiled potatoes. No salt—just plain boiled potatoes.

Then one day the guards came in and told us that they were going to surrender to the Americans. They said they would tell them where we were located. We never saw the guards again. The next day, May 3, 1945, American troops from Patton's 3rd Army showed up. They took us by truck to the river and then across the river in boats.

We were in the camp for a couple of days. They deloused us and gave us new clothing. I got some salve for my feet and some hot food.

A couple of days later, they flew us by C-47s to Camp Lucky Strike. I stayed there for about three days. We got to eat five times a day. Boiled chicken, eggnog, and almost anything else we wanted. We did have to watch the rich food, though, because our bodies would not take it.

A lot of the guys got to fly to England to catch a ship home, but I was shipped to another camp. This time it was Camp Phillip Morris. It was more of the same at this camp. Lots of food and medical attention. I got treatment for my feet, and they got much better in the few weeks that I was in the camp. When I regained most of my weight, they shipped me home on the *Comrade Wiser.*

I arrived home on June 8, 1945. It was the happiest day of my life. After sixty-seven days at home, recuperation in Florida and short assignments in New York and Virginia, I was discharged on Thanksgiving Day 1945.

TEC/3 John M. Hancock

U.S Army
Troop C-106 Reconnaissance Squadron
Captured in Rauwiller, France
Prisoner of War
November 24, 1944–March 27, 1945
Stalag XIIA

---

*John was inducted into the army in March 1943. He received his
basic and communications training at Fort Riley, Kansas. He joined
the 106th Cavalry Recon Group on maneuvers in Louisiana. Six
months later John shipped out from New York and landed in Scotland.
John fought in campaigns at Normandy, Northern France, Central
Europe, and the Rhineland. His unit's main responsibility was to
gather all the information possible about the Germans. As a result his
unit was often out in front of all of the combat units. These forward
operations resulted in his capture by the Germans.*

We had been out in front of the combat units all the way across Europe.
In November we joined the 2nd French Division under the command of General de Gaulle. We were getting ready to attack a town. We knew the Germans were in there. We were on the outside of town, making plans on how we were going to attack. I had not been so nervous in all my life. I didn't predict that anything unusual was going to happen, but I was really nervous.

We attacked the town and took it. We found out that a Panzer tank division had been in the town, but they were gone. We thought we had them on the run; but what actually happened was they had pulled to the outskirts of town into a wooded area to regroup. Just before dark they launched a counterattack. We were ordered to pull out of the town and withdraw to a town a few miles back.

Our captain had promised us turkey for Thanksgiving. He had ordered the trucks up with the turkey. I had already pulled my duty on the outpost and was just getting ready for my turkey when they called me back. The men at the outpost couldn't operate the gun, and they thought we were going to be attacked. I went back up, and sure enough, the Germans were coming. I got the captain on the phone and told him what was going on. He said that

60

TEC/3 John M. Hancock with his wife, Lucille Hancock. (Courtesy of John M. Hancock.)

we should pull back to this other small town. We did and found out that there was already an infantry battalion in the town. They told us not to worry because they had everything under control. About that time all hell broke loose, and we fought for hours. We were down to fourteen men out of a platoon of forty when the fighting stopped.

We had just gone into a building where we had an armored car. We were in the car looking for a flashlight, and we heard tracks coming down the road. The lieutenant said that it was probably that tank we passed that they were trying to fix. We kept looking and I kept listening. I told the lieutenant that the tracks were iron tracks and that our side had rubber tracks. He said, "Well, they must have captured a German tank and are taking it back to the rear." So I looked out, and I could see that the tank was all buttoned up. I thought that if it was Americans coming in they wouldn't be buttoned up like that. I told the lieutenant, and he said, "You're right. We better get out of here." We tried every exit in the building, but they all were covered. The Germans knew we were in there, so the lieutenant thought that the best thing we could do was surrender.

We stayed in the building all night, and early the next morning the Germans shot a few rounds into the building to let us know that they knew we were in there. One of our men could speak German, and he told them that we were ready to surrender. We took everything off that might be of informational value to the Germans, and one by one we walked out of the building with our hands up. It was November 24, 1944.

They loaded us on trucks and moved us out. There was about three truckloads of us. They took us back to a small town and put us in a schoolhouse. We stayed there the first night. The second day they marched us to a second town, which was about twelve miles from the first. They took us to another schoolhouse, which was being used as a headquarters by the Germans. They interrogated us there, and although they didn't bother me, some of the guys were beaten pretty badly. When they finished the interrogations, they took us to a small building where we stayed overnight.

The next day we went to another town, and that's where we got our first solid food. It was something like rice, but it had been made out of barley. It had no seasoning, but it sure tasted good. It was the first food we had been given in three days. We still didn't get any water.

The following day they took us into this railroad station and loaded us on "forty and eights." They crowded us in so much that all of us couldn't lay down. We had to take turns standing up and laying down. They gave us one can of meat, about the size of a pork-and-bean can, and two loaves of bread, which had to be divided between ten men. They left it up to us to divide the food. Once again we got no water.

We were on the train for three days and nights. There was no place to use the bathroom, and they never let us off the train; so we had to use our steel helmets and throw it out of the car the best we could.

Their railroad stations were busy moving supplies and equipment. They used us to stop a lot of the air attacks. They had POW written in big letters on top of the box cars, and they would stop our train in the middle of the yards a lot of times to stop the planes from attacking.

We finally reached Stalag XIIA. It was a transit camp where all the POWs captured in the area were registered. They took our steel helmets and anything else they thought they could use. Then they assigned us each to a barrack. The barrack didn't have any furniture in it. There was straw on the floor for us to sleep on. We each got two blankets. We could have used several more because it was really cold in December and there was no heat in the buildings.

We weren't forced to labor. The main activity was falling out on the hill twice a day for roll call. They didn't care about our names. We all had a number. My number was 079779. They knew how many heads they had, and that's what they were interested in. If there was one man missing, we stood out there until he was accounted for. Sometimes we stood for hours in the cold winter.

There was one barrack of men called A Company that did the work. It was this unit that cleaned the barracks and made things as comfortable as possible for the rest of the prisoners. I asked to be put in that group because they got an extra bowl of soup. I had heard of the Red Cross packages, but I had never seen one of them, and I was getting weak from so little food. We normally got a slice of bread in the morning with a cup of malt coffee. Potato soup for dinner. That was it, except on Saturday, when we got sauerkraut, and on Sunday, when we got potato soup with the jackets still on. They let me in the work party, and I was able to get some extra soup.

In late December I came down with a sore throat. They had a doctor there, and I went on sick call. The doctor had to report everything and was afraid that I had diphtheria so they placed me in an isolation ward. The build-

To protect the prisoners from Allied bombing raids, the letters "P.O.W." mark the roof of a barrack at Stalag XIIA near Limburg, Germany. (Courtesy of Mr. and Mrs. David Schneck.)

ing I was in was right next to a building where they kept the officers. The Germans said that there were eighty-two officers in the building.

On December 23 the R.A.F. flew over and targeted the rail station in Limburg. It was about three miles from our camp. They dropped flares first, before bombing. I was in the yard talking to an officer, and telling him what a pretty sight it was for Christmas. What we didn't know was that the wind was causing the flares to drift toward our camp. By the time bombers got there, the flares were over the camp and they bombed us. We ran in the building and got under a table. The bombs were getting so close that they were blowing the doors open. We would run and shut the door and then run back and get under the table again. A bomb hit our building, and the whole building caved in. I was under the table, and I looked up and could see some light. I guess you might say that was the light at the end of the tunnel. I was pinned in by the table legs. I was trying to get through a hole in the rubble, but my hips were too big. I strained and finally got out. I don't remember whether I got out frontwards or backwards, but I can remember crawling through the rubble. There were fourteen of us in the building, and we all got out alive.

One of the bombs hit the officers' building next to us, and they weren't so lucky. All of the officers in the building were killed. I don't know how many were in the building at the time of the bombing. There were different numbers, but from fifty to eighty men were killed.

I guess there is a little humor in everything that happens. The Germans had let us go back up to the compound to see if we could salvage any of the medical supplies. We had gotten another prisoner in our compound that day, and he had ear trouble. In the excitement the medics had forgotten all about him. When we got back up there to see if we could find any of the medical supplies here was this guy with his head sticking out of the rubble. He said, "Hey, you think this thing might catch on fire?" We got him out of the rubble and then salvaged what medical supplies we could.

Before the bombing incident happened when we would hear the planes going over we would run out in the yard, yelling and cheering them on. After the incident, when the bombers came over, I got a fear that I can't explain to this day. None of us left the buildings to cheer after that.

The Germans had promised us that we would get extra rations for Christmas, but after the bombing they told us that all the extra rations had been destroyed. Of course, after we were liberated we found out that they had been lying.

We started getting prisoners from the Battle of the Bulge. There were too many to handle. There were a lot of sick ones. Some were so bad that they couldn't stand for roll call, so they would have to sit up in bed for roll call. I had worked my way from the labor group to helping as a medic. I would get their food for them and help take care of them.

On Christmas Eve, I was with the prisoners that were the worst off. I was talking to one of the prisoners about Christmas and home, and someone suggested that we should sing some Christmas songs. We didn't know how it would work out because some of the guys were so bad, but we started, and as we sang, others joined in. Then someone suggested that we say the Lord's Prayer. Everyone joined in, and as we finished you could hear men all over the barrack continue to mumble their own prayers. It was really emotional.

After Christmas we just took it a day at a time. It was so cold, and the snow got waist deep. We had a lot of cases of frostbite. A lot of guys' feet would be completely black. When they bent their toes, the skin would just break open and you could see the bone.

Each day we prayed for nightfall to come so we could go to sleep and not think about the constant hunger pains. We had been deloused in the showers—which was a scare because we had heard about the Jews being gassed, but the delousing only worked temporarily because the lice were everywhere. Right before bed we would go to the windows, so we could get as much light as possible, and pick as many lice off of us as possible. Some of the guys had gotten so bad that you could see their clothing move.

The diarrhea had gotten so bad that the guards brought thirty-gallon buckets into the barrack at night for us to use, because they wouldn't let us go out of the barrack after dark. We tried to keep the place as clean as possible, but eventually the floor was caked with stool from the men tracking it. The odor became almost unbearable.

Anytime that something bad happened to the Germans, like the bombing raids, they would turn our water off and then tell us it was because of the raid. It was their way of getting to us.

Some of the guys never made it. We would clean them up and try to feed them, but they were often in too bad of a shape to make it. About eight weeks after the prisoners arrived from the Battle of the Bulge, we had to bury about thirty-five—of course, it was mass graves. The Germans would bulldoze a trench and mass-bury them. The Americans always got picked as the burying party. It was hard for me to feel sorry for myself because I was feeling so sorry for the dead. As I look at it now, it's like it was a movie I saw—not something that actually happened to me.

On March 25, our boys came by and bombed the railroads. The next day the Germans ordered everyone who could walk to leave the buildings. They were going to march us out of there the next day. There were two American medical officers who wanted to keep me there to help them with the prisoners who couldn't walk, so they hid me in a corner. When the Germans came through the second time to see if anyone was hiding, they spotted me; but the officers talked them into letting me stay. There were several other men who hid in a tunnel they had dug for an escape. The tunnel was covered, and the Germans didn't detect it. Altogether there were sixteen of us who stayed.

On March 26, they marched all the other prisoners out. That night the Germans gave us guns. They didn't turn their guns over to us, but they did turn the camp over. There were some White Russians in one barrack that got out and started destroying everything. They tore down the latrine and got into our garden and started destroying that. One American and one regular Russian soldier got them back in the barrack and guarded them so they couldn't do any more damage.

We found out later that all the prisoners who were marched out of the camp were being taken to a railroad station in Limburg to be shipped to another camp. About five miles out from camp, one of the American sergeants told a German officer that he knew the war was almost over. He asked the German officer why he didn't just give him his pistol and turn the prisoners over to him. It would be a lot better for him if he turned himself over to the Americans. The German officer looked at the sergeant and reached down and pulled his pistol out like he was going to give it up. Then he put it to his own temple and blew his brains out. Then they turned around and came back into the camp.

On March 27, we were liberated by an artillery unit. That's how fast the Americans were moving. Instead of us being liberated by a front unit, it was a rear unit that relieved us. We went down to the munitions compound and found a building full of Red Cross packages. Here we had been starving, and the Germans had been holding the packages back from us.

We got a supply of new underwear for the sick men. We had to delouse them and put them into new clothes. We got some Red Cross packages, which we should have been getting all the time, and started handing them out. I was one of the last to get clothes, and they were out of underwear tops. So I was running around in underwear bottoms and no top in the middle of March. I was happy though.

They started the evacuation process. They moved us to an airfield, and we got some good food and more new clothes. After a couple of days, they flew us out to England. I wanted to see the English Channel as we flew over, but I was too sick. I didn't get to see any of the country until we landed. It sure was a pretty sight.

I spent three weeks in a hospital, recuperating. I had lost forty-seven pounds, but I was able to stay on a regular diet. A lot of the guys were so bad they were given a special diet because their stomachs had shrunk so much.

After three weeks in the hospital they sent me to London to catch a ship home. I was there for a month, but I enjoyed myself. We had the run of the town, and the MPs were told to leave us alone unless there was something real drastic. I tried to behave myself, but it was a great feeling to be free.

On June 1, I caught a ship back to the States. It took us eleven days. I came home, and my wife and I were married on June 24. I spent sixty days at home, and then I went back to Miami, Florida.

Part of a group of 1200 American soldiers who escaped from Stalag XIIA shortly before the camp was liberated. (Courtesy of John M. Hancock.)

After my records were updated, I was sent to Fort Riley, where I worked as a technician until I was discharged in March 1945.

For years after the war, people would ask me about my experiences. I have always told them I wouldn't take a million dollars for the experience that I had in the prison camp, but I wouldn't go through it again for ten million dollars.

Part III

THE BATTLE OF THE BULGE

LOW IS THE SUN

Days have their worries,
Nights have their flurries;
But in between time it's dull.
I hate to dream alone,
Evening brings such a lull; for—
Low is the sun as slowly it leaves the sky;
Low is the sun as night draws nigh,
So is my heart whenever the day is through,
Once a day every day, evening brings thoughts of you.
Each long shadow whispers you are lonely too,
But my heart keeps saying, Don't go back, you're through.
So, in the dusk when I sit alone just for fun,
It's to think of you only, lonely, when low is the sun.

—From a Kriegie's diary

Corporal Walter B. Young, Jr.

U.S. Army
110th Infantry Regiment
Captured During the Battle of the Bulge
Prisoner of War
December 16, 1944–May 7, 1945
Stalag IVB

On December 7, 1941, Walter was home from school over the week-end. The radio was on, and the program was interrupted with the news that the Japanese had bombed Pearl Harbor.

When Walter returned to his fraternity house, all the guys were talking about what program they could enter in order to serve the country and continue their education. Walter told them, "I am overweight and flat-footed; they won't take me! I won't get into those programs. I'll be standing on the porch waving good-bye to you guys."

On March 17, 1943, Walter was inducted—one of the first among his classmates. When he left they stood on the porch and waved good-bye to him.

Walter was assigned to the 78th Lightning Infantry Division. He stayed with them until May 1944 and then was reassigned to a replacement company. After thirteen days of zigzagging maneuvers in the Atlantic Ocean to avoid U-boats, his unit arrived in England.

I went first to England and stayed there until June 13, 1944, when I landed in an L.S.T. on Omaha Beach. This was seven days after the WACS had landed, so I felt pretty secure. On the first night, soldiers were digging foxholes. "The front is too far away; I'm not digging a foxhole," I declared. So I slept on the beach the first night, through a couple of air raids. I wish I had dug a foxhole!

After the Allies pushed through St. Lô (inland from the Omaha beach-head), I was assigned to the 28th Division, 308th Regiment, anti-tank company. One day I was in the hedgerows, which were large hills with brambles to keep in the livestock. I was getting acquainted and mentioned that I was from Southern Illinois. A fellow popped up his head from the other side of the hedgerow.

"Who's from Southern Illinois?" he asked. It was Tom Land of Carmi, who was a jeep driver for an intelligence officer.

His officer censored Tom's letter to home about our meeting. But my letter got through, and the story of the two hometown boys meeting in France over a hedgerow made the newspaper.

After the war, I would visit the Land home. Mr. Land would always ask me to tell him about how Tom and I met in France. "Well, I can't understand why Tom never wrote us about that!" he would say.

We did not get into battle until after the liberation of Paris. Our division was rested and clean, so we were placed in the liberation parade. We were eight trucks abreast, going down the Champs Élysées. At the Obelisk, half went to the right and half went to the left.

The French were so happy to see us that they brought flowers, champagne, and Benedictine. After we passed the reviewing stand at the Obelisk, where de Gaulle and Eisenhower and the big brass were, we opened the champagne and benedictine and passed it around until it was gone. In a little while, we had three fights on the truck between guys who didn't think they were getting their fair share.

We went on north from there, near Aachen. On September 14, 1944, we passed into Germany through the Maginot Line. There were roads through the pilings of concrete that the French had built to keep tanks from getting through.

Come to find out, we were too far ahead of our line, so we had to back out in order to let our right and left flanks catch up. We had not yet met with opposition.

In November 1944, we were in Hurtgen Forest for twenty-one days. Being in the anti-tank outfit, we were behind the lines. We had no warm food, very little water, and no baths. We were in a holding position—the Germans across the line were holding us down in foxholes. We kept guard and took patrol duties.

Just after Thanksgiving we got our first baths. Furloughs were issued. We were on a 30-mile front in Luxembourg and ordered to hold there. We believed that Intelligence was correct that there were no enemy in the area.

On December 5, I received a three-day pass into Luxembourg city. (I was due for my pass to Paris in late December.) It was a free city. We stopped into a hotel and ate in the hotel dining room. We were always aware of the war, but it seemed a long way off. At this time they were celebrating "Father Christmas" in Luxembourg, as is their custom in early December.

There was a Catholic church in the little town in Luxembourg where we were based. Our platoon leader was Sergeant Grimoldi, and he went to confession two or three times a week. He wanted us to go to church with him. In the church, the men sat on the right and the women on the left. The kids sat up front and the older folks in back. We all sat in the back on the men's side without our weapons. I sat next to an older man who kept looking at me because he could not understand why I (a Protestant) was not kneeling and genuflecting.

On the morning of December 16, 1944, we were awakened by artillery shelling. We had taken over a little corner cafe on the town square as our headquarters. We had out three 57 mm tank guns in place. One gun was facing the wrong direction. One was being repaired. Only one gun could fire at the Germans as they came at us, wave after wave in their snow-white camouflage uniforms.

While we were out with the gun, the sergeant was at the cafe. I had received packages from home. One of the prize things I had was a can of sliced pineapple that my aunt in Evansville, Indiana, had sent. The sergeant decided

Corporal Walter B. Young, Jr. (Courtesy of Walter B. Young, Jr.)

that we were all going to be killed, so he and his corporal ate my pineapple.

The town in which we were stationed lay in a bowl and was surrounded by hills. When the Germans descended, they all carried automatic weapons. One man from our squad picked up a Browning automatic rifle and ran down the road to mow down Germans. They got him right there.

The fighting and the shelling continued until about dark. The word came to us to surrender because we were surrounded. The Germans had gotten behind us. Major General Cota only escaped by flying out his Piper Cub plane.

I suppose that was the most traumatic time of the whole experience. We destroyed our guns. We had a new colonel who had been recently shipped over from the Pentagon. He was really "G.I." Everything had to be according to the book, with every man outfitted with his correct weapon. In our squad (there were three per company) there were three rifles and six or eight carbines; the rest of us (including me) had one .45 pistol each. Several of us had picked up dropped guns from battles. I had a .45 caliber "burp" machine gun and an extra clip, which I had in my hip pocket. In the excitement of the capture, I forgot to pitch the clip of ammunition.

After we surrendered, the Germans gathered us all in the town square. We stood there with our hands behind our heads, wondering what would happen next.

That's when they pulled me over to one side by myself and began talking to me, in German naturally. They finally made me understand that they were looking for the gun that matched the clip they had found on me.

I didn't know much German, but I knew enough to tell them it was "Kaput"—gone. When they first took me aside, I thought that they were going to make an example of me and that I was long gone.

That first night of capture, they put us in a barn, the only building in town with a lock on the outside. We lined up in the only space available—behind the dairy cattle. You talk about being knee-deep. There was only about three feet behind those cows; we spent the whole night sitting on our steel helmets.

The next morning we were taken to an interrogation bunker. They called us in one by one. Now, I had missed the instruction session on what to do if captured; I had been assigned to K.P. duty. So I told them that before the war I was a student in Carbondale, Illinois. They knew that Carbondale was a rail center and had a small college.

On December 24, 1944, we were in a warehouse, and we were given Red Cross packages. The Germans had nothing to feed us. Each package was for ten people and contained raw rice. There was nowhere to prepare it. Some guys ate the rice raw. They did feed us a little soup of potatoes, cabbages, or rutabagas, stuff. I didn't know what would happen. I just decided to bear with it and go along.

We were marched from place to place during the night, and we would be kept in warehouses or other cover during the day. Two or three times American warplanes strafed us during our night marches; they could see columns along the roads. We were afraid of being hit by friendly fire, so we'd jump in the ditches, which froze during the nights and were wet and muddy during the day.

That Christmas Eve night the road along which we were marched was bombed and strafed.

Christmas was just another day. We realized what day it was, but there wasn't much for us to celebrate and no way to do it. We did spend a lot of time fantasizing about all the food we were missing. One fellow mentioned that his grandmother made the best baked eggs he had ever eaten. I'd never heard of baked eggs.

After the first of the year, we were put in boxcars with straw floors. It was terrible. People were sick. The Germans would let us stop once in a while, but not enough.

We were taken to a big camp, Stalag IVB, where our clothes were painted with red triangles. They did give us baths, but they took all of our clothes and put them in a gas chamber to kill any of the lice we might have brought into the camp from the boxcars.

We were put into a big shower area with no towels. We went out from there and sat on marble slabs and were given overcoats and the clothes that had been decontaminated.

In our barracks we slept on the floor. We were so close there was no room to turn over. In the back, a soldier was cold and put his overcoat over his entire body, covering his head. The gas from the decontamination killed him during the night.

Two or three soldiers' feet turned black when the shower water hit their frostbite. Some had their feet amputated.

After being in this camp for three days, we were assigned work details and trucked into the town of Freiburg, Germany, where we worked in a factory. Our work was to grind up old uniforms and clothes, which were then made into felt-like material. The material was baled and then rewoven into cloth for recycled clothes.

We started out working around the clock, in shifts. Later we were all taken to work at day, and there was no night work after that.

In the factory there was a stove where we might cook a little hamburger once a week to accompany our soup staple.

An Italian, Charlie, was captured at the same time I was. He was barely five feet tall, and he was thirty-five years old. He looked after me and shared his cigarettes, which he had gotten by selling the ruby-stoned ring his wife had given him. After the war, Charlie came to visit me. He went outside on the pretense of locking his car and called me to follow him. He told me not to tell his wife that he had sold his ring for cigarettes. He had told her that the Germans had taken it. I learned a little Italian from Charlie, but was reluctant to use it, not being sure it was acceptable in mixed company.

We had a seventy-year-old German first lieutenant in charge of marching us back and forth to work. Sometimes in town the Germans would jeer at us. Our German lieutenant's sergeant was between forty and fifty years old and had one eye. We called him "One Eye." He knew a little English so we didn't call him "One Eye" to his face.

One Sunday we had the afternoon off. We went to the country, to a town with a cafe. They had paid us enough to buy German beer, which was dark and hot, tasting more like sour root beer.

In the factory where I worked, there was a twenty-five- or thirty-year-old Russian woman who had been there for some time. We shared a machine together. One day, she motioned for me to go with her to the common toilet. Behind the screen she pulled up her skirt. I didn't know what was going on. Then, she pulled out a sandwich of dark bread and butter and gave it to me.

The Russians had been there for some time. This was at the end of the war, and the Russians were better at managing their food. The Russian woman was friendly, and we got along well. We were fond of each other.

But by this time, the Germans were so afraid of the Russians (for they had treated them so badly) that they took them away. When they took the Russians away, my friend didn't come back to work. I don't know what happened to her.

I heard through a soldier who had been on sick leave as a POW that the Americans were within twenty miles of where we were. But they had to stop and wait for the Russian Army to catch up from the other side because of the military agreement. On May 7, 1945, the Germans turned us loose. The old lieutenant stayed behind, but "One Eye" led us part of the way to the American lines.

We walked all day long and finally got to our lines. I was sitting on a curb and resting. "Beetsie" Tuck of Carmi walked by. I hollered, "Hello, Beetsie!" He just kept going on, and we didn't see each other again until we were together at Camp Lucky Strike in France.

The Red Cross was at the camp, serving nonalcoholic eggnog. We first went to breakfast and then took our canteen cups to the large tent and lined up for eggnog. After we had our cup filled, we went back to the end of the line to do it again. This went on until lunch and all through the afternoon until supper.

With my first money I bought a whole box of Hershey chocolate bars and ate all of them. When I was captured I weighed 210 pounds. I don't know what I weighed when I was released, but when I got home I weighed 150 pounds. When I got off the Big 4 train in Carmi at the end of May, they said, "There he is!" But my mother said, "No, that's not him."

That summer of '45 they sent us as close to home as possible to serve out until our discharge. I went to Fort Sam Houston, Texas, to be reassigned. They sent me to Camp Adair, Oregon. It was close to Portland.

I was finally discharged on November 5, 1945, at Camp Beale, California. In Sacramento, a lady who had worked with me in the A.P.O. said that she could get me an air ticket home. She had worked for the airlines, and her husband was in service. I told her I wanted to take the train back home with my buddies.

Well, the fleet had just arrived from the South Pacific. So when I got on the train, there were no seats. I had to stand up all the way to Omaha, sleeping in the vestibule between train cars.

I left Chicago at 10 P.M. one night and arrived at 7 A.M. the next morning on the Big 4, home for the second time. That December, I reentered school, at "that rail center where there is a small college."

Private Walter F. Gurley

U.S. Army
Company H, 110th Regiment, 28th Infantry
Captured During the Battle of the Bulge
Prisoner of War
December 19, 1944–April 17, 1945
Camp Leipzig

Walter was working in a parking garage in Chicago, Illinois, when he received his draft notice. He quit his job and reported for duty. After the physical exam was complete, Walter was sent to the marine recruiter and asked which branch of service he wanted: army, navy, or marines. Walter chose the army. The recruiter stamped "marines" on his papers and sent him to a navy man. He asked Walter what branch he wanted, and Walter said, "The army." The navy man stamped out "marines" and put "navy." Walter figures that he was lucky to get the army recruiter last, because that recruiter stamped out "navy" and put "army," which is what he had wanted all along.

Walter was trained as a mortar gunner and then shipped to Europe. He arrived in Liverpool, England, in June 1944.

We were sent to the front, which in August was in France. That's when I saw my first combat. We all lost several friends, and several were wounded. One friend of mine was killed only thirty-five or forty minutes after we went into our first combat. He was the same age as me, a fine guy, and always good for a laugh. Whatever he told, he could make it funny.

Several months after we went into combat, myself and another guy were assigned to an outpost. We were both as green as grass about communications. Neither one of us was trained in communications. We were at a cross-road outside of the town of Bastogne, France. We were dug in, and we could hear the Germans. We went back to the company to get away, and the company commander told us if we didn't get back up to the outpost we were going to be court-martialed. So we went back to the outpost.

It was December 19, 1944, when we were overrun by the Germans. We got down in a hole and covered ourselves up with blankets, grass, and leaves to camouflage ourselves. We were doing fine until a German medic came walking around, looking for souvenirs. He stepped down into the hole where we were hiding and stepped right on my shinbone. I flinched, and he started yelling, "Hands up! Hands up!" We came out hands-up since everything around us was Germans. They shook us down and then walked us down this road for about two miles. This jeep came along with a spare tire hanging on the back like a Lincoln Continental. I sat on the tire, and the other guy sat

Private Walter F. Gurley. (Courtesy of Walter F. Gurley.)

on the bumper and clung to me. Unsheltered, in freezing weather, they hauled us to a collection point.

At the collection point, I saw many men from my division that had been captured. The Germans were taking us one at a time into this dairy barn to interrogate us. They used one crib as an office and tried to get information from us about our division—where we were coming from and how many men we had—but we weren't suppose to give out anything other than our name, rank, and serial number. They tried to put the pressure on when the men wouldn't tell them anything by placing them against a wall and threatening to shoot them if they didn't give the information. Some men were beaten, too.

When I went before this German interrogator, he wanted to know my name, rank, serial number, and what division I was in. I told him everything but the division. I told him I didn't know what division I was in because I was a new recruit who had come in as a replacement. I didn't know anything about the unit. He asked me what my A.P.O. [American Post Office] number was, and I told him I didn't know. He said, "Well, you will know." I said, "I'm just a new recruit, and I've told you all I know." He let me go after that. I guess he believed me. The next guy was a sergeant, and they liked to beat him to death.

A couple of days passed, and they moved us out. We marched 125 miles in the freezing weather with no food. They strung about three hundred of us out down this road when we started the march. There was snow on the ground—and it was a good thing too, because snowballs is what we ate for the entire 125 miles. We were at the mercy of the maker. There were about twelve men who just couldn't walk any further. They would collapse, and the Germans would come up behind them and shoot them. They weren't taken to any hospitals.

We finally reached this small town, and after an overnight stay we were loaded into railroad cars for transportation to a prison camp. These cars were called "forty and eights," meaning they could each hold forty men and eight horses. However, the Germans crowded seventy-two of us into these cars. We huddled in the cars for four days and five nights with no food, no water, and no bathroom facility. There was one small window in the car, and it was covered with barbed wire.

On January 4, 1945, after passing through Berlin, we arrived at a camp of sorts, in a rural area near Brandenburg, Germany. That's when we got our first food in captivity. It was soup. It was green and looked like old green scum off of a pond. We use to call it "grass soup without the grass." It looked bad, but it was warm, and we had been so cold. That was the first meal we had had since December 19, and that soup tasted great to me.

After about three days they separated me and the guy I was captured with. I never saw him again.

In another few days I ended up on a work detail in Leipzig. I worked in a sawmill, where green pine was milled into lumber. We built walls and floors from the wood and then bolted them together to form refugee barracks for German citizens.

When I first started working, one day I was working in one of the lines of the factory smoking a cigarette. This superintendent of the factory had this big leather club, and he hit me upside the head with it. It almost knocked me cold.

He started to hit a Russian that was working there, and when he drew back that Russian motioned for him to come on. He didn't care whether they killed him or not. I was just trying to get by and live. The injury to my jaw left a big lump. I carried it for years, and finally had to have it worked on in 1988.

I worked in the mill until it burned down in an air raid. After that, I moved to construction, scraping old mortar off of bricks to rebuild the multistory Central Theater of Leipzig. We worked day after day until the theater was finished. The day after it was finished, we were supposed to clean the theater and then we were told that we would be able to watch a movie. But the movie was never shown. The night we finished it, to the delight of all us prisoners, the theater was leveled by Allied bombs.

During all this time, we refused to take shelter during bombing raids unless the guards forced us into air raid shelters. I can remember standing in a rain of glass from shattered windows, refusing to go in during a raid. We told them that we were not afraid of Allied bombs.

The Germans themselves were deadly. Prisoners were taken out, lined up, and shot by firing squads. We could hear the shots, but we did not know what was going on.

I was taken out to be shot, but right after they lined us up a passing officer ordered the German soldiers to stop. "The Allied forces have more prisoners than we do," he said, "and we need every prisoner to keep for possible exchange."

I only faced that squad once, but I know of prisoners that were taken out more than once, called back in, and taken out again.

Throughout our imprisonment we were poorly fed. I ate everything I could get my hands on, but I still lost fifty-five pounds in 119 days. A small, hard loaf of heavy, dark bread, about twelve inches long and six inches wide, had to feed twelve of us. In the morning we would get one cup of what they called coffee. At noon, we received a tin can of soup. Sometimes, the soup was as green as grass from the dehydrated spinach or other greens cooked in it. Once a week we got cole slaw for a meal. It was a welcome change. On Sunday and on German holidays we received a pretty good soup, although it had very little meat in it. The Germans were near the end of their resources by then and they nearly starved us.

There was one guard we had who had a restaurant in New York. He had gone to Germany from the United States to visit his family, and they put him in the German army. His wife and two children were still in New York. If it hadn't been for him, there would have been a lot of us guys who wouldn't have made it. He would do anything he could for us. He stole food and supplies for us; he let us get by with things that nobody else would. If he had ever been caught, they would have killed him. But, as luck would have it, he never got caught.

Health care in the prison was nonexistent. I went without a bath for four months. We all had lice. Once, right after I was captured, there was a bunch of us lined up in front of a large, barnlike building to be deloused. Our clothing was placed on hangers and sent through the building, where chemicals were supposed to kill the lice. I was overcome by fumes and passed out. The Germans thought I was dead and tossed me into the snow. Later someone saw me move, and I was recovered.

There was no clothing allowance in the prison. As the toes of my knee-length socks wore out, I pulled the socks farther over my toes, folding the ends underneath my foot. By the time I was released, those kneesocks were down to anklets.

We were moved deeper into Germany to provide labor when the front line moved closer to our camp. Based on a radio report heard by a British prisoner, we decided to go on strike at one point and refused to march farther. But German machine guns changed our minds, and we marched on.

On April 17, 1945, American forces overran the camp and freed us. I was selected to help shake down the guards and take their guns away. It was one of the best days of my life. The guards that had been bad to us never said a word as we shook them down. Except for one doctor. He told me that he was a doctor, and his people needed him at home to help them. I told him that I didn't know him, and I told him that my people had needed me at home for a long time, too. I told the German guard who had stolen food for us that I was his friend and that I was going to do everything I could to help him. We all let our commanding officer know about his situation and how he had helped us.

All of us had food on our minds. But the doctors had warned us not to overeat because our systems would not handle it. There were coffee and doughnuts available all the time. The doc told us to get a doughnut and break it in half. Eat half of it and throw the other half away. One prisoner didn't listen. He ate several doughnuts and later died from it.

A couple of days after we were liberated we were trucked to an area that had been set up for us to get hospital care. We got a bath, a haircut, and a shave. That first shave I got, I was afraid of. It was by a German woman, and she was using a straight razor. I wasn't sure about it, but it all came out okay.

Then they started putting us on rosters of twenty-five men each. Each day C-47s would come in, and a roster of men would be flown to Camp Lucky Strike. When my group got flown out, we hit a storm and landed in Paris. We had to take a train from there, but we finally made it. Once we were there everybody wanted to see everybody else. I was going through these tents and found my lieutenant. We were sitting on the floor of the tent talking, when one of the other officers came up and said, "Don't you know it is against regulations for that enlisted man to be in here?" My lieutenant told the officer he didn't give a damn about regulations—we had something to talk about. That's all that was said.

At the separation center I helped make preparations for discharging servicemen, until I was finally discharged myself on November 26, 1945.

When I got home I had a little more press coverage than some of the other guys. I managed to nab the $100 war bond offered by the local newspaper for being the first prisoner of war to return home. I barely made it, because another prisoner of war came in just two hours after I did. We both laughed about it, and the other guy always said that I owed him half of the bond.

In June 1945 the local newspaper reported: "Just released from a Nazi Prison Camp, Pvt. Walter F. Gurley has been taken prisoner again. But he doesn't seem to mind his latest capture. This encirclement is not barbed wire, but a wedding ring."*

---

* Walter married Verna Fick on June 7, 1945. They were presented with the $100 war bond the next day.

Sergeant John P. Wilson

U.S Army
121st Squadron, 106th Cavalry
Captured During the Battle of the Bulge
Prisoner of War
January 1, 1945–April 29, 1945
Stalag VIIA

John was inducted on January 13, 1942, and sent to Fort Riley, Kansas, to take his basic training. After that, he was stationed at Camp Livingston in Louisiana for about a year. He then was sent to Fort Hood, Texas for further combat training.

In February 1944, his unit was given orders for overseas. The ships were originally bound for England. But during the trip, John's ship was constantly followed by German U-boats, and the ships had to take a route in the North Sea to dodge them. They finally landed at Glasgow, Scotland, in early March 1944.

We were sent to a little place called Dobbington Park, and we were there until the first part of June. At that time they moved us to Mount Hampton. We didn't go over on D-Day, but a few days after the landing we went over to France and did reconnaissance for General Patton. We were strictly a recon outfit, and when they made the breakthrough they sent us out way ahead of the regular units.

We had this major, and he was crazy. He decided that we were going to be the first unit in Paris. We started toward Paris and got to Versailles and ran into a bunch of Tiger tanks, and we didn't have any way to stop them. The major was killed by a booby trap. We never did get to Paris, and it took four days to get some other units up to us for some support.

Then they moved our unit across France to the Belfort Gap on the Swiss border. We stayed there until Christmas Day 1944. On Christmas they moved us to the border of Germany. They put us on an outpost by the Saar River. We were across the river from the other units. We had relieved a ranger outfit that had dug foxholes and covered them over. We normally used radios for communications, but they had a telephone system set up, and we decided to use it.

One night we were sitting there, it was about ten below zero and the sky was clear with a full moon. The Germans were just about a half-mile from us. There wasn't much going on. The Germans were dug in, and we would try to call artillery in, but we couldn't get to them. This went on like that for several days.

Then, on New Year's Eve, we could see some activity. We were the furthest outpost. It was an old coal mine. It was a pit dug down below the ground level and a tunnel that run under the hill where the mine was located. Our C.P. [Command Post] was in the pit, and we had our outpost set on the banks around the pit. We had a couple of artillery shells hit US at about 1800 hours [6 P.M.], and we were told by the C.P. to keep on the alert. It was pretty quiet until just before midnight, when all hell broke loose. The Germans started dropping artillery in on us.

After about an hour of constant artillery bombardment, the Germans made a ground attack. They were so close to us that we had to call in artillery on our own position. That cut our telephone lines so we didn't have any communications. The Germans were coming in on us and the men on my post were forced down into the C.P., where the lieutenant was at. I told him that we needed to get out before we were all killed, so we started crawling up this

Sergeant John P. Wilson (right) with an Army buddy. (Courtesy of John P. Wilson.)

2 ND J 42   GOVT

WASHINGTON DC   624P JAN 16

MRS PEARL WILSON

RR 1 BOGOTA ILL

THE SECRETARY OF WAR DESIRES ME TO EXPRESS HIS DEEP REGRET

THAT YOUR SON SERGEANT JOHN P WILSON HAS BEEN REPORTED MISSING

IN ACTION SINCE ONE JANUARY IN GERMANY IF FURTHER DETAILS OR

OTHER INFORMATION ARE RECEIVED YOU WILL BE PROMPTLY NOTIFIED

DUNLOP ACTING THE ADJUTANT GENERAL

823AM

Telegram to the mother of John P. Wilson.

bank. Just as we got over the bank, we ran right into a German machine-gun nest.

They were only about thirty feet from us, and they opened up. I had five bullet holes in my clothes, but I was only hit once, in the groin. They took all of us prisoner.

They started taking us back to their lines, and the other boys were trying to carry me. It hurt so bad that I couldn't stand it. I stood and walked for about a mile, until we got to a six-by-six truck. They took us back to an interrogating station. They separated all of us and started interrogating us. I was there by myself because I was wounded. The German who was trying to get information from me told me that I needed to go to the hospital and that he would take me if I would tell them what they wanted to know. I told him that according to the Geneva Convention I had a right to go to the hospital. He stood there looking at me silently for a minute or two, and then he called an ambulance to take me to a hospital.

I laid there for several hours before the ambulance got there, but when it did they loaded me in the ambulance along with several wounded German soldiers. The ambulance had racks in it, and they slid us in like you would slide a pan in an oven.

It was the next evening when I finally arrived at the hospital. The doctor came in and started working on my wound. He couldn't find the bullet.

He was poking and poking and I was really getting sore. He told me that he would just leave it if I wanted, because he couldn't find it. I told him to leave it.

They took me to a ward. There were a bunch of wounded German soldiers in the ward. I was the only American. There was a German soldier in the bed next to me, and he could speak English. He asked me where I had come from, and I told him. He said that he was one of the guys I was fighting. He said that he had gone through the entire war without getting wounded, and during this fight he fell down an embankment and broke his leg. He never had a bit of bitterness toward me.

A while later this nurse came in and bumped my knee. It sounded like she said "aput," but it was in German so I couldn't understand. She said it two or three times, and I thought, "Well, what does she want?" Finally this German soldier told me that she wanted to know if my bowels had moved. I told her yes. A few days later they brought some more Americans in, and she asked me how to ask them if their bowels had moved. I couldn't think of anything, so I just said, "Shit." So she would go around to them and just say, "Shit?" It was funny, because at first the Americans didn't know what she was doing, so they would get mad and she would get mad, but it finally worked out.

They brought a bunch of Russian soldiers into the hospital, and one of the nurses noticed that there was a louse crawling on my sheets. She said that the Russians had lice and that they were going to move me. They did, into a private room.

This one nurse came into the room one day, and she had her four-year-old daughter with her. I had gotten a chocolate bar and tried to give it to her, but she wouldn't take it because she was afraid of me. Her mother told her it was all right to take it, and she did. After that the nurse would come and see me often.

They treated me real good there, just like I was one of them. The doctor would come in every day and check on us. He could speak English real well. He got off every night about six, and he would come in there when he got off and talk to me every night until about 11 P.M. He said, "I don't know why the Americans don't come on. They have already won the war." He said that he wanted to brush up on his English a little bit before they came. He asked me if I had gotten a letter home to my folks, and I told him I hadn't. He told me to write a letter to them, and he would see that they got it. It was in March when they got it, but it was the only letter they ever got from me.

The hospital was really short of medicine. One of the Germans soldiers had to have his leg taken off, and they did it with no antiseptic. They had a box that looked like a carpenter's miter box. They would put the leg or arm in there and cut it off.

I was at the hospital for eighteen days, and then they moved me over to a railroad center near the Saar River. They loaded us on trains and moved us to Fellbach, Germany. While we were waiting for another train, this German soldier told us that we couldn't wait there, that we were going to have to get out of there. The Americans had bombed Fellbach the night before, and the Germans were really upset.

We started out on foot. It was really foggy, and we got about six or seven miles down the road to where the train was located. By now the fog had cleared, and our planes came in and blew that train to bits. If we had been on it, we wouldn't be here.

We finally caught another train and got to the hospital in Freising. There were two American doctors in the hospital, but they were worse than any German I ever saw. They wouldn't take care of the patients. We didn't want to do what the Germans wanted, but they would do anything for the Germans to get favors.

We didn't get much food at all. They would bring in a coffee in the morning. It didn't have much of a taste; it tasted like it was made out of some grain. It would be cold by the time you got it. They would give us small portions of boiled potato with it if we were lucky. At noon we would get a slice of bread. Then in the evening, if we got anything we were lucky.

When we moved out of there, they started us out on foot. There was this wagon that was loaded with German equipment, and I never could figure out what this equipment was for, but we had to pull it. There were some Russian soldiers, and they wouldn't do anything with it. On the second day out, we found this old mare, and we rigged her up to the wagon. We pulled and pushed with the mare as we moved along the road. We moved at night so we would not be strafed during the day by our own planes.

A few times we ran across SS troops, and we would have to hide from them. The German guard told us that if they spotted us they would kill us. As a matter of fact, the guard was scared to death of them. He said they were crazy.

We also ran across some of Hitler's kids. They were just as bad. They were young kids, and all of them had guns. They would stand and just shoot their guns in all directions without regard for the safety of anyone. Not even their own people.

This German guard we had was good to us, but he was a little off, too. He would lay down when we were resting and shoot his rifle straight up in the air, and just lay there to see if the bullet would come back down.

One day when we stopped to rest, some German soldiers came up on us. They had a horse, and the officer that had been riding it, was walking at the time. They stopped to rest, and our guard tried to steal the officer's horse. It was funny because this officer jumped on another horse and chased him. He finally caught him, but you never saw such a horse race in your life.

They had given us a loaf of bread and a one-pound can of meat when we left the hospital. We opened the can, and it was lard instead of meat. We pulled that wagon twenty-five miles a day for ten days on one loaf of bread and a can of lard.

Along about the tenth day, we came to a farm and ran across an old cow that had been killed in the bombing. We found an iron kettle in the barn, and we built a fire. We cut a hindquarter off of it, threw it in the kettle, and cooked it all day. It smelled pretty good.

About the time that we had it cooked, the guard moved us out, so we threw the meat on the back of the wagon. We would walk along, and grab a handful of the meat, and eat it. Well, the meat was spoiled, and we got dysentery. We were right by a British prisoner of war hospital, and they took us in.

They treated us pretty good. The day after we got there American planes came over and dipped their wings for identification. The hospital wasn't marked as a hospital. We told the Germans that they had better get out there and mark the hospital because the planes would come back and strafe us. "No.

Representative John M. Voyrs (R-Ohio), a member of a congressional committee that had been studying evidence of German atrocities in concentration camps, stands up in his jeep to talk to a group of liberated American prisoners from Stalag VIIA near Moosburg, Germany. U.S. Army Signal Corps photo by Tec/4 Merge (first name not recorded). (Courtesy of the National Archives.)

No. They wouldn't do that." Just a few minutes later, some P-51s came over and strafed. They killed all the German guards in the towers and a whole squad of British prisoners that were lined up in a column for a work detail. I was in bed, and the guy in the bed next to me was killed by a bullet. When the raid was over, the Germans was really moving with buckets of red paint to get crosses painted on the buildings.

The day after the raid, the Germans moved us out to Stalag VIIA. They had more POWs than they had room for. They had some Red Cross packages that they handed out to us. That was when I got my wound to heal. The packages had sulfur power in it, and I put some of that in the wound to heal it. Before that it wouldn't heal, it would just drain constantly. The Germans had not had the medicine to heal the wound.

The conditions were bad. It was overcrowded, full of lice, and there were a lot of sick prisoners. The beds were like a box with straw in them. The straw was lousy.

All we got to eat was a piece of old, green, molded bread and a small boiled potato. I did get about a third of a Red Cross package once, but we got so little food that I lost sixty pounds.

The toilet facilities was the worst, though. The bathroom had toilet stools setting over a pit that was probably twenty feet by twenty feet. Everything just flushed down into the pit. Most of the guys had dysentery, and it was impossible to keep the stools cleaned.

They only had one water faucet for about five hundred men. We often stood in line a half a day, just waiting to use the water—that is, when they hadn't turned the water off.

Every day they had a burial detail to bury the dead prisoners. Most died from disease, but a few died from starvation.

The Nazi guards made us stand in the snow without shoes for four hours because we refused to salute the officers. Prisoners were sick from the treatment, but we didn't give in.

One of the things that kept us going was the radio news about the war. Some of the guys had made a radio, and we were getting the news about the war. Someone would stand guard while we listened; we knew we were going to win. It was something to look forward to. I was lucky that I was only there for about four months.

Then on April 29, 1945, the 14th Armored Division liberated us. They took us to an airport at Eichstatt shortly after the war ended in May. While we were waiting to load on the plane, a Nazi fighter plane came over. We thought he was going to attack. I crawled under a gasoline truck, which is the worst place I could have gotten. One of our antiaircraft guns opened up on him, and he threw a white sheet out of the plane and landed. He surrendered.

They flew us to France. The first thing I wanted was a Coke and a candy bar. You would think that a man who was starved would want something else, but that's what I wanted. This one officer told some troops that when they called for chow they had better get out of the way because the POWs would run over them. They were right. We were starved to death.

We had to be careful about what we ate, though. They gave us bland food for a while until our systems got used to the food.

We were all lousy, and they sprayed us with a special spray to kill the lice. Then they gave us showers, and that was the end of the lice.

On May 11, I was sent to England. I borrowed some money from the Red Cross and took a tour of London. I went all over for three dollars. We were there for a few days and then caught a ship home.

I landed in New York on June 21. Four days later I got home. I sure was glad to be home. I can say that I was one of the lucky ones as far as treatment as a POW. I wouldn't trade my experience—but make no mistake, I wouldn't want to go through it again for anything.

Part IV

BOMBING RAIDS OVER GERMANY

THE GREATEST DEBATES
IN BULL SESSIONS

Resolved: that
  I. We could have stayed out of the war and still survived (*con*)
  II. Russia was prepared for the war (*pro*)
  III. Russia will attack Japan (*con*)
  IV. An aircrew member should marry regardless of the definite prospect of being shipped overseas in a very few months (*pro; later, con*)
  V. In the game of billiards, English can be imparted to the object ball (*pro*)
  VI. B-17s are better than B-24s (*pro*)
  VII. The two end legs of a pool table will leave the floor first when a sufficient upward force is applied to an exact corner (*pro*)
  VIII. In a "no limit" poker game, a skillful player with an average run of cards will win over a less skillful but very lucky player over a considerable length of time (*con*)
  IX. You can give your own car a better grease job than a skilled mechanic (*con*)
  X. Any kind of a standard college education is a good thing for a girl (*pro*)
  XI. Over 70 percent of the females of marriageable age are virgins (*pro*)
  XII. Mr. Churchill was right in harping on unconditional surrender in the early part of the war (*con*)
  XIII. The war will be over by Christmas 1944 (*pro*)
  XIV. A prune is a dried plum and not a dried prune (*con*)

—From a Kriegie's diary

Technical Sergeant
Gordon K. Butts

U.S. Army Air Forces
451st Bomb Group (H), 725th Bomb Squadron, 15th Air Force
Shot Down Over Mostar, Yugoslavia, During an Air Raid
Prisoner of War
April 17, 1944–May 7, 1945
Stalag Luft III; Stalag VIIA, and Stalag XIIID

Gordon Butts enlisted in the U.S. Army at South Bend, Indiana, on October 29, 1940. He was sent to Fort Benjamin Harrison in Indianapolis for his basic training. After his arrival by bus, he received his first army meal: a bologna sandwich and a glass of milk.

From Fort Benjamin Harrison, he was sent to Maxwell Field in Montgomery, Alabama, where he was introduced to what would become commonplace: six-man G.I. tents constructed with wooden floors and frames. He was also introduced to southern-style cooking. One morning at the mess hall, he covered his "cream of wheat" with sugar and milk, only to discover it was grits.

Gordon was sent to a couple of bases in the south before embarking on a troopship for several ports in Central America, debarking at Rio Hata, Panama, to build a technical school to train aircraft mechanics, and at Albrook Field as a clerk in the inspection division.

In October 1942, Gordon heard about an air cadet examination that was being given. Anyone could take the exam. A buddy told Gordon that he couldn't pass the exam because it was designed for college graduates. Gordon was a high school graduate with six months of business college. Gordon took the exam anyway and passed by one point. Then, after passing a battery of physical and psychological exams, Gordon was on his way. He began flight training at Harlington, Texas, and washed out of flight school. It was the low point in his career. He was given a choice between training as an officer in the infantry or being a corporal in the Army Air Corps.

Gordon trained for the next couple of months before being assigned as a gunner on a B-24H and heading for Europe.

Technical Sergeant Gordon K. Butts. (Courtesy of Gordon K. Butts.)

In December 1943, our group started overseas. The ground support personnel of the group went by ship. Each individual aircraft was to fly by itself to Africa.

We flew to West Palm Beach, Florida, stayed a couple of days and then traveled to Puerto Rico. We landed on the south side of the island. The next day we continued on to Georgetown, British Guiana. Then to Belém, Brazil. The next day to Natal, Brazil, and all I can remember is flying over jungle. We stayed three days in Natal, and I spent most of the time checking over the aircraft, mainly the four engines. I took off all of the engine cowling, making sure nothing on the engine was rubbing against another part. I don't swim, so I didn't want to ditch in the ocean.

We took off in the early morning, over the Atlantic, headed for Dakar, Senegal, in West Africa. The navigator gave us an E.T.A. [estimated time of arrival], and he was within ten minutes of the time. We were ten minutes early, and glad to have made it over 2,000 miles of ocean. We had an extra rubber gasoline tank in the bomb bay but had not had to use it.

When the airplane landed, we heard the loudest noise. We thought something was wrong with the plane. It was the metal lattice runway we were landing on. These are metal pieces hooked together to provide a hard landing surface. Each piece is about twenty inches wide and ten inches long, all the pieces are hooked together. They were used in most of the fields we were to land on.

We stayed at Dakar until all our group was in Africa. One day while we were training, word came down that one of the planes had lost some engines. The plane was about five miles out from the base. We watched for them and could see the plane coming in on one engine and a prayer. The runway was cleared, and it came straight in. We never thought the plane would make it, but it did.

Most crews had a picture and a name painted on their plane. The crew that brought the plane in on one engine had been an exception, but not for long. They named their plane *Three Feathers*. There was a whiskey named Three Feathers, so the crew painted a young lady holding a bottle of Three Feathers whiskey.

One other time while we were at Dakar, President Roosevelt returned from a meeting with Churchill and boarded a cruiser in the bay. I had binoculars and watched the president being put aboard. I didn't know he couldn't walk and was in a wheelchair. I didn't know because the news reporters always took photographs of him from the waist up, and they never wrote about him being in a wheelchair.

As time went on, our crew decided that they wanted a picture and a name painted on our plane. We met and chipped in $10.00 to get the job done. After several days of discussion among the crew, the pilot finally decided we had discussed it enough and named the plane *Honeychile*.

From Dakar we flew to Marrakech, Morocco. On the flight we had to fly over the Atlas Mountains. While flying over the mountains, the carburetors on a couple of our engines iced up. We turned the de-icers on, and the engines quit missing just about the time that the wings started icing up. When wings ice up, they lose their lift. The wing de-icers, which are located on the leading edge of the wing and move in and out to crack the ice, were turned on and the ice was removed. It was a busy time for a while.

On the early part of the trip, we flew over the Sahara Desert at about one hundred feet, looking for a B-24 that was missing, but we saw nothing. Years later the plane was found, and the story was in *Life* magazine. They found no bodies, and the plane was in good shape. It had landed but not crashed. Another mystery.

We stayed in Marrakech until an airfield was captured in Italy and we

The B-24H, the type of plane on which Technical Sergeant Gordon K. Butts served as a gunner. (Courtesy of Gordon K. Butts.)

could fly in. Marrakech had a population of over 100,000 and was a tourist vacation spot before the war. There were major hotels and many gambling casinos. I saw my first French Foreign Legion soldiers there. Before they entered a cafe, they would stop and salute. This was in case there were any officers in the cafe.

There was actually two parts to the city: a European section and a native section, called Medina. The native section was off limits to GIs. Being the good GI that I was, I wanted to see why we shouldn't go in. The native section was a walled city with large gates. The gates were closed at sundown. I went to the native part of the city and stayed too long. I was caught in the city when the gates closed. What to do? How to get out? I saw a load of hay being pulled by on a cart. Most of the natives could speak some English, so I stopped the carter and asked what he would charge to take me through that gate. We settled on ten dollars, and he hid me under the hay. He took me through the gate without trouble. It was the best ten dollars I ever spent, because I didn't want to lose my stripes.

In December of 1943, we moved to Italy. We landed in Gioia delle Colle, Italy. We had tents, an open mess hall, tent showers, and a wash bench with cold water faucets. It is cold in December in southern Italy. Our landing strip was again steel grating linked together. We flew a few practice missions and were ready for combat. Our first mission was at the Fier radar station on the coast of Albania. We were excited and a little afraid. We circled a few times, trying to find the target. We had no flak and saw no fighters.

Now, we were combat-wise, we thought. But no fighters, no flak. Why? We had missed the target by five miles and had dropped the bombs in an open field. Mission One was over, and we had only forty-nine to go.

The next missions were directed at radar stations and a marshaling yard [railroad yard]. Then we had a mission to support troops. We had flak, but very little trouble with fighters.

Mission number six was to support the ground troops at Anzio. We had a lot of flak and a few fights, but we were not hit.

On mission number ten we bombed a marshaling yard and then a Messerschmitt aircraft factory in Regensburg, Germany. This was the toughest mission up to that time. Our group led the mission with 40 aircraft, we flew without fighter escort. We were attacked almost continuously by the Luftwaffe ME-109s, and there was intense antiaircraft flak from batteries near the target. During the aerial battle, our gunners shot down sixteen ME-109 fighters, but we lost six B-24s.

I shot down my first ME-109 on this mission. The fighter tried to fly up and through the formation. I was manning the top turret. When I saw him, he was about one hundred and fifty feet from us. I could see the pilot in the cockpit clearly. I fired. Other planes in the formation saw the plane explode. You had to have verification from other crews to claim a kill.

We were so beat up that we landed at Foggia Airfield in Italy, about fifty miles from our home base. That night I couldn't sleep. All I could think about was the German pilot's mother. War is hell.

I had another experience with 109s later. We were on a mission, and there must have been a squadron of them. In your turret you have two .50 caliber machine guns. In order to charge the round into the barrel, you pull a cable with a handle on it, then let go. This puts a round into the chamber, and you are ready to fire. My left gun jammed and would not fire, the right gun quit firing. I tried to charge the right gun and the cable broke. Each gun has a sear pin. It is a safety device; the end of the pin sticks out about three quarters of an inch. I reached down, got a spent casing, and stuck it into the sear pin and pulled. I was able to charge the gun so it would fire; I continued to fire this one gun for the rest of the fight.

When we landed, I tried with one hand and then with both hands to charge the gun. No luck. This shows what you can do when your adrenaline kicks in during a fight.

The next mission we hit Foulon submarine pens in France, then marshaling yards in northern Italy. The yards were in a valley, and the sky was black with flak bursts. We received some flak damage, but nothing serious.

Our next mission was on March 15, 1944. We bombed the city of Cassino, Italy. The German ground troops used an old church ruin to dig in. Only part of the group dropped bombs because of cloud cover. This turned out to be a difficult time for me. We were over the target, and I was told to go to the back of the plane. The bombardier had opened the bomb bay doors. Since I had to walk through on the catwalk, I closed them. I had just got into the back of the plane when the bombardier let the bombs go. The bomb bay doors were closed, and the bombs took the doors with them. I still had to walk back to the cockpit and my turret; all I could see was open space and the earth below.

As flight engineer you never wore a parachute, just a chest parachute harness. If you wore a parachute, you could not get around inside the plane. I hung on to the bomb racks and walked the catwalk back to the cockpit.

I thought I would catch hell when I got back to base, but no one said a word about the doors. The next morning we had a set of new bomb bay doors and were ready to go again.

From March 7 to April 4, 1944, we flew a mission about every day, unless we were grounded for repairs. We bombed a variety of targets in Romania, Austria, Italy, and Hungary.

On the morning of April 5, 1944, the target was the Ploiesti oil refineries in Romania. This was the most heavily defended target in Europe; this refinery provided the greatest source of fuel for the German war machine. The Germans were determined to protect it and keep it operating. The last raid on Ploiesti had been in August 1943. The mission had been to go in at ground level. General Brereton, the commander of the 1943 mission, had told the airplane crews that they expected 50 percent loss of planes. The crews were not happy. The losses were not quite that high. Of the 177 planes that went in, 54 failed to return.

The air corps felt that if only 5 percent of the planes were lost on a raid, it was a successful mission. But the catch was that you had to fly fifty missions to go home. Fifty missions at the 5 percent rate is 250 percent. What chance did you have to come home?

What actually happened in my squadron, the 725th, was that one full crew of ten and four members from other crews got home. Of course what kept you going was the belief that it wouldn't happen to you, just to the other crews.

We lived in a tent city, separated from the ground maintenance and other personnel. By April, every crew around us had been shot down. We were a jittery crew.

In crews shot down, some of the men who bailed out were captured and became POWs. If it was going to happen, we hoped this is what we could do.

The next mission was going to be the big one, Ploiesti. We all knew what had happened on the last raid. This was the group's twenty-fourth mission and our twentieth—only thirty more to go. The only thing that we felt good about was that we were going in at 20,000 feet, and we felt we had a chance. This was a major effort. Several groups from Italy would be bombing the target from different directions. We expected a rough fight, and it happened. We encountered many ME-109 fighters on the way to the target and more fighters as we came off the target. While over the target, there was major flak. We received flak damage, but it could have been worse. I shot down two ME-109s on the raid, one going into the target and one coming off the target. We lost four B-24s over the target. For this raid we received our second presidential citation.

One of the things most people don't realize is the ways the German air force attempted to shoot us down. We were bombed while in flight by German aircraft dropping bombs into our formation from above. This was not very effective. We did fear having ME-109s around with rockets trying to hit us. I only saw two bombers hit with rockets, and they exploded on contact. The Germans would flip in back of our formation, out of range of our .50 caliber machine guns, and lob rockets into the formation. This was scary, but again, not very effective.

After the Ploiesti raid we made raids on marshaling yards in Yugoslavia and Romania and on airdromes in Hungary and Romania. It was a busy time in April 1944: four targets in four days.

Dawn, April 17, 1944, another raid—this one was to bomb the Belgrade Zemun airdrome in Yugoslavia. This was the group's twenty-ninth mission and our twenty-third.

It was a normal mission to the target, some ME-109s on the way and some flak over the target. We were hit by flak. We had bombed at 20,000 feet and were letting down to about 14,000 feet over the Karst in Yugoslavia. The mountains were about 10,000 feet. Intelligence had not told us that the Germans had 88 mm antiaircraft guns on top of the mountains. We were literally flying down their barrels. They opened up, and we were hit. The first hit was on the number three engine. This is the engine that has the main hydraulic pump which enabled the pilot to control the aircraft.

At that time I was standing between the pilot and the copilot. I saw the pilot go through the regular check of all controls. No response. The bail-out order was given.

I had my chest-parachute harness on. I hooked on my chute, checked to make sure the two snaps were secure, and got down off the main flight deck to the deck below. That was the last thing I remember. I think the airplane exploded and blew me clear. The next thing I remember is floating in space with my parachute open. What made the chute open, I do not know. Maybe the explosion opened it, or I may have had a reaction, for we often practiced bailing out after a mission, when we landed and stopped rolling. It will always be a mystery why more men didn't get out. There were four men in the tail of the plane, but only the tail gunner and the back-turret gunner bailed out. The last thing those two men remembered was that the two waist gunners were fighting over who would open the bottom escape hatch. I often wondered why they didn't go out the open waist windows.

Of the ten men in the plane, three bailed out: two of the four from the tail end and one, myself, from the cockpit end. The rest went down with the plane.

On the way down I was machine-gunned by an ME-109. The silk of my parachute was full of holes, but I was not hit. I landed in a tree, and my feet were about three feet off the ground. A German soldier came over and pointed a luger at me and said in broken English, "For you the war is over." I agreed.

S/Sgt. Sanborn and S/Sgt. Tittle were on the ground when I landed. We were all taken to a jail in Mostar.

The flying crews never wore a gun, or even a knife, into combat. Why wear a gun? If you bailed out, were you going to fight the whole German army with one gun? If you had a gun and landed among civilians who had shotguns, pitchforks, and clubs, were you going to win a fight with them? It was better to be taken to a POW camp, where they had to guard you and feed you. In a POW camp your chances of survival were better.

We were in jail in Mostar for three days. We were interrogated. We had been trained only to give name, rank, and serial number. That's what we did. After I was interrogated, the German captain told me more about our group than I knew. He knew our group by our crashed plane.

When our group had flown about fifteen missions, one of the tail gunners had bailed out over Germany. We were told later that he was interrogating downed airmen at an interrogation center in Germany. I would say he was a spy.

We were taken to Sarajevo. There was a large German garrison there. In the jail we would watch the new German recruits learning to march and do the goose step.

Our jail was okay, food fair, but we could bathe and wash our clothes. We had only our flying suits.

At Sarajevo the three of us were put on a train with three guards. On the train we went through many towns and cities we had bombed. A grand tour at German expense.

The next stop was Budapest. We stayed there a couple of days, then to Vienna.

In Vienna we were held in the mess hall at an army camp. We slept on the floor. We had been given two German army blankets, one to sleep on and one to use for cover.

Our next stop was at our POW camp at Sagan, called Stalag Luft III. The camp was situated in a pine-wooded area outside the city of Sagan. It is in northern Germany, near the old Polish border. There were four compounds of American Army Air Corps prisoners and three of Royal Air Force officers (British, Australian and Canadian). Each compound had fifteen buildings. Ten were barracks or blocks, each housing from eighty to one hundred and ten men. The higher ranking officers had from two to four men per room—normally there were ten men to a room. The blocks were one-story, much like the barracks we had had in the U.S. Beds were double-decker bunks.

When we entered camp, the prisoners lined up on each side of the road, looking for someone from their old outfit. I found no one from our group.

We were taken to the supply building and issued new clothing. The clothing had been sent here from Switzerland, where supplies had been stockpiled. The uniforms were enlisted men's uniforms, even though this was an officers' camp. They issued us one overcoat, one pair of gloves, one pair of wool trousers, one belt, one GI blanket, two German blankets, one blouse, two pairs of winter underwear, one sweater, one cap, two wool shirts, two pair of socks, one pair of high-top shoes, and four handkerchiefs.

I was assigned to the enlisted men's room in a block. All the men were sergeants, for all air crews were that rank. They were expected to take care of the block—clean the bathroom, which only had sinks and stools, and clean the hall. We were dog robbers; officers could not work. This was the reason that the camp had to have some enlisted men.

I was lucky to end up in an officers' camp. In the enlisted men's stalags, the housing conditions were bad and the food poor—not that ours was good.

I was assigned to a room of ten men. Two men did the cooking, two men did the dishes and cleaned the room. Each man was responsible for his bunk and the surrounding area. Sometimes duties were rotated. The rest of the men were assigned to block duty.

After I had been there a few days, I was assigned to the compound's first-aid room. I had had some Red Cross courses in first aid before joining the army. There were three of us manning the first-aid station.

There were no doctors in the compound. In the central compound was a hospital manned by German, American, and British doctors for seven compounds of men. If we couldn't take care of a patient we sent him to the compound hospital. All new prisoners coming into camp, if they were wounded or ill, were examined by us and, if necessary sent to the hospital.

The Germans furnished very few medical supplies. What supplies we had, we received from the Red Cross. In 1944 we received some much-needed sulfa powder. We mixed this with iodine, and this made a paste that we could put on wounds and cuts. It worked.

Sanitation was poor. Bathing facilities were extremely limited. In theory the camp shower house could provide each man with a three-minute shower weekly. But if we got one a month, we were lucky, and it was with cold water.

I was housed in the west compound. Our American senior officer was Colonel Darr H. Alkire. His duties were to run the compound and he was our contact with the German Luftwaffe, who ran the camp. Again, we were lucky to be held by the Luftwaffe, rather than by the German army.

The camp was operated like a military base. We had appel [roll call] twice a day, morning and evening. In some cases there were special appels—when they wanted to search the blocks, for example. There were guards stationed in guard towers, armed with rifles and machine pistols. The guards were fourth-class troops, either peasants or too old for combat duty, or young men convalescing after long tours of duty or wounds received at the front. While we were in the camp, they had no contact with the POWs.

In addition to uniformed sentries, soldiers in fatigues would hide under the blocks, listening to conversations, looking for tunnels, and making themselves generally obnoxious.

Occasionally, the Gestapo descended upon the camp for a long, thorough search. The only way we could get back at the guards was passive resistance at appel. Instead of falling in, we milled about, smoked, failed to stand at attention, and made it impossible for the Germans to take a proper count. This was not done often, for they would bring in German regular soldiers with rifles and machine guns.

There was an escape committee operating in the compound, and men did escape. Any individual that wanted to try an escape had to have permission of the committee.

The Germans did supply some hot food, about 1,900 calories a day. This was insufficient. What they provided was mainly brown bread and potatoes, and meat three days a week, vegetables twice a week, and watered-down soup on alternate days. To supplement the German food, we received Red Cross parcels. Most were American, some British or Canadian. This was food like we had at home and was greatly appreciated. These parcels came out of Switzerland and were delivered to the compounds in GI army trucks. These trucks were driven by Swiss civilians. We were to get one-half parcel a week, but as the war went on the normal ration was one-half parcel every other week. Some of the items in the parcels were Spam, corned beef, salmon, cheese, dried nuts, crackers, Klim [powdered milk], orange powder, liver paste, and a chocolate bar. The chocolate bar became money. If we wanted to trade with anyone for something, the question would be how many bars of chocolate for the items.

Each compound had an athletic field and a volleyball court. The sports equipment was provided by the Red Cross. POWs built a theater with materials furnished by the Germans. Musical instruments were brought in by the Red Cross from Switzerland, and several orchestral and choral groups were formed.

There were bridge tournaments, and a school was set up to teach a wide range of cultural and technical subjects, manned by the former teachers. There was a library, which is where I spent my time.

The Germans and the officers who ran the camp wanted to keep the men busy for morale purposes. Busy people don't cause trouble or try to escape.

I was lucky because I had a job at the first-aid room. I worked six mornings a week and part of the afternoons. Some of the time I would take patients to the central hospital, which gave me a change of pace.

Most of the prisoners were interested in keeping in shape. The most common exercise was to walk the compound circle. Starting from the outside guard fence, there were two more barbed-wire fences, which had coils of wire between them. Then, inside of the prison was a space of about ten feet wide, which was a no-man's-land. If you were in this area, you could be shot. Just in front of the no-man's-land was the walking path, which was about five feet wide. This was wide enough room that three people could walk abreast. There were always people walking, except at night. At night we were locked in our block. If you went out, you could be shot.

Walking the path was interesting, for often you would find fresh dirt on the path. This was a clue that someone was digging a tunnel. The tunnel diggers would carry the dirt from the tunnel in their pockets or in small bags and dump it on the path. We would never ask about the dirt.

Of course, the Germans also watched for new dirt on the path. So the hunt would be on to find the tunnel. This was the camp from which the British soldiers attempted an escape in the film *The Wooden Horse*. They were caught as they came out of the tunnel and shot. Their ashes were in urns in the central hospital as a reminder not to try to escape.

In April when I arrived, some of the blocks were planting gardens with seeds sent from home. Fresh vegetables would be a welcome addition to our diet.

We did receive some mail from home, and packages could be sent every three months. I received one package while at Sagan. My mother said she had sent three. These packages were often pilfered. We could send one letter a month, and my mother did receive some letters. All mail was read and censored by the Germans.

The International Red Cross made all the extras we received possible. To a man we gave thanks to them.

One day when we were walking the circle a twin-engine German fighter flew low over the camp. It made a lot of noise but had no propellers. What made it fly? Then we realized that this was the new jet fighter, the ME-262 which the Germans were building. They started production too late to make a difference, thank God.

There was always a "friendly" discussion between the fighter pilots and the bomber crews. It went like this: Fighter pilot says, "You bomber crews shot me down. I was looking for protection, for I was having trouble, and when I got in formation, you shot me down." Answer: "You pointed your nose at us. We had a standard rule, if any plane pointed his nose at us, we shot it down." This discussion could go on for days.

The explanation for the bomber crews' standard rule was that the Germans had rebuilt some of the American fighters from the planes that had crashed. They would come up and get into the formation and fly with us. Then all of a sudden they would kick their rudder and start firing. Whenever a fighter came into our formation, we always trained our guns on them.

We knew that the Russian army was not too far away. We knew from radio broadcasts, mainly the BBC, picked up by our canary [an illegal radio in a prison compound]. In a room next to the first-aid station was a map of Europe. The map would show where the Germans battle lines were. On the same map the Americans would put on a line where the BBC and the Allies said the battle lines were. The Germans would come each day and look. They knew there was a radio in camp. They searched for it. Sometimes I think they didn't want to find it. The canary was never a topic of conversation in camp. It was understood that you did not ask questions. Just enjoy the map. The lines were put up with yarn and pins.

The big question was would the Germans move us out before the Russians captured us? We received an answer at 2100 hours [9 P.M.] on January 25, 1945. All compounds received German orders to move out on foot within thirty minutes. Colonel Alkire had told us two weeks before to be ready to move on short notice.

In knotted trousers used as packs and makeshift sleds, we packed clothing and all the food we had. The Germans issued one Red Cross food parcel per man. We abandoned books, letters, and camp records, took our over-coat and blankets, and left.

By 2400 hours [midnight] all the men, except some that couldn't walk, marched out into bitter cold and snow in a column of threes. Destination unknown. Our guards from the camp went with us. They carried rifles and machine pistols.

We marched all night, fifty minutes of marching and a ten-minute break every hour. German rations consisted only of black bread and margarine, obtained from a horse-drawn wagon—the camp kitchen. Each compound marched separately, and each could tell a different story.

We slept in unheated barns, empty factories, and on the ground. After the first twenty-four hours, we were given a thirty-hour rest for recupera-tion. I am not sure where we were at this time or where we were going. The guards from the camp were old men and had trouble keeping up.

The GIs told the guards that they would carry their rifles for them. They knew we couldn't escape in this kind of weather.

At the first river we came to, we dumped all the rifles in the water. We had some very angry guards. We had a good laugh.

Later we were loaded on unmarked "forty-and-eight" freight boxcars, fifty men to a car. There were four boxcars of prisoners. They locked the doors.

We were in the boxcars for three days and nights, with no water and no sanitation. One corner of the car was reserved for a toilet area. But who could go in a corner with forty-nine men looking on? Our greatest fear was that our train would be strafed by our P-51s or P-47s. At that time of the war, the fighter planes were sent out to shoot up trains or any other target of opportunity.

On the third afternoon we de-trained at Nürnberg.

After being in the boxcars for three days, we needed to relieve ourselves. Having no place to go—the guards kept us together in the marshaling yard—we looked at each other, took down our trousers, squatted down, and let nature take its course. What a relief. Some picture: 200 prisoners getting relief.

Conditions at Stalag XIIID at Nürnberg were deplorable. The barracks had recently been inhabited by Italian POWs, who had left them filthy. There was no room to exercise, no supplies, nothing to eat out of, and practically nothing to eat. No Red Cross parcels were available upon arrival. German rations were 300 grams of bread, 250 grams of potatoes, some dehydrated vegetables, and margarine. A few days after our arrival, Red Cross parcels started to arrive by truck.

Toilet facilities during the day were satisfactory, but the only night latrine was a can in each sleeping room. Since many of the men now had diarrhea, the can had insufficient capacity. The floors were soiled very soon.

The barracks were not heated. The morale of the prisoners dropped to its lowest ebb.

At 1700 hours [5 P.M.] on April 3, 1945, we were told to evacuate the Nürnberg camp and march to Stalag VIIA at Moosburg. The Germans agreed that the Americans would take over the march. The Americans were responsible for preserving order, and we marched only twenty kilometers a day, about twelve miles.

On April 4, 1945, each POW received one food parcel, and we started south. While we were marching through a marshaling yard near a highway, some P-47s dive-bombed the yard. Two Americans and one British soldier were killed; three others were wounded.

The next day a large replica of the American Air Corps insignia was placed on the road, with an arrow pointing in the direction of the march. This ended the bombing of the column.

Many of the men were very weak and had difficulty keeping up. This is when we started the "flying wedge." The weaker prisoners were allowed to drift back through the column as we marched. Then a group of the stronger prisoners would take the weaker prisoners to the front of the column during the ten-minute break. This was repeated every hour.

Colonel Darr H. Alkire was now in charge of the column. He was an excellent officer and was responsible for many of the improved conditions during the march. The German guards were aware of how close the American army was, and this helped. Even though the Americans were in charge, the guards went with us.

On the third day of the march, diphtheria broke out among the men in the column. Since I was the medic, I did what I could, which wasn't much. A couple of days later, I had the disease. I could hardly talk. My throat was beginning to close.

We were camping near a barn. I climbed up into the hayloft. I thought I had had it, and the hay was a soft place to lie down. Later in the day, I heard Colonel Alkire asking where Sergeant Butts was at. They told him I was up in the hayloft. He shouted for me and wanted to know what the problem was. I crawled out to the opening and tried to answer. He couldn't understand me, but realized I had caught the diphtheria. He said to lie down and stay there.

We had been getting Red Cross parcels on a regular basis, for we were near the Swiss border. Since Colonel Alkire was in charge, he told the German captain that we needed more Red Cross parcels, *now*. The German captain called Switzerland to send a truckload of parcels right away.

The truck was there the next morning. They unloaded the parcels and told the driver to take me to the column ahead of us, for there was a doctor with the column.

The driver did this. When we got to the column, they found the doctor.

I had worked with him at Sagan. He had been stationed at the central hospital. He asked what was wrong, and when I tried to answer, he knew.

In his medical bag he had some diphtheria serum, and he gave me 1,000 units and told the driver to take me to Stalag VIIA. It was down the road about twenty miles.

When I arrived at Moosburg, they put me in a barracks. This was where they dumped all the sick prisoners. There were no German or American doctors, no medical personnel at all. I don't remember much for the next few days. I had gone into a coma and just laid in my bunk. An army corporal took care of me as I came out of the coma. He fed me, gave me water, and looked after me. I don't even know his name. This nameless corporal saved my life.

The sanitation was unbelievable. When I was able to move, I would crawl to the latrine. The latrine had a sloping floor, with holes in the floor. The holes took care of the human waste. There were no stools or sinks. When finished, I would crawl back to my bunk. I was very weak.

This was near the end of April. General Patton's 3rd Army and the Germans fought a battle with the camp in the middle. Bullets flew like mad in the barrack. A British soldier in the bunk next to me was killed in his bunk by a stray bullet. It hit him in his mouth and came out the back of his head. We had talked, and he had told me he didn't want to go home. He had been captured in North Africa.

From the barrack we were taken to an evacuation field hospital for seven days. The rule was that after seven days you had to move up to another hospital. I was the last one to leave from my old barrack. At that time I was paralyzed in both legs and arms and my throat, and I was down to about 105 pounds. From the evacuation hospital we were flown out on a C-47 hospital plane. We were on the ramp, waiting to get on the runway. The first plane took off. The second plane taxied to the runway, tried to take off and crashed at the end of the runway. We taxied to the runway and took off through the smoke of the crashed plane. I was afraid, for the last time I had been in a plane, it had gone down.

They took me to a hospital in Reims, France, where I stayed for a few weeks. I began to get stronger.

The next stop was Camp Atturbury near Franklin, Indiana, at Wakeman General Hospital. At Wakeman I was given a lot of vitamins and all the food I could eat.

I was a RAMP [Released Allied Military Personnel] and treated very nicely. When I started to walk and could move around, I went down to the recreation room to watch a ping-pong match.

I noticed a young lady, also in hospital clothing. I asked if the chair next to her was taken, and she said no. This was the beginning of a life-long experience. She was a WAC, recovering from an appendix operation. We were married in the hospital chapel on September 7, 1945.

We have just celebrated fifty years of marriage. We have three children and six grandchildren.

I was discharged with 100 percent disability. A few years later, it was reduced to 60 percent and then to 10 percent which I still have.

I went back to school, received a B.S., an M.S., and an Ed.D. I taught at Southern Illinois University for thirty-three years, and I am now retired.

2nd Lieutenant Carl W. Remy

U.S. Army Air Forces
8th Air Force 95th Group, 336th Squadron
Captured During His Second
Bombing Mission Over Germany
Prisoner of War
September 28, 1944–May 1, 1945
Stalag Luft I

In 1942 Carl had two years of college under his belt at Oklahoma University. The war was going strong, and a program was offered to college students to allow them to finish college before going into the service. Students could enlist in the reserves and get a two-year deferment. Carl and a bunch of his buddies joined and were sworn into the Army Air Forces reserves in October 1942. All their papers were stamped "Deferred for Two Years" in big red letters. Four months later, they all got orders to report for active duty.

Carl went to Wichita Falls, Texas, for basic training, and then to a college-training detachment at San Marcos, Texas, for officer training. From there he was shipped to West Texas State Teachers' College for aviation training. After completing this training, he was sent to California for cadet school. After several other training schools, Carl became a bombardier B-17 officer. He was now qualified to locate and mark targets, test and inspect the equipment, and in emergency to navigate by means of dead reckoning pilotage. Then he was given orders for England.

We took the new B-17 from the east coast and flew it to England. It was exciting flying over the North Atlantic. We flew inside of Greenland and landed in Iceland for an overnight stay. The next day we flew to England.

We had had a lot of training on formation flying and simulated bomb dropping, but that was it. Then, on September 27, 1944, we flew our first mission. It was on the Main River near Frankfurt, Germany. It was a milk run; there weren't any fighters to deal with. In England you flew ten missions in the first ten days—that was shaking you awake at 1:30 in the morning, taking off about daylight, and heading for Germany.

108

The next day, on September 28 we were up and at it again. Our mission was the Merseburg oil refinery, which was deep in Germany. This was the twenty-fifth time this place had been bombed. We took off early, formed up above the clouds, and headed for Germany. We cleared our guns over the English Channel. We were near the target about 11 A.M. We made the turn and began the long bombing run at an altitude of 27,000 feet. The accuracy of the German flak batteries was uncanny, even though we were five miles high with a cloud layer under us. Besides the ordinary 40 mm and 88 mm stuff, there was a terrifying rocket, which left a dense black exhaust trail all the way up and then exploded, leaving a black ball of smoke that gave the thing the appearance of a giant cobra.

Prisoner I.D. card of 2nd Lieutenant Carl W. Remy. (Courtesy of Carl W. Remy.)

Being a deputy-deputy [lead bombardier], I had the bombsight set up; but since the clouds did not break, I knew it would be a P.F.F. [path finder flight] run. So I turned the sight off and glued my eyes to the bomb bays of the lead ship a few feet above and ahead of me. The idea is, of course, for the entire group of planes to drop its bombs at the instant the lead ship does.

The flak gunners simply seemed to have our number. When flak bursts so close you can hear it inside the plane and can see that the black puffs have wicked, furry, orange centers, that's damn close! A flak suit can't be worn over a parachute; but with all that stuff hitting us, I felt inclined to wear my chute anyhow, so I just kind of draped the flak jacket over my shoulders. As I crouched there with the bomb-release button in my hand, I could hear the showers of flak bursting against the ship. The near misses tossed the ship around; and after one of them burst almost in my face, there was a hole in the Plexiglas right in front of me. I knew I wasn't hit, and I glanced back at Swann, the navigator, and saw that he was okay.

That was only the beginning. For the first time in my life, I was earnestly praying. I was concentrating on the bomb bays of the head ship, but that didn't keep me from knowing what was happening to our ship. The number two engine was hit and began to wind up to a high-pitched scream. Heath, the pilot, fought the controls and did an excellent job of holding formation. Flak literally rained through the nose, creating a fine mist of glass particles and dirt from the floorboards. The tail gunner reported that both handles of his guns had been blown off by flak that had ripped through both sides of the armor-plated tail, but he wasn't touched. The waist gunner reported flak holes in the waist, but he was okay. The ball-turret was blown to hell. Lucky for the ball-turret gunner that he wasn't in the turret. The glass was shattered in the top turret, but the engineer, Younts, was busy elsewhere. After a close burst at twelve o'clock high, Heath told Eastman, the copilot, to take over the controls. One fragment had knocked Heath's helmet askew, broken his goggles, and inflicted a wound over his right eye. Then a burst over the right wing blew holes in the wings and the number four engine; flak shattered the glass in the pilot compartment.

Heath and Younts were trying to feather the number two engine, which was still running away at a terrific speed and causing the ship to shudder. Runaway engines sometimes throw their props, and that screaming propeller a couple of feet to my left was a real concern.

Finally, after an eternity, I saw the bombs leave the lead ship, and instantly I hit the bomb release, at 1205. Lights flicked off on my control panel, indicating all bombs dropped; but when I said on interphone, "Bombs away," the armor gunner, Curtis, reported that one five hundred pounder had hung up. At the same time we veered sharply in the turn off the target, catching hell from the flak worse than before. Our crippled plane lost speed and altitude and was wandering crazily around the sky. The interphone crackled and popped, and I couldn't understand what was being said. We couldn't keep up with the formation, and Heath and Eastman were working hard to keep from being rammed by the onrushing groups of bombers behind us.

There was another B-17 badly hit, careening crazily around the sky, leaving a trail of smoke. It finally leveled out and disappeared in a southerly direction. The pilot was probably trying to make Switzerland—a greater distance than France. I've always wondered how that crew made it.

Heath ordered, "Prepare to bail out." As if I weren't ready.

Eastman radioed the lead ship of our group, telling them we were okay but bailing out. Their lead navigator acknowledged: "Good luck." Then we were all alone over Germany.

I told Curtis, the armored gunner, to kick out that hanging bomb. He was a well-trained boy and did it with ease, even waiting for the proper moment when he thought he could splatter a small German village below. He certainly got a big kick out of personally bombing Germany.

We dropped lower and lower—easy prey for German fighters—and there was no sign of an American fighter. Eastman was radioing over and over for "little friend" [P-51s] to come and help us. Our fighters usually protect lone, crippled fighters.

We were out of the flak by this time. There was no fighters—just us. At this time it began to soak in that we probably wouldn't get back to England. My main reaction was that this can't be me in an airplane that's going down in Germany. This must be a picture show. This sort of thing happens to other guys, but not to me. I must be dreaming. I'll awaken in a minute—wonder what Mom'll think—I told Betty I'd be home for Christmas—dear God.

But I wasn't dreaming. Heath said to throw everything that could be torn loose out of the ship in order to lighten the load. I remembered the story of the guy who bailed out in order to lighten the plane enough for his buddies to fly home. He was brave.

Out went guns, ammunition, flak suits, and among other things thousands of dollars worth of radio equipment. The navigator kept his G-box [bombsight equipment], and I kept the bombsight.

The fatally hit four engine caught fire, and Eastman feathered it. By transferring all the fuel from two engine, Eastman was able to stop the runaway two engine, but it was still windmilling—holding us back.

Eastman was still calling for fighters. We were dropping fast; and Swann was fighting maps and instruments, trying to plot us a flak-free course to the Alsace, in France. He measured distances to Switzerland, to Sweden—too damned far.

Heath again ordered the crew to get ready to jump.

Swann reported that at our present rate of descent we'd be on the ground before we ever reached France, so Eastman dropped flaps, and we mushed along at a stalling speed; one hundred miles per hour, and started holding an altitude of a little over sixteen thousand feet. My hopes soared till Swann told me we were bucking a head wind of over sixty miles per hour. Then I knew we'd never make it. The straining one engine and sputtering three engine would never get us there.

Fighters were dogfighting about three miles to our left. A little later some P-51s came to escort us.

We were still mushing along on a prayer when the ball gunner reported that three engine was on fire, so Heath said he guessed it was time to jump. As Heath feathered three engine, the interphone went out and we went into a shallow dive. I thought the pilot and copilot must have jumped out, so I ripped off my oxygen mask and other entangling equipment and scrambled past Swann up to the pilot's compartment—to find them still there, looking scared. There were holes in the windshield, and both Heath and Eastman had little holes in their jackets and were covered with Plexiglas dust. Heath, with a little blood trickling down his forehead, was smoking and gave me a faint smile. Eastman looked relatively cool and collected. Heath said, "God-dammit, we've had it," and told me to go around the ship and tell every man that if he wanted to bail out, to go at once, but that he, Heath, was going to land the ship and that all who wanted to stay could do so.

I didn't have to make up my mind. I was staying for sure. I'd heard too many true stories of how lone airmen, parachuting into Germany, were beaten, pitchforked, burned in oil, dragged behind a truck, castrated, and I figured we'd be a little safer all together.

I crawled back down in the nose to find Swann still working on his maps. It was hard making him understand that we were positively going down. He seemed kinda numb or something.

We made our way back to the radio room, and Carlsen, the radio operator, said he would stay with the ship. Curtis, the armored gunner, and Shull, the ball gunner, said they had rather crash-land. With the ship diving, the interphone dead, and his guns knocked out, the tail gunner, Goodshed, was still at his position, just like the hero in a movie. I had to send Shull back to get him. While Younts cranked the wheels down—we had no electrical power—the rest of us popped chutes and prepared padding in the radio room for the crash.

Meanwhile, we had broken through the overcast and were at a very low altitude. Heath, suddenly worried that Swann and I were still in the noses, sent Eastman down to see. He barely made it back to his seat—didn't even have time to fasten his safety belt for the landing.

I looked out of the little radio room window and saw that the terrain was very rough and wooded. But Heath picked a field, circled, and went in for a landing. Suddenly a brick house and a telephone pole loomed up ahead. Straining one engine with our last surge, the plane cleared the obstacles, and I felt the wheels touch ground on the plowed hillside. Eastman immediately cut all power. As we bucked along the rough field, the plane suddenly swerved, and I felt Swann, lying on top of me, brace himself. He, too, thought we were nosing over. That swerving was Heath skillfully maneuvering the plane to miss a German girl working in the beet field.

We finally rolled to a stop with the plane smoking and steaming like a tea kettle—oxygen hissing and number two engine on fire. I felt that I couldn't get out fast enough because the plane was due to blow any second. So everyone in the back ran down the waist and jumped out the back door. It was 1305 [1:05 P.M.].

I fully expected a reception of swarms of Germans, but the peasants working in the field where we landed just stared or kept on working. The navigator gunners and I ran about a hundred feet from the plane, while big Heath dropped out of the nose escape hatch. Eastman didn't appear for a few seconds, and with the pilot's compartment filling with smoke, I was afraid we'd have to go in and drag him out. But he soon came out. When I first saw him, he had a big flak hole though the right shoulder of his jacket, and I thought, "God, he's been hit!" But I was mistaken. He hadn't been wearing his jacket, but had just put it on before he jumped out of the plane.

About that time my nervous tension dissolved, and I felt weak as a kitten. Tears came, and I wanted to break down and cry hard. But then I looked at big Heath and he had big tears too, so we all laughed instead. Rather hysterically, I suppose.

It then dawned on me why no Germans were bothering us. Our American P-51s were flying patrol over us, occasionally letting go a burst of machine-gun fire. You might call it local air superiority.

I had just decided to go back to the plane and set off a fire bomb to completely destroy the ship, when one of the P-51s made a pass at our B-17, shooting at it. Obviously, he was intent on destroying it, so we had to get out of there at once. I still had my chute harness on; and wired to it were my escape shoes. We all started running over the hill, and I skinned out of my chute harness, leaving my shoes—my first mistake.

We made it to the woods and ran a little ways in. It was afternoon, and we found a low spot. There were a lot of leaves on the ground, and we pulled them up around us to hide until dark. Then, when it was dark, we started walking. We had maps and some food that we were supposed to ration out over a few days. We ate it all right then.

We could hear Germans or somebody in the woods, and we were afraid they were going to get us, but they didn't. We evaded them all night. We left the woods the next morning at 0500 [5 A.M.], stopped on a hilltop, and stayed under cover until nightfall. Then we walked again. By then we all had colds and were extremely tired. We were walking along this road about fifty feet apart and a German armored column came down the road. We all leapt to cover in the ditch. After they passed we couldn't find all of the men. They were so tired that they had fallen asleep as the Germans were passing.

On the third day we didn't much give a damn. We were so tired and hungry that we were walking on the road in daylight. We even passed some people who were uniformed and gave them a "Heil Hitler!" We got to the small village of Herbstein, Germany. To go around the town would have been too rugged because it was semimountainous country, so since we had gotten by with so much already, we decided we would walk through the town. There we were in American flier uniforms. We got most of the way through and then were surrounded by the *Folksstrom* [village guard]. They took us to the courtyard and lined us up against the wall. They operated the bolts of their guns. We were standing there with our hands up and thought they were going to shoot us, but they didn't. Instead, they searched us and then took us down to the woods at the edge of town. We were sure they were going to shoot us then, but they had taken us down there to use the toilet. Then they brought us back and put us in the Herbstein jail. We were then moved by train to Geissen Prison, where they had a dungeon in one of the buildings. They put us there for the night.

Sometime the next morning, they boarded us on the train to Frankfurt, Germany. We spent the night in solitary. They took us to an interrogation center the next day. We got a little soap and water, but not much at all to eat. They took me in for interrogation. The Nazi officer told me to answer just three questions and I would get to see the Red Cross, get some warm food, and even go to bed and get some sleep. The first question was, "How was your armament for your new tail gunner?" I told them that I had no idea. They knew our target was Merseburg.

The second question was, "Could you see the target?" I told them I didn't know because we dropped in on radar anyway. They brought some pictures in and showed us a photo of the tail section of our plane and a photo of a woman who was supposed to have been killed by the P-51 strafing. They knew the bomb group. They knew my mother's maiden name. I didn't tell them anything, and I didn't get to see the Red Cross or get any food or any sleep. I don't think they ever asked the third question.

They put us on a passenger train, and we moved out. After a while we came up on a passenger train that had been bombed by American bombers. It was terrible. There were women and children who had been killed, and they were trying to get them off the train. There was blood everywhere. The German guards took us off the train and marched us around the wreckage, and we were almost mobbed by the German people. But we got on another train, and we finally reached Stalag Luft I at Barth, Germany. There were ten thousand officers at Luft I. About three thousand were British. We were organized as a wing of the air force and in groups and squadrons. The wing commander was Colonel Spicer from Texas. He was a fighter ace.

We started our hitch in the POW camp. The camp was right on the Baltic and the Baltic sea was kind of warm, which helped in the winter.

We were not tortured. We were not forced to work. We never got out of the camp for anything. The food in the morning consisted of grain cereal; We made our own lunch from Red Cross packages; and in the evening we ate rutabagas and potatoes.

When we started out there were about twelve to fifteen men in a room that was about twenty by twenty feet. In the end we had twenty-four men in the room, and there were triple bunks all the way around and out in the center of the room.

There was very little to do. We had a library and could read all we wanted. A lot of people get headaches when they don't get enough nutrition. I'm one of them, so I couldn't read much. I didn't want to exercise, either, because I wasn't getting enough to eat. I had lost about twenty pounds.

We fell out for a head count twice a day. We would line up in front of our barrack, and the Germans would come by and count heads. I will never forget: there were 158 of us, and the German would come by and say, "Ein hundert acht und fünfzig" [158]. They would do these head counts every day to see if anybody had gotten away. During the seven months that I was there, no one escaped or tried to escape. Everybody knew the war was going to end and that it was just a matter of time. We got in the camp in October 1944, and the Americans were already at the Rhine River. So we were just going to wait it out. We weren't sure we were going to get out alive, though, because we had heard so much about the Nazis killing POWs and Jews.

KRIEGSGEFANGENEN

MEMOS

OF

Carl W. Remy
2nd Lt. A.C.

FROM

SEPT. 28, 1944

TO

IF LOST, MAIL TO:
CARL W. REMY
1717 N. W. 20th
OKLAHOMA CITY, OKLA.
USA

— Feb. 1, 1945
I predict that the war will end on or before April 15, 1945. Last September I thought the war would be over by Christmas.
————— So you never can tell —.
April 15, 1945 Dammit, I missed again!

Above and on following pages: Three pages from the diary kept by Carl W. Remy during his imprisonment.

We would get a shower once a month. That was nice. It was warm water. They would turn the water on for a minute, and we would lather up. Then they would turn it on for another minute, and we would wash off. But after the war, hearing about what they did to the Jews, I wondered just how safe we really had been.

We had one barrack in the camp that was just Russians, and the Germans would never let them out. They were the meanest people I have ever heard of. The Germans would send the dogs in after them, and they would just kill the dogs.

RATIONS

THE MAIN DIET OF A
KRIEGIE CONSISTS OF
THE CONTENTS OF THE
11 LB. RED CROSS FOOD
PARCEL. THESE PARCELS
ARE DOLED OUT AT THE
RATE OF ONE PER MAN
PER WEEK IF ENOUGH
IS BEING RECEIVED. WE
ALSO RECEIVE PARCELS
FROM THE BRITISH AND
CANADIAN RED CROSS.

AMERICAN
RED CROSS

CONTENTS OF THE
AMERICAN PARCEL

1 CAN SPAM - 12 OZ. ____ 90 pts.*
1 CAN CORNED BEEF - 12 OZ. ___ 70
1 CAN SALMON - SMALL ____ 35
1 CAN MEAT PATÉ - SM. ____ 35
1 CAN MARGERINE - 1 LB. ____ 0
1 CAN POWDERED MILK (KLIM) ___ 90
1 BOX CRACKERS (K-RATION) ___ 50
1 CHOCOLATE D. RATION ____ 60
1 BOX PRUNES - 1 LB. ____ 40
1 CAN SOL. COFFEE ____ 60
5 PKS POP. BRAND CIGARETTES __ (VARY)
* STANDARD FOOD-ACCO VALUATION POINTS. (SEE NEXT PAGE)

(Remember the month of March!!)

1 BOX SUGAR ½ LB. ____ 60
1 BOX VITAMIN TABS. ___ 0
1 CAN JELLY - SM. ___ 60
2 BARS SWAN SOAP ____ 0
1 BOX CHEESE ½ LB __ 60

If the Germans wanted something changed in the POW camp, they would issue an order to Colonel Packer. If it was reasonable, he would issue orders down the line and get the change made. If he thought it was unreasonable, he would refuse, and they would put him in solitary confinement. That's where he stayed most of the time.

We went to bed as usual one night, and the next morning, on May 1, 1945, when we got up there were Americans in the watchtowers. The Germans had begged to be taken prisoner, but they were told to get the hell out. They just left us. We had no particular reason to get out. I kept a diary, and this is what I wrote:

BETS

(7/)

	Debit	Credit
January, '45-Bet 10 dollars against 10 with Jackson C. Johnson that the end of the war would not occur between the dates of April 1, 1945, and June 30, 1945.	Lost / Paid	
January, '45- Bet 10 dollars against 10 dollars with Joe Revitz that the war would end before April 1, 1945.	Lost / Paid	10
February 11, 1945 - Bet 10 dollars against 25 with Robt. H. Ahrens that the war would be over by March 4, 1945.	Lost / Paid 10	
February 26, 1945 - Bet 10 dollars against 10 with Robt. H. Ahrens that the war would be over by July 15, 1945.	Won / Paid	
March 9, 1945 - Bet 10 dollars even with Robt. H. Ahrens that the the Americans would break out of their Rhine B/hds within six weeks.	Won / 10 Paid	

April 30, 1945—Everybody is nervous. Himmler, the Nazi Butcher Boy, visited the camp. Half the German guards left the camp last night. It's rumored that the rest will leave tonight. The Germans plan to take 1500 POWs and go west to escape the Russians. The Germans have been destroying the air field and flak school—big demolition explosions all day. Early in the morning we began digging networks of trenches around the barracks for protection. Used Klim cans, knives, and sticks for tools. We completed trenches by nightfall and dived into them at every explosion. German strafing expected. Russians now twenty miles away. Civilians stealing Red Cross food. At midnight, all Germans left the prison camp.

May 1, 1945—All Germans except five left for U.S. lines. A major and German staff stayed as our POWs. Our American Col. Zempkes now in charge of camp. Camp life as usual. Still confined for safety. Russians now less than ten miles. The battle can be heard. Germans still blowing up own equipment. All shops in Barth closed. Barth citizens passively awaiting Russians. They say "no resistance." We have plenty of food. Russians should be here today. I Hope! This is the strangest, most precarious predicament I have been in for seven months. Here are 9000 POWs unguarded on the Baltic coast in Nazi Germany. Four miles to the south of us is a German air field swarming with all types of German planes. Then a little south of there the Germans and Russians are fighting. I never could understand this prisoner of war idea. We are now free men. Aren't we fair game now?

There are four armed parties of around fifty (Kriegies). They've taken over the flak school, Barth Power System, and the air field. The Germans cleared out of the air field before the American Kriegies arrived.

10:00 P.M. May 1, 1945—Advanced Russian Patrol arrived at this camp! Only two Russians. They say the main body of the spearhead is about five hours behind. Be here about dawn. Burgermaster (sic) in Barth who has been cooperating with us committed suicide. His life wasn't worth a dime.

May 2, 1945—Situation is still a very confused state. The two Russians who got here last night arrived drunk with women in a confiscated German automobile. They said the rest of the Army is drunk and ought to be here soon. This POW camp is still pretty well under control. MPs have been appointed from our numbers and we are still prisoners—of our only guard.

There are almost no weapons in camp. I feel pretty helpless. About fifty American ex-POWs armed with a few old rifles went south to try to contact higher Russian authorities. They were disarmed, "captured," and returned by the Russian Shock Troops. Another body of Americans that had taken over the Barth Air Field were handled likewise by the Russians. Another party of Americans and British from here struck out for Rostock which is probably by now in Russian hands. The air field is very heavily mined.

More and more Russian troops are arriving in parties numbering five to fifty men. One Russian tank driver wanted to run his tank through the camp fences and liberate all the prisoners so they [could] sack the town of Barth.

Two Russian colonels arrived here at 3:30 P.M. They told one of our American colonels that he should be happy and overflowing with joy to have been liberated by the Russians. To keep the Russians in good humor, the colonel started hugging and kissing and crying over them. They were satisfied.

But they weren't satisfied for long. These two Russian colonels said we shouldn't still be behind barbed wire, but should be out raising hell. Our commanding officer, Colonel Zempkes, said, "No!" The Russian Colonel leveled a gun at his head and said, "Yes, you will tear up the prison camp."

So the camp went stark raving mad. Nine thousand ex-prisoners tore down the barbed wire and guard towers with their bare hands. These Russians we were dealing with were not the crack Russian spearheads but the Terror Troops which fan out and create havoc, demoralizing the Germans. Human life—their own and anyone else's—is worth nothing. I could hear shots all over the place. In a few seconds, the entire camp was emptied.

I went over to the German flak school. This establishment is huge and modern covering about a square mile. Civilians and French and Polish ex-prisoners had been through the place before me. The Germans had blown up part of it—mainly radar equipment, and the civilians finished off the rest. There were millions of fur coats, boots, and jackets stored there and still undamaged. There are no young German males left, and the few old men along with the women and children were living in the flak school buildings setting up housekeeping.

There were a lot of the Polish, French, and Russian whores living near the flak school. There are always a lot of these captured women near German soldier concentrations. The Germans believe a mistress is necessary for morale. Some of these women were nice looking and apparently of high class.

This may seem like a mess of senseless scribbling, but the way things are happening accounts for it. I wonder if I'm losing my mind.

I went on into the outskirts of the town of Barth. The civilians were white and trembling—scared senseless of the Russians and afraid but to a much lesser degree of us. Russians were shooting and raping civilians for no reason at all. In one spot I saw three women, a child, and a baby, all with their brains blown out. I saw the little white baby buggy near the dead woman, and wondering where the baby was, I drew back the little pink coverlet over the top, and saw a little soft, fat, German baby, all tucked in, in a little lace nightie. The only thing amiss was that his brains were blown all over the little white pillow.

I was almost sick and returned to camp. The Germans murdered Russian women and children, so why shouldn't the Russians do likewise?

At about five o'clock, the Russian told Colonel Zempkes to have the prison camp ready to move out by six o'clock. Col. Zempkes said, "No," that we would wait for Americans to fly us out. The Russian drew his pistol, and said, "You will move!" So we began a mad scramble to roll packs and get ready. We were each given three red cross parcels, thirty-three pounds of food. Then Col. Zempkes pulled a fast one on the Russian. He passed the word around for everyone to scatter out all over the countryside so that the confusion would be so great the Russians couldn't move us. You see, the Russians had no definite plans. They just wanted to see us out and free, so we could go along with the Russian army to loot and raise hell.

I was in town again and got a close-up of the Russians' fighting men. They were all drunk and I was kissed and hugged till I was weak. There was a Russian woman soldier with a huge machine gun slung over her back. She stopped me and since I understand a little German and no Russian, and she spoke nothing but Russian, I was unable to give her much help. Later I saw her again and she asked, "American Flieger?" I said I was. All the Russians wanted to give us a bottle of whiskey. Americans were stealing and getting drunker than the Russians. They didn't exactly steal; they just asked the trembling German civilians for cars, bicycles, motorcycles, etc., and the Germans, fearing for their lives, gave up everything.

German men in civilian clothes came up to the camp gate begging to be taken prisoner. They were ex–German guards who fled this camp last night. We turned them away. Let the Russians get 'em.

Things began to settle down after that. We mainly lived day to day, awaiting word that the Americans were coming for us. A couple of us did go to a factory in the nearby town and found a couple dozen Jews who had been worked as slave labor. They had been forced to work at a dead run with little to eat. If they couldn't keep up they were shot.

We went in and got them some soup and a hunk of bread. They were a pitiful sight. They all had TB. I have always wondered if any of them lived.

Then we got the word that the planes would be coming to take us out of the camp. This is what I wrote:

> May 13, 1945—Mothers Day—Sunday—Boarded a B-17 at Barth Air Field at 12:15 P.M. Arrived at 4:00 P.M. 8 km. south of Laon, France. No fear of flying, no air sickness. Transported by G.I. semi-trailer truck to a tent city. Supposed to get showers, delousing, and new clothes.

Lieutenant Arnold Samuelson of Tacoma, Washington, gives food to hungry Russian slave laborers who were liberated when elements of the 9th Armored Division took Limburg, Germany. Carl Remy encountered similar slave laborers after his own liberation. U.S. Army Signal Corps photo by TEC/4 W.D. MacDonald. (Courtesy of the National Archives.)

We were at Camp Lucky Strike for a month getting medical checks, good food, and new clothes. Then they put us on troop ships and sent us home. We arrived on June 20, 1945. It was a wonderful day that I will never forget.

The entire crew got home alive. The pilot visited me some, and the copilot wrote to me. Now it is hard to believe that about half of them are dead. When I think of them, I think of them as young men. People don't realize that these were nineteen- or twenty-year-old kids flying these bombers. Most people think men flew those bombers. We were kids.

Sergeant Forest L. Wilmouth

U.S. Army Air Forces
95th Bomb Group
Captured During A
Bombing Mission Over Berlin
Prisoner of War
October 6, 1944–May 2, 1945
Stalag Luft IV

Forest was deferred for over a year at the beginning of the war in order to care for his sisters and widowed mother. In early 1943 his deferment expired, and he was sent to Chicago for induction. They wanted to assign him to the navy, but he told them that he couldn't swim. He was told that that would be the first thing they taught him. Nevertheless, he was assigned to the army and sent to Fort Custer in Battle Creek, Michigan, in June 1943.

Forest scored high on his aptitude test and mechanical test and therefore was assigned to the U.S. Army Air Corps. After finishing basic training at Wichita, Texas, he was sent to Amarillo, Texas. There he was trained in mechanics for the B-17 bomber. Then he went to Kingman Air Base in Arizona for flight and gunnery training. He got his first flight in the Grand Canyon.

He went to Lincoln, Nebraska, where he was assigned to a B-17 crew. His assignment was mechanic/gunner. There were four officers and six enlisted men in each crew. Later the enlisted men were reduced to five. At the age of twenty-four, he was the oldest member of the crew. The pilot was twenty-one and the copilot only nineteen. He was the crew chief and nicknamed "Pop."

The crew was sent to Dyersberg, Tennessee, and underwent rigorous training, ninety-six hours straight, with only about six or seven hours off each day for meals and sleep. When the training was complete, they were assigned a brand-new B-17 and immediately went on twenty-four hour stand-by.

We would have left for Europe immediately except for a hurricane that was going up the east coast of the U.S. After a three-day delay, we finally took off. Our first stop was Manchester, New Hampshire. From there we flew to a Canadian base in Newfoundland. Our next stop was in Iceland, where we encountered some really foul weather. We had the best navigator in the army, and he brought us down through the clouds right over our destination. We stayed there one night and set out for northern Iceland. This was the B-17 depot and we left the plane there.

We went by ship across the Irish Sea and then on to the 95th Heavy Bomber Base near Horam, England. It was at this base that the first bombers to hit Berlin were stationed. We were assigned to a B-17 there that was named *I Dood It.*

Our first assignment, shortly after D-day, was to fly over the North Sea and English Channel searching for downed flyers. The British bombed at night, and the Americans during the day. Many planes went down in these waters, and it was always a race between our forces and the Germans to see who could get to them first. When we spotted their lifeboats, we stayed with them until a navy launch could pick them up.

We then flew some decoy missions, which were designed to confuse the German radar while our gliders landed troops in France. Our first bombing mission was at the very end of September 1944, and it was uneventful. Our third mission involved bombing a German Red Cross train in the railyard of a German city. Our intelligence told us the train would be in the yard at ten o'clock in the morning.

It was a hospital train all right, but loaded with munitions headed for the front. I have never seen such explosions as when we hit that train. There was very little left of the entire city.

On our fourth mission, October 6, 1944, we bombed the Daimler-Benz aircraft engine factory in Berlin. We had completed our bombrun and were headed for home when a German antiaircraft shell severed a large oilline on our number one engine. Oil sprayed back onto the exhaust manifold, which is red hot, and caused a fire in the engine. The B-17 has three CO_2 fire extinguishers, which can be selectively activated toward each engine. The first activation put out the fire temporarily. But the oil kept spraying out and reignited. Eventually our CO_2 was exhausted, and we knew the oil was also spraying back into the wing fuel tanks. It was just a matter of time before the fire reached the fuel tanks.

It was time to get out. We were at 24,000 feet, where the temperature is -55 degrees F, when the pilot said to bail out. The ball-turret gunner yelled over the intercom, "Wait for me." I kicked the door over the bomb bay open and could see that most of the crew was already gone. I went back to the flight deck and saw that only the pilots and I were left. I bailed out and the pilots followed shortly.

It was the first time I'd used a parachute, and I hit the ground hard. It was windy, and I was dragged along by the chute. I learned years later that both my collarbones were broken when I hit. German civilians saw me come down and came running out to me. I was really afraid of what they intended to do to me.

When I hit the ground, I immediately began trying to get out of the harness. Almost immediately there was a German VW Jeep there with a soldier holding a submachine gun. I had thrown away my .45 when coming down. We had been told to do that if we knew we had no chance when we reached the ground. I was able to convince the German I was unarmed. He put me in his jeep, and it was then that I realized the German civilians cared nothing about me, but were after the silk and nylon in my parachute.

I was taken to a German air base and put into jail with several other airmen, including two members of my own crew. They interrogated us at length, wanting to know about the black boxes in the tail of the B-17. Nobody knew except the navigators. We didn't know, and they didn't press us too hard.

As our navigator was trying to get his parachute harness loose, one of the guards, a very young German, thought he was going for his pistol and shot him. The bullet went right through the flesh of the navigator's side and out. It did little damage—didn't even bleed much. But the German boy went to pieces when he realized he had hit him.

The ball-turret gunner had quite a frightful experience. Where he came down, there was a deep valley with hills on each side. Running between the hills were some high-voltage power lines strung between two towers. Shortly, our gunner, came down right on these lines and the big snaps on his chute harness clipped right onto the power line, suspending him several hundred feet off the ground. The Germans cut off the power and tried everything possible to reach him. Finally they shot a line up to him somehow and were able to pull him over to one of the towers and get him unhooked. He had hung there for several hours.

We were sent to Stalag Luft IV, a prison in eastern Germany right near the Polish border. The officers were sent to a different prison camp, because the Germans wanted to keep the officers and enlisted men separated. I found out after the war that all of my crew were captured and all survived.

I was in this prison camp from October 20, 1944, until February 6, 1945. All of the prisoners there were airmen, and most in my barracks were British. The bunks were full, so I had to sleep on a blanket on the floor. We never got enough to eat. Two or three times a week the Germans would give us a few vegetables like turnips and kohlrabi. Never any meat. We would make a soup out of the vegetables—pretty thin. Occasionally we would get a Red Cross food parcel to divide up between four or eight men. It was these that probably kept us alive.

Some of the men had been in this prison since the early days of the war—over three years now. Somehow they had managed to get one of the radios from a downed B-17—probably by bribing a German guard with chocolate from the Red Cross packages. So we were able to get news from the BBC on an irregular basis.

In December 1944 we began to get word of the Battle of the Bulge. This was terribly depressing news as we could see ourselves there for a very long time. Shortly after Christmas, though, we began to hear bombardments to our east. The Russians were advancing through Poland and into Germany.

Some of the British prisoners were really Polish airmen who had flown their planes to Britain when the Germans invaded Poland in 1939. They flew for the British Royal Air Force and wore the British uniform, but with a special insignia indicating their Polish origin. When news came of the fall of Poland to the Russians, we thought the Polish airmen would be elated. But they weren't. They said that one aggressor, the Germans, had merely been replaced by another, the Russians.

About February 1, 1945, the Germans began removing us from the camp. On February 6, I left with about six hundred other prisoners, mostly British and Canadian. We each had the clothes on our back and two thin blankets. We spent almost three months on the march from one prison to another, but never staying very long at any one. We were at Stalag XI near Fallingbostel, Germany, for about ten days. We slept mainly in barns along the way, and the lice and bedbugs were horrible. It was winter, and we were cold and wet much of the time. It was really miserable. Most of the guards were very old men and didn't mistreat us. We just got so very little to eat. Once there were about two hundred of us in a barnyard. There were several chicken troughs around, and the German farm woman brought out five or six large kettles of oatmeal. She had cooked and poured it into the troughs for us. It was not very elegant, but it was one of the most memorable meals of my life—nice and hot.

We were marched north from southeast of Berlin into northeastern Germany (Eastern Pomerania, the Reich's breadbasket), then west across northern Germany and through an area called Swinemünde. This was near the Oder River and was one of the areas from which the Germans were launching the V-2 rockets on England. They moved us through there very rapidly.

Once we were stopped near a German airbase. A British plane was attacking the base and flew right over us as it was firing its cannons. One of the spent shell casings fell and hit the ground about a foot from one of our men. It would undoubtedly have killed him had it hit him in the head.

The fighter plane was shooting at a German fighter that was taking off. As soon as the plane came into view, we could see that it was on fire. The pilot flew his plane straight up until it stalled out. He then turned it on its back, and he dropped out, opening his parachute. As he floated down, the plane almost came down into the fire. We were watching from about five hundred yards away. The last we saw of the German pilot, he gathered up his chute and started walking back to the airbase.

During the march we stopped at a barn near a small town. The barn was not large enough for all of us, so the guard let some of us sleep outside. About midnight, the R.A.F. dropped a flare that turned the town into daylight, and it hung in the air for nearly an hour. A large railyard was on one side of the town and a canal was on the other. The R.A.F. bombed the town, the railyard, and the canal. I had a close-up view of the fireworks. The next day they marched us past the town, and we could see the total destruction. But there was one building that remained almost totally untouched. It was a church building. Another time we marched past a railroad yard that was filled with several dozen steam locomotives, all with blown boilers—the work of the R.A.F. and American fighters.

About a month before we were liberated, we stayed about three days in one place. The weather was a little warmer, and the sun was shining. There was a clear mountain stream. I removed all of my wool clothes and attempted to take a cold water bath—no soap, no towel. I went back to the fire we had going, and I turned all my clothes wrong side out and passed them through the flames to attempt to kill the body lice. It helped a lot as I didn't notice so many at night.

The night that we were liberated, we were near a small town. We were asleep in a barn when the door opened and a voice said, "Blokes, give me your attention. I'm Dixie Dean." He was a POW who was trusted by the Germans to travel around and work for the good of all POWs. He said he had talked to the commander of the British army, and he said they would be through the town where we were at about nine o'clock the next morning. Dixie Dean gave us instructions to lay low and not to fight the guards.

The next morning we noticed the guards had dropped their rifles, and all the houses had white cloths hanging out the windows. The tanks came in about 9:30, and we were free. We discovered some cows that had not been recently milked. So we milked some and had lots of warm milk. The hen eggs also had not been collected, so we did that and had eggs for breakfast. It was May 2, 1945.

We were liberated by the 101st Airborne Division of the British 2nd Army, near Lauenburg, Germany, on the Elbe River. We had marched nearly five hundred miles in the three months since leaving Stalag Luft IV.

The British troops who liberated us pointed out several nice homes on the bluffs overlooking the Elbe River and told us to pick one out and go to sleep in it. We chose a fine brick home and went up to it. There was a sign in German and English on the wall saying that no civilians were allowed to occupy these homes. They were reserved for liberated Allied prisoners. We found an old couple sitting inside in the dark and told them to get out. They ran out the back door fast. The next morning the fellow who had spent the night with me in the house got up early while I was still asleep. At the foot of the hill, he had found a damaged German truck that was filled with Red

Cross food parcels—what a find! He brought three boxes—all he could carry of the food parcels—back up to the house and dumped them on top of me. That woke me right up.

We opened up the parcels and were preparing to make some breakfast. About that time a young woman appeared at the door mumbling about *Essen* [eat] and *Kinder* [children]. I told her to get lost. My buddy went out to the woodshed to get some wood to start a fire. He found the old couple sitting in the woodshed. He motioned for the old man to build a fire in the stove, and for the old woman to cook the oatmeal from the Red Cross parcels. She cooked enough to feed a platoon. We ate all we wanted and gave the rest to the old couple.

With the little German I knew and the little English the old woman knew, she learned that I was twenty-four years old. With that she began to cry because she had a twenty-four-year-old son who was in the German army and had been sent to the Russian front. They had not heard from him for a long time. Soon the old man came in with the young woman and some kids. It turned out that the young woman was their daughter-in-law, and the kids were her children and they lived next door. The young woman was crying because her children were so hungry. We took the chocolate bars and left the rest for them.

The night before, we had taken an old Chevrolet from a couple of German women. In the morning it was gone, and a bicycle had been left in its place. We walked down to the fields along the river. The fields were filled with thousands of German soldiers. The British were marching them across the pontoon bridge to the other side of the Elbe. Any German who was wearing an SS insignia was pulled out of the line and taken around the corner of a building by the British troops. There were shots, and the Brits came back alone. The British didn't fool around with any trials for SS men—killed them on the spot. Many of the SS escaped, though, by discarding their SS uniforms and insignia.

My buddy and I got a ride in a British jeep. The German soldiers had been told not to walk on the pavement, but on the side of the roadway. Some of them disregarded this warning and stayed on the pavement. The British jeep driver hit several of them and knocked them off the pavement. Probably killed them.

In Lüneburg the British had set up a processing center for liberated prisoners. The first thing they did was give us a shower in the coldest water I've ever been in. Everything except our personal items was taken from us and burned. We received new British uniforms and were flown out to Brussels, where we were turned over to Americans.

We were sent to Camp Lucky Strike near one of the French harbors. We were fed five times a day in an effort to restore our health. We sailed from France on the troopship USS *Weehuck*, a converted German luxury liner. We were in a convoy that arrived in New York harbor. Before we docked, the ship's captain sailed us around the Statue of Liberty. Men knelt down and cried, they were so happy to be back home.

I went to Camp Kilmer, New Jersey, and the next day I left on a train for Fort Sheridan in Chicago. I got home on June 8, 1945, to spend sixty days of convalescent leave. It was during this time that Margaret and I were married.

I wanted to remain in the Army Air Forces and specialize in engine mechanics, but I failed the physical exam. I was given the choice of hospitals in which to receive treatment for ulcers and my nerves, which were shot. I chose the hospital in Colorado Springs, where I spent several weeks. At the end of this treatment, I was discharged, on September 26, 1945, with a 50 percent disability.

On October 6, 1974, thirty years to the day after our plane was shot down, seven members of my crew had a reunion at a hotel in Chicago. One of the men was unable to make it, and the copilot who had remained in the air forces had been killed in a plane crash in 1952. But the rest of us had a great time reliving our memories.

Technical Sergeant Claude E. Harper

U.S. Army Air Forces
323rd Bomb Squadron, 91st Bomb
Group (H), AAF Station 121
Captured in Köthen, Germany, After His
B-17 Was Shot Down During A Bombing Mission
Prisoner of War
November 2, 1944–April 15, 1944
Laz Hildbnrghausen—Laz Meiningen

On March 22, 1943, Claude was called to Chicago for a physical examination for induction in the U.S. Army. He wasn't worried about it because he was sure he wasn't physically fit. During his high school days Claude had been taken off the track team after being diagnosed with a heart murmur. To his amazement, however, he was not only found to be physically fit, but he was assigned to the Army Air Forces, which required the most physically fit because of assignments to high-altitude bombers.

For the next several months Claude went through training—first basic training at Keesler Field, Mississippi, and then radio training at Scott Field in Belleville, Illinois. Claude considered himself more fortunate than many young men while at Scott Field because he and his new wife, Wilda Elizabeth Parker, were able to spend almost three months together.

After his completion of radio training, Claude was sent to Yuma, Arizona, for aerial gunnery training, then to Salt Lake City for crew assignment. He was assigned to crew 4496, consisting of pilot, copilot, navigator, bombardier, crew chief, radio operator, ball-turret gunner, two waist gunners, and tail gunner. For two months the crew studied maps of Italy and Southern Germany. The crew was told their base would be Foggia, Italy.

During this time, Claude's first son, Donnie, was born. Claude requested emergency leave to see him, but was denied. He was able to see him before shipping out, but by then Donnie was over a year old.

129

Technical Sergeant Claude E. Harper (in rear, second from left) and crew. (Courtesy of Claude E. Harper.)

We traveled by train to New York for a troopship to England. We sailed from New York on July 1, 1944, arrived at Liverpool on July 13, 1944, and were sent by military convoy to Bassingbourne Airfield, near the city of Cambridge, arriving on July 16, 1944. The Bassingbourne Airfield had been the "air force academy" for the R.A.F. We had brick, three-floor buildings to live in, with tile baths and showers—just about first class. On the day of our arrival, the group was returning from the raid on St. Lô, in which our front lines were accidentally hit by our bombers. We had two weeks of intense study in formation flying, then we were ready to fly combat.

On August 3, 1944, crew 4496 flew our first combat mission, to Mulehouse, Germany. It was a rather routine flight. No German fighters came at our 91st Bomb Group nor was there much flak. The mission lasted almost seven hours, five at high altitude. The 8th Air Force was escalating their bombing missions. Between August 3 and August 9 our crew flew four missions. On August 8, 1944, the 91st flew to Caen, France, to assist the Allied troops in their advance. Our flight encountered the worst flak that I saw in all twenty-four missions. The 88 mm guns were zeroed in on our altitude, and the sky was completely black with the burst. It seemed you could walk on the black bursts. If the shell burst in the vicinity of the B-17, it bounced the plane as if we had hit a severe "updraft," but our plane didn't get a scratch.

As we progressed through these early flights, we became "wiser and dumber" as to the workings of B-17s at high altitude, where the temperature was sixty below zero. Instructions were to fire all the guns on the B-17 as a check before reaching enemy territory. We did this procedure on our first two missions, but didn't encounter any German fighters. Nevertheless, you had to take the guns apart and clean them after the mission. We decided that was a lot of work for nothing, so we didn't check all the guns every time. We learned pretty quickly that the air force had expertise that we should have listened to. About the fourth mission we did encounter some enemy fighters, and some of our guns were frozen. The firing at high altitude cleared the lubricant from the gun; otherwise, it could freeze. We always cleaned all thirteen guns after that mission.

Another little lesson came to our attention also. During the long flights nature's call has to be answered. The B-17 was equipped with a relief tube in the bomb bay area for urinating. We found out that the urine freezes at fifty or sixty below zero. So the first guy was O.K., but the tube was frozen for the next guy. So we decided to use the bomb bay when we had to urinate because we were going to drop the contents of the bomb bay on the Germans anyway.

On August 9, 1944, we were sent to Munich area. One of the radio operator's duties was to check the bomb bay to see that the doors opened when we started the bomb run. As we started the bomb run, Lt. Carlini blurted over the radio, "Bomb bay doors open." I checked, and they were not. I could see the problem was that frozen urine had sealed the doors. Hurriedly I climbed onto the catwalk and swung down to kick the doors open. It worked, and I got back on the catwalk. I could hear Capt. Farris say, "Get Harper out of the bomb bay. We're going to drop in five seconds." Sgt. Knapp was trying to pull me out, but my chute harness was hung on the catwalk structure. I just hung on tight as the bombs fell away. Capt. Farris later told us, "I was afraid it was bombs and Harper away." All was well, but we listened to the more experienced crews from then on.

On August 12, 1944, we flew a short mission to Bû, France. This was a large commercial airport outside of Paris. Sgt. Knapp was knocked down by a piece of flak, but it hit him in the chest and the flak suit deflected the metal. No damage, just a scare.

One of our hairiest flights was on August 13, 1944. We were to bomb a bridge across the Seine River at Rouen, France. Our crew had been flying just any plane that was available, but we were assigned an old olive-drab plane named *Mary Lou*. A colonel who had been the first pilot of the plane had named it after his wife. This was to be our plane. As we made the turn for Bassingbourne, at rather low altitude, we ran through a flak field and got the nose of the *Mary Lou* almost blown away. The navigator, Lt. Passenger, took a piece of flak in the neck, but not a serious injury. No one else got a scratch.

Another burst hit in the bomb bay and damaged some of the hydraulic lines. Another damaged the controls on number two engine. We fell out of formation and were on our own. The pilot dropped low, to avoid any fighters that might see us. Capt. Harris reported our condition and headed for Bassingbourne. By throttling the other engines up to match the runaway engine, we were able to keep up with the formation, only below them. As we came near to Bassingbourne's airspace we reported our problem to the tower. They cleared us for a straight in. We cranked the landing gear down, knowing that we needed to save all the hydraulic fluid we had. Capt. Farris had us all get in crash position, and then he made the approach. As the plane touched down, the hydraulic system failed. We had no brakes and the number two engine could not be controlled. The pilot and copilot cut all throttles. The plane, with number two out of control, pulled off of the runway to the left and made about three tight circles before number two burned out of gas. We jumped out and got away as fast as we could. The emergency crews were there to assist. Nothing happened. We surveyed the damage, and we all decided that was it for the *Mary Lou*—it was a mess. In about three weeks we were told, "Your new plane is ready." We were surprised: The *Mary Lou* had been repaired. It was the only olive-drab plane in the 91st. All the rest were silver. We flew the *Mary Lou* another eighteen missions without a scratch. One day when we were not on a mission, someone flew the plane up to Ireland and came in with the landing gear up. That was the end of the *Mary Lou.*

On August 17, we flew to hit an aircraft factory at Halle. It was deep into Germany, almost to Leipzig. Those were really long missions. The German fighters were very much present when we ran out of fire cover of our fighter planes. The German fighters hit the 91st Bomb Group pretty hard. We lost a number of our friends that day.

On August 28 the mission was to Poleitz. The way we had to fly to get in and back made it the longest mission I ever flew. The next day we flew to Brux, Czechoslovakia.

Our next mission was to Kiel. This was one of the first 1,000-plane missions I flew on. The Germans were ready for us with a massive concentration of flak. I saw one of the B-17s in our squadron take a burst of flak that tore off one-fourth of the left wing, but he was able to fly back to base. On September 11 we flew to Merseburg (near Leipzig) for the second time. This was another of the 1,000-bomber raids. The allied fighters shot down 110 Nazi planes.

One of the largest concentrations of Allied planes was put into the air on September 26 to bomb Ludwigshafen, a major rail center. About a year before, only one plane, *Hi Ho Silver,* had made it home from a raid there.

On September 29 we made the long flight back to Merseburg to hit the synthetic fuel plant. The group just in front of us and the one behind us were completely wiped out by German fighters. On October 20 the B-17s flew back to Ludwigshafen to continue the destruction of the rail system.

During the rest of October, the weather accounted for many "stand downs" of the heavy bombers from the 91st Bomb Group. Also during this time, our crew did not have a plane assigned to us, so we only flew when another crew was on leave. On November 1 we were scheduled to fly deep into Germany in a new silver B-17 that only had seven missions on her log; however, the mission was scrubbed. On November 2 we were briefed on the same mission: back to Merseburg again. The plane assigned us was *Sherry's Cherries*. It was the same new plane from the day before. Painted on the nose was a topless blonde with a large bust and shiny, red nipples.

As the English fog cleared away, we took off for the fourth time. The flight was pretty routine until we came close to the Merseburg-Leipzig area, then it all came at us—flak, planes, and whatever else was available. As we headed on the bomb run, a burst of flak took out our number three engine. The pilot was able to adjust and pretty well keep up with the group. We were in the lower squadron, near the tail end Charley position. After dropping the bombs, the pilot cut across the gap to the left to intercept the group as they headed back to England.

Being out by ourselves, we were fair game for the FW-190s. In seven minutes they had *Sherry's Cherries* on fire, with two crew members dead and myself wounded. All the wounded were in the rear of the plane, where the FW-190s could just hang out there and fire. I was using the left waist gun when I was knocked down by something. I thought I had been hit in the head. I got back to the gun, but only one hand had hold of the stock. My left arm had been hit and was hanging down. As I looked out the waist window, I could see the right wing was almost engulfed in flames. I yelled at the other gunner that we had to bail out. I pulled out the pins on the waist door and was ready to jump when that plane started spinning in a downward spiral. The force of the spin held me flat on the floor, I had seen a number of B-17s spin a few times, straighten out for a few seconds, then dive nose-down out of sight. I said to myself, "When she levels out, I'll jump." But it never leveled out. There was an explosion that blew me out of the open door. I rolled over in the air and saw the four engines falling below me.

Forgetting the instructions to free fall until you are near the ground, I pulled the rip cord. I was glad it opened, but then I saw the error of my ways. When the chute opened, it popped off both my boots. It's cold at eighteen to twenty thousand feet. I would warm one foot in the bend of my knee and then do the other foot the same way. Probably there was some good in my action because it slowed down the flow of blood from the wound in my left arm.

A strange fact was that my chute was only hooked on one side. On an earlier flight, a plane just above the radio hatch, a B-17, had disappeared in a burst of smoke. I reached down and hooked my chute on the right chest hook. I always flew that way. It saved my life. I'm almost sure the other gunner did not have his chute on when the plane exploded. However, after I was back in American hands, I learned that one strap won't hold you in a jump.

About 5,000 feet above the ground, I could see a FW-190 crisscrossing about 2,000 feet below me. That made my heart skip some beats. I was sure he would see me, and I'd be his next target. As I got nearer the ground and below a low cloud cover, I could see that I was going to land in a small town. I could see quite a bit of activity. I saw two chutes lying on top of a flat-roofed building. They weren't moving. I don't know if they had died from the fall or had been killed in some other way. There were a couple of uniformed people there, too. As I got almost to the ground, I saw a bunch of kids playing in a playground; and that was where I hit. They sure were excited. The largest two kids only reached to my shoulders. They asked if I had a pistol. When I shook my head and pointed to my useless arm, they became somewhat braver and crowded around. With the two largest kids on each side and the rest following along, I was led down the main street toward the main part of town. There they turned me over to some soldiers, and I'm sure were telling how they had captured an American flyer.

They put me in a cell and locked it. After dark, someone with some medical knowledge looked at my arm and then left. I could feel the blood still seeping around my rib cage and down my sides. It must have just been a slow leak. Sometime later, they put us in a truck and transported us away. I later learned that we were taken to a small hospital in Köthen. There they put some dressings on the wound, showed me a bed, and locked the door. We would see someone three times a day, and then at dusk they turned out the lights and left us. At first, the nurse and a guard would come in to check on us; but after they realized we weren't going any place, the nurse started checking on us by herself. One of the things that sticks with me today is the memory of a young nurse that checked on me from time to time. She was a beautiful young blonde. When she was checking me one day, I saw lice crawling up her neck. They were big lice. But that was just part of life in Germany. It didn't seem to bother her a bit.

One fellow in the hospital had a broken leg, and they set it. They didn't have any painkillers for anyone. They just held the guy and set the leg. At the same time, they were amputating a German's leg, without any painkiller.

The twenty days in Köthen were mostly a blur of pain and dark, sleepless nights. My arm was shot up, and I laid in bed without a sling or cast on it. But I felt lucky compared to some of the other prisoners. I really didn't know you could stay awake and in pain for so long and still exist, but you can.

The rest of my crew that were not killed had been captured by the military, and their crews' families had been notified that they were prisoners of war. I was the only crewmember captured by civilians, and for twenty days—until I was released from the civilian hospital—no one in the United States knew that I was a prisoner of war.

One morning they came in and said "We are going to move you." They put us on a small train. It must have been a hospital train because the car we were in had beds in it. On the back of the train, the Germans had mounted an 88 mm antiaircraft gun. At night the heavy bombers would come over from England. The train would stop and fire that gun. It would almost knock us off of the rails. This went on for three nights. Then we arrived in Frankfurt, and they loaded us on a small van. After we were loaded, the driver raised the hood and lit a match. I thought, "What in the world is he doing?" I found out later that that was the way he started the engine. The van ran on corncobs dipped in some kind of fuel. I don't know exactly how it worked, but it would start. The van would putt-putt along. We started up a mountain at Frankfurt to an interrogation center that all air force personnel went through. The van putt-putted along, and about half-way up the hill the driver jumped out to pour more corncobs in the engine tank. I bet that van had thirty gears in it. The further up the hill, the steeper it got, and the more the driver geared down.

We finally reached the interrogation center. The Germans were waiting on us. They took us in a room and sat us down. The first thing that they did was ask us if we wanted something to eat. It was the first decent food that I had seen in a long time. Naturally we said that we wanted food.

The second day that I was there, they called me in for interrogation. They asked me where I was from. I knew they already knew where I was from, so I told them that I was from Illinois. The German responded, "Ah, Chicago." I said, "No, Chicago is a long way from where I live." The only thing that he knew about Chicago was Al Capone. He said that he had a cousin who was a barber in Chicago. He continued the small talk for a while, and then he asked me where we were flying to the day we were shot down. I told him that I didn't know. He said, "You are their radioman, and you didn't know where they were going that day?" I told him that I had missed briefing that day. We discussed things back and forth for a little while, and he excused himself and left the room. While he was gone I looked over on his desk, and he had a list of my crew. He already knew that I was a part of that group. So when he came back, I asked him what the marks were by some of the names on the list. He said, "Those are the ones that are dead. The rest have already been shipped to prison camps." I said, "Well you know more about me than I know." That pleased him, and he said that's all.

A couple of days later, they shipped me out to a hospital at Meiningen, the main prison hospital in western Germany. At this time I had my arm in a sling. The first day that we were there, I asked them if they had anything for pain. They gave me some medication, and I slept for two days. I hadn't slept much for the entire time I had been captured. I was out of it, but I could hear voices. I heard them say that they were going to have to rebreak my arm. They broke and reset it and put it in a cast. The pain was gone. So after I was alert enough, I asked them what type of medication they had given me—it was aspirin. It had just enough kick to it that it relaxed me. After we were able to get around, they would let us out into the regular area of the hospital, where the other patients were located. They didn't have any heat, and it was in December. Early each morning, we could go out and pick up sticks and whatever coal we could find, and we would build a fire in the fireplace.

We had one fellow in the hospital who was an old man. One day he was showing a picture around of this beautiful young blonde. I asked one of the other prisoners if that was his daughter. He said, "No it is his wife." Come to find out, the old man was only twenty-seven years old. He looked like he was sixty-five. I asked what was wrong with him, and they told me it was a broken leg. He had pitied himself so much that he had just gotten old. I saw two other guys who each had a leg off. They were on crutches and all the time cutting up. One day they were on the road rooster-fighting. They were having a ball. They had a good outlook. But here was this guy with a broken leg, and he was worse off. I learned after I left that the doctor came in one day and got real mad at this guy. He told the guy, "I don't care what you do, just go ahead and die." After that he got well.

That's where I got the body lice. They shaved my head and all the hair off my body and put some blue ointment on me. Everybody had them. You were there for a few weeks, got the body lice, and then they treated you. Then, when you came into contact with the lice again, they would go through the same procedure. I stayed at Meiningen until they saw that my arm was going to set okay, and then the Germans moved me again.

I was sent to Hildburghausen, which was about thirty miles from Meiningen. Hildburghausen was a small hospital that had been moved into a three-story home. There was a large yard with big trees. The entire place was surrounded by barbed wire. There were only about thirty-five or forty prisoners there. A German corporal was the commander of the hospital.

One of the things that I learned at Hildburghausen was to eat everything that I could get my hands on. Of a morning they had bread that was made out of some rye and wheat. It was black and dry, and you couldn't hardly eat it. It had a terrible taste to it, but we had one slice of that bread for breakfast with acorn coffee. At noon we got a bowl of turnips. In the evening we would have a piece of bread and marmalade, and that was it. I found out that the turnip soup had a lot of good nutrients in it. On warm days we could walk out in the compound, and whenever one of the other prisoners didn't want their soup I would eat it. But that was our diet for the whole five months that I was there. One time the bombers killed a horse, and they did let us have part of that. But it was the only time we got any meat.

The International Red Cross would check on these hospitals, and they would send little packages with cigarettes, a couple of candy bars, and toothpaste for the prisoners of war. We got one of those every couple of months. I found out that cigarettes were the best gold you could have. I could trade them for anything. One of the English prisoners had been at the prison camp for five years. He could speak German very well and had been kept at the camp as an interpreter for the English and Americans. He had connections with a guard who would go downtown and buy you something if you had something to trade. I accumulated cigarettes and would give them to the guard through the English interpreter. We would get enough bread with one pack of cigarettes to feed thirteen people.

The Germans also liked the chocolate bars. I traded my cigarettes to the other prisoners for the chocolate bars and accumulated a large quantity. The guard would get a chocolate bar, and he would return from town with something for us to eat. This went on for about two months until the guard got caught, and that ended the trading.

People have often asked me if we were mistreated. I don't think we were. It was getting on into 1945, and the war was almost over. They simply didn't have a lot to give us. One of the stories that I was told about the bread we were given was that some of the bread we received was baked in 1938. It had been rolled in sawdust. When it was delivered, it was on a rack and stored in a central location. That was the German soldiers' rations also. They got a loaf of bread a week and some kind of meat that we might call a summer sausage. So I think they gave us as much as they could.

Several nights while we were there, the English had bombing raids. We didn't pay much attention to it at first, but then they kept getting closer, and we had to go into the basements during the raids. We would be there until two or three in the morning.

During the day I would sit in the window and let the sunlight warm me. There was no heat at all except in the commandant's room, and I was there a few times. That was during the Battle of the Bulge. The commandant was listening to the reports and let us come up to listen. The Germans thought this was the turning point of the war. It was going their way, according to Hitler, who always had a secret weapon. This was the secret—the Battle of the Bulge. So they were sure the war was turning around. The commandant would let us come up and listen. I just went where I could get some heat. I knew we were going to win.

Each day that I could, I would go out and walk around and around in the compound. I was in good physical condition except for my arm, and I wanted to stay that way. The guards didn't bother us except when we were playing ball. If we got the ball too close to the fence, we had to let the guards know before we retrieved the ball; otherwise they would shoot.

After several big bombing raids, the word got out that the Americans were going to bomb every town that had a rail station in it. We had a rail-road running through our town. One day we were out in the yard exercising, and we heard these planes. We looked up, and there they were—B-17s flying in low. We saw them open their bomb bay doors, and we ran for the basement. It looked like they were going to hit us, but they actually hit about half a block from us. After that, when the bombers came over, the commandant opened the gates to the compound and let us go out into a graveyard that was close. He would send one guard with us each time. The bombers were concentrating on the buildings and railroads and always passed over the graveyard.

The Germans knew the war was close to the end. Patton was moving quickly across the country, and they knew he would be there soon. Orders came that the Germans were to move as many of us as were physically fit closer to the Russian front. There were thirteen of us that was able to move. So they brought a German sergeant in and put him in charge of us. The sergeant had three of the home guard to help him, all older men. We each got a cart and put what belongings we could carry in it and started out. He told us that we were "just going to start walking, we are going to take the back roads, and the Americans will catch us." About the second day one of the home guards, in his sixties, just give out. So one of the prisoners carried his gun for him, and we put him in a cart and pushed him along. If people could have seen us prisoners carrying the guard's gun and pushing him they would not have believed it, but he was our protection.

The German sergeant and myself were the same rank, and we usually walked together at the front of the column. He hated the SS troops. They were supposed to be the elite, and they were always putting the regular army down. The regular German army respected any army personnel from other countries. The SS did not. The SS did not care for life at all. The German soldiers were true soldiers.

We stopped in a little town one day to get some bread. The sergeant came out into the street, and two SS troops were with him. This lieutenant from the SS and the sergeant were screaming at each other. I couldn't understand what they were saying because it was all in German. One of the old guards told us to take off. The sergeant pulled his pistol and stuck it in the stomach of the lieutenant as we started walking down the road. The sergeant showed up about fifteen minutes later. I heard him tell one of the old guards that the SS officer wanted to kill us. The sergeant told him that he had left the compound with thirteen prisoners and that when the Americans arrived in a few days he was going to have thirteen prisoners.

We traveled for thirteen or fourteen days through Germany. We went through part of the Black Forest. One day we were walking along there, and I looked back into the forest from the road. There was a whole tank division that had pulled back about twenty yards into the forest. The planes couldn't see them from the air. I had heard of the Black Forest, but I didn't realize until I saw it that it was that dark.

We passed the forest, and the sergeant told us that there was a prisoner of war hospital in the next town. "The Americans will be here any time. I am going to put you in the hospital." So when we arrived in the town, he took us to the hospital. The next afternoon at two o'clock, Patton rolled into that little place and took it over. They came into the hospital and asked if there were any Americans in the hospital. There was seven of us. They told us to come with them. The commandant of the hospital told him that we couldn't go. The American officer that came in looking for Americans said, "Not anymore. They are ours."

He took us down to the headquarters and fed us our first meal. I had some bread and stuff. One guy decided that he wanted two eggs. They fixed them, and he tried to eat them. As soon as the food hit his stomach, it came back up.

The next morning at daylight, we got up and looked around. There was no one left but a lieutenant and a corporal. The lieutenant asked us where we needed to go, and we told him that we needed to get to Frankfurt. He told us that he didn't have any transportation, but he could write us an order allowing us to hitchhike. Then you can get there the best way you can. So we started hitchhiking.

We left and caught any vehicle we could that was headed that way. We traveled all day. We stopped at some depot, and we found another truck that was going on west. I looked for all the guys, but we had lost one of them. So we went ahead anyway, and lost all but three of us at the next stop. I had orders for all of us, but when we arrived in Frankfurt there was only three of us.

I took the cast off of my arm and cut the heads off of the lice that were under the cast. They grew about like ticks do on dogs. That's how big the body lice had gotten.

I was taken to the aid station, and the doctors found that my elbow was moving when it should have been stationary. There was no joint there for it to move, but it did and the doctors couldn't figure out why. They decided that I should be sent to Paris to have my arm taken care of. So they flew me out, and I stayed in Paris for about twenty days. In Paris the doctors decided that that wasn't the place to do the work either, so they flew me to England. So I spent fifteen days in the hospital in England doing whatever I wanted to do. They still didn't do anything with my arm, but decided that I should be sent to the United States. In New York they looked at my arm and said that there was a place in a hospital in Springfield, Missouri, which had experts that could look at my arm. In Springfield there were supposed to be orthopedic experts on staff, but there weren't. They sent me to Vaughn General Hospital in Chicago, claiming there was an expert there. When I arrived, they asked me if I had been home. I told them no, so the doctor told me that they were going to send me home for thirty days because they couldn't do anything at the time anyway. After thirty days I went back up there and they told me that they had decided there was nothing they could do for my arm. So they put me on disability, discharged me, and sent me home.

Part V

THE INVASION
OF GERMANY

HIT PARADE

Low Is the Sun
Embraceable You
Rockin' at Aachen
I Walk Alone
It's Foolish But It's Fun (from *Spring Parade*)
Dear Old Girl
Close to Me
My One, My Only
Hit the Bottle
Half a World Away

—From a Kriegie's diary

Lieutenant Paul H. Smith

U.S. Army
Company D, 314th Infantry
Captured During An Ambush While
on Patrol Near the Rhine River
Prisoner of War
August 1944–October 1944
Stalag XIIA

Paul has done many things twice in his life. He has been killed in action twice and lived to tell about it. He was wounded twice and received two purple hearts. He received two Bronze Stars for bravery, and he received the Silver Star once—for saving the life of a wounded soldier when he carried him under intense gun fire from a bridge. It is worth mentioning that he did the same deed a second time without receiving a medal. He was captured by the Nazi soldiers during World War II, but he escaped and made his way to freedom. Years later he was taken prisoner in Korea. Again he escaped and found his way back to American troops.

Each time he was captured, his mother was notified that he had been killed in action. Each time, it was months before she learned otherwise. Eight years after the war ended, she received a letter from the Veterans' Administration for death benefits that had recently been approved for Korean veterans.

At the age of twenty-two, on January 2, 1943, I was drafted into the service. I didn't pass the medical exam because of problems with my teeth. The next day, when I got home, I went down to the army recruiter and told them I wanted to join up. I took the exams, and I was accepted.

They shipped me back to Chicago, and I joined the guys that I had originally went up with for induction. We all went through training together.

After training, I was shipped to the European theater, in May 1944. I trained with the 76th Division, but I fought with the 79th Division. I was captured during the Battle of the Bulge. There was a group of us. They marched us during the night, and during the day we holed up in barns and schoolhouses.

Straw-strewn floor at Stalag XIIA where Paul Smith and other prisoners slept. (Courtesy of Paul H. Smith.)

We didn't have any problem with water because the snow was several feet deep, but we did have problems with food. Some of us had a little rations on us, and the Germans allowed us to keep them. But we marched for days, and they never gave us any food at all.

I had received a battlefield commission and was separated from the enlisted men when we arrived at Stalag XIIA. The conditions were bad. We were crowded into a barrack with straw beds to sleep in. There was no heat in the barrack.

When you were sick, you didn't dare go to the doctor because you didn't know if you were going to be used as a guinea pig or not. Hitler's SS troops were inhumane. They had no consideration for life at all.

We had Mexicans who had volunteered in the American army, and their fate was at the mercy of Hitler's Third Reich. They were treated like the Jews, considered to be an inferior race because of their dark skin. They were taken away and gassed.

I've seen men shot, stabbed, burned, and buried alive. The Nazis would dig a big trench and just keep filling it with bodies. It was pure horror.

We got little food to eat. In the morning we got some colored water the Nazi guards called coffee. Most of the time it was cold. A slice of barley bread to go with it if we were lucky. At noon we got potato soup. At night a hunk of bread.

The Nazis needed food for their troops, and manpower was very short for the Germans, so a lot of the prisoners worked taking care of the farms. We grew potatoes and cabbage, but we weren't allowed to eat any of it. If a prisoner got caught eating produce, he was really in trouble.

Officers didn't have to work, but I volunteered. I got to go out on a farm. I knew that I would get more to eat because the workers got an extra bowl of soup, and I also knew that I would be able to consume some of the crop without the Nazis catching me. It also gave me an opportunity to start making an escape plan. I could determine the directions by the sunrise and sunset so I always kept that in mind. Then I set my sights on something that I didn't think would get blown up when I took off.

I watched for several days while I was working out in the field, and I spotted some woods. It was along the edge of a field a couple hundred yards from where I was working. One evening, when it was getting close to dusk, I watched the guards. They had not had anybody try to escape, so they were pretty relaxed. They were across the field from where I was, so I took off. I made it to the woods without them spotting me. I hid there until it was completely dark, and then I took off. I moved through the night as fast as I could. I wanted to place as much distance between me and the camp as possible.

I ran as much as I could, but even when I stopped running I continued to walk. I never stopped all night. The next morning at about

Lieutenant Paul H. Smith. (Courtesy of Paul H. Smith.)

daylight I spotted a barn, and I hid in the hayloft. I was dead tired, hungry, and scared to death. I fell asleep and woke up in the afternoon.

That night I took off again. I spotted a garden near the barn where I stayed, and I got some raw vegetables and ate them. Then I started across country again. I ran and walked all night. The second morning I found an old, empty building and stayed in it all day.

That night I started out again. I walked all night. I found a stream along the way and got water, but I didn't eat the second night. On the third morning, I stayed in a barn again. By now I thought I was getting close to France. I slept most of the day, but the hunger pains were starting to get to me. I was getting weak.

That night I walked all night again. I didn't find any food or water, but by the next morning I was on the outskirts of a village. I thought I had made it to France. I went to one of the houses and knocked on the door. I asked them in French for some milk. The lady looked at me strange and went back inside her house. A short time later she came to the door with a glass of milk. It tasted so good, and I was happy because I was sure that I had made it. What I didn't know was that her husband had gone to get the Heimwehr [home defense force made up of mostly old World War I veterans]. I was still in Germany.

A couple of the old guard took me at gunpoint to a small building and locked me inside. I stayed there for most of the day until some of the Nazi soldiers from the stalag arrived. They took me back to the prison camp.

It was the worst time in the prison camp for me. I was beaten with a wooden club on my back, legs, and buttocks. I found out years later when I had some X-rays taken for back trouble, that my neck had been cracked during the beating. They took my pants and shoes and threw me in the cooler [solitary confinement]. I was in the hole for thirteen days without food or water. I had to concentrate on something other than my present conditions, or I don't think I could have survived. So I figured out another escape plan.

A couple of times during the thirteen day period they would bring me out of the hole and ask me if I had learned my lesson. I would tell them I had. They would beat me a time or two with the club, then put me back in the hole. Finally, they let me out after the thirteenth day.

I was really weak from the lack of food. My feet had froze while I was in the hole, too. The other prisoners took me into the barrack and took care of me. They gave me extra rations and water.

We were not usually allowed to have water for a shower, and when I got out of the hole we had none. Some of the prisoners had been washing potatoes, and they kept the water and used it to clean me up.

The Nazis would let us pick up some loose timber outside the camp for firewood, but if they thought that you had too much, they'd take it away. They didn't want you to be comfortable at all. The guys had some extra wood, and they built a fire to get my feet and body warmed up. They did a good job getting me back in as good a shape as could be expected in a prison camp.

They wouldn't let me out to work on the farm after I got out of the hole, so myself and some of the other prisoners got together and played baseball, basketball, and volleyball. If we were playing baseball, we didn't dare go toward the fence. If the ball got loose and went toward the fence, you'd better make sure a guard in the tower knew it. You'd have to yell at him and point to the ball. He'd let you go get it, but all the while you were near the fence, he'd have a rifle pointed at you.

Some of the guards were friendly to the prisoners. They would talk with us, but they had to be careful not to do it too much because they would get in trouble for collusion with the enemy. The German guards had to watch the SS troops because "they are crazy," as one guard put it. Even the Germans were afraid of being shot by them.

I was able to write letters home, but I found out later that my mother only received one letter and it was all cut up. The Nazi guards read every letter, and if you said anything negative about the conditions or how you were being mistreated, they would cut it out of the letter.

A month or so after I got out of the hole, they let me go to work on the farm again. It was a life-saver because I was on the farm working when the British air force flew a bombing mission over the stalag and bombed the camp. There were a large number of POWs killed in the raid.

One day we were working near some timber. As soon as the guards were looking the other way, I slipped into the timber and ran. I ran till I dropped.

To keep from being caught this time, I decided not to talk to anyone. I had a plan. You know, if someone is crazy, you don't like to be around them. Every town has their town drunk or town idiot, and nobody wants to associate with them. So when I got out of the camp, I just acted like I was crazy. Some people would yell at me, trying to find out who I was, but I would just wave at them and keep walking.

I slept in haystacks at night. During the day I would walk. Along the way I spotted a motorcycle, and I stole it. I had never rode a motorcycle, but this one had a sidecar to it. I rode it, but I couldn't get it to go very fast for some reason. I don't think I ever got over fifteen or twenty miles an hour. I drove it for a day until I ran out of gas. Then I ditched it.

I started walking down the road again. Every time I heard something, I would hide. I heard this car coming, and before I could get off the road they had spotted me. I saw their helmets, and they looked like the Kaiser helmets. They stopped and asked me who I was. I was so scared I couldn't talk. I just mumbled, blah, blah, blah, blah. They took me back to the car, and I tried to talk again, but I couldn't. What I didn't realize was that it was a French command car. It was one of ours.

They took me back to the American lines. I got all I wanted to eat, was deloused, and got new clothes. They sent me to the hospital, where I stayed until I recuperated.

I got the greatest Christmas present in my life that year. It was a day late, but that was okay. On December 26, 1944, I boarded a ship for home. I arrived on January 11, 1945.

Private First Class
Phil Trapani

U.S. Army
10th Infantry Battalion, 4th
Armored Division, 3rd Army
Captured Approximately 100 Miles Inside
Germany While Caring For Wounded Soldiers
Prisoner of War
August 25, 1944–May 15, 1945
Stalag VIIA and Stalag IIA

Phil Trapani entered the army on June 21, 1943. After complet-
ing basic training and training as a medic, he was sent to the 42nd
Division in Oklahoma for six months. While he was there, he had a
conflict with a noncommissioned officer. Although Phil was not a vio-
lent man: he had had all he could take and hit the noncom. He had a
choice-court-martial or orders for Europe. Needless to say, he was sent
to a rifle company as an infantryman in England on June 13, 1944,
a week after D-day. No one, however, remembered to change his occu-
pation on his orders. As soon as the commanding officer saw that he
was a medic, he was sent as a medic to the 4th Armored Division in
France.

I joined the 4th Armored Division just as they broke out of St. Lô,
France. That's where I saw my first dead. It was a German soldier, and he
had been dead for about three days. Seeing that alone is enough to make a
person want to go home.

We had a lot of battles, but most of them didn't last over two days at a
time because we were driving the Germans ahead of us. Patton was really
moving us.

We had been moving for about a month, taking one town after another.
Then on August 22nd, we were about 150 miles south of Paris, and the rumor
was that we were going to take Paris. We left that morning, and after about
three days one of my buddies said that he couldn't wait to get to Paris. I told
him that if we were going to Paris, that we wouldn't be looking at the sun

148

every evening. We were going west, not north. He said, "I didn't think of that." Next thing you know we are at Troyes.

It was August 25, 1944. At about 4 P.M. Patton decided to take the town. We had the 4th Armored Division and 300 men from the 35th Infantry Division. A fourth of the tanks were out of gas. My jeep was on empty when we attacked. We thought the Germans would run just as soon as we attacked, but they didn't. They stood and fought.

We took several wounded soldiers back to the aid station. While we were at the aid station, Patton regrouped the units and attacked the town again—without any medics. When we returned from the aid station, our troops were gone. So we

Private First Class Phil Trapani. (Courtesy of Phil Trapani.)

tried to find them. During our quest we ran into about 250 German regular army troops. They surrendered to us. Here we were, eleven medics with no guns, and we had all these prisoners. We were treating some of their wounds, and me and my buddy got to talking. We figured that the next day's newspapers would have us in the headlines as heroes. It wasn't to be.

After a while we started moving out, and we got about a mile down the road and ran into thirty-five or forty SS troops. They were mean. They killed an eighteen-year-old driver in the first truck. They killed our doctor, our captain, and his driver. They hit me and another guy in the next jeep. We rolled out of our jeeps, and we still didn't surrender. The SS were in a row of buildings, and they kept firing at us. We were behind our jeeps and still wouldn't come out. We saw a row of American tanks way down the road, and we thought they were coming our way; but they didn't see us, and they turned and went another way. We still wouldn't give up. We waited and waited, and then we heard one of them holler at us. They had set up a .30 caliber machine gun behind us, not a hundred yards away. We were looking down the barrel of that gun, and we had no guns ourselves. So we had no choice but to surrender.

We stood with our hands up, and they marched us inside of town. They were going to kill us. They had us lined up against a wall. The firing squad was in front of us, and the SS lieutenant was standing with his pistol in one hand and an ax in the other. I knew I was dead. He asked if I wanted a cigarette. I didn't smoke, but the guy next to me took one. He still had to keep his hands in the air while he puffed on the cigarette. He was so scared that he was perspiring heavily; there was so much that it run onto his cigarette and put it out. He looked over at me, and I said, "When they kill us, I hope they shoot us because I don't think I can stand to be killed with the ax."

The lieutenant walked over to us and wanted us to beg him not to kill us. I wouldn't do it, but two guys did. They got on their knees. I told them, "Don't beg, men." One of them said, "You're just as scared as I am." I said, "I am more scared than you are, but don't beg. Be a man. Get up off of your knees." About that time the SS captain came over the hill. He walked down and called the lieutenant over and they started arguing. I told the guy beside me that if he could pray, now was the time to do it. "Pray the captain wins the argument, because he doesn't want to kill us." He won!

There's humor even when you are scared. They moved us to the third floor of this empty building. We started taking artillery from our own troops. I was really scared. I was the youngest one there, and one of the men knew I was really scared. He crawled over to me and said, "Hey, Trapani! They say that a mortar shell costs about $18.75." I said, "Yeah, I guess, but I don't know what you are getting at." He said, "Well, I think I am going to ask that German guard out there for a letter so I can write home to my congressman and tell him to stop my payroll check, because I don't want to buy any more ammunition to get shelled." He was trying to cheer me up.

We stayed on that third floor, and it was the first time I talked back to a German officer. A German doctor came up, and he started to bandage my wound. I grabbed his hand and threw it. The SS soldier started toward me, and the doctor told him that it was all right. I told him that I didn't understand why they killed our doctor and the other men. The red cross was flying, and they knew we were medics. He apologized and said they shouldn't have done it. He said that he was deeply sorry. He told me that they were going to move us to a bunker and that the next morning they were going to leave us when they left. I thought, "Well, one night as a prisoner of war isn't so bad," but he had lied to me. They weren't about to leave us.

The next day they moved us out. We walked to Nancy, France, and they kept us there for about a week. Then they loaded us on trains for Nürnberg, Germany. We spent part of the time shaking our coats out the window when our planes would come over so they wouldn't bomb us. Once they saw us they would tip their wings and fly by.

When we got to Stalag VIIA at Moosburg, I got in trouble with the Germans. The only thing that I had left by now was a bandage around my head, and I was in good shape otherwise. It was sick camp where I got off the train. I looked around and thought, "This isn't too bad if I have to spend the war here." So I got off the train. I was really disgusted when I realized that my buddies hadn't gotten off and that I would be separated from them.

About two weeks after I got there, we had an inspection. We had to strip to the waist. The doctor said, "I can't figure out how this horse got here," and that was the end of this camp.

The next day they put a bunch of us on a cattle train and sent us as far as Leipzig. In Leipzig, it was the second time we were almost killed. The night before we arrived, the town was bombed. There were a lot of people killed. Some of the houses and buildings were still burning when we pulled in. When we got off the train, there was a mob of people. They wanted to kill us for the bombings. The officer in charge of us told us that they wanted to kill us and that he had orders to protect us. He said that he was going to put the guards around us as we moved, but that he wouldn't shoot his own people. If they broke through the lines, he wouldn't stop them. He went out and got the mob settled down, and we moved to another train without incident.

They had to put us on a passenger train because they didn't have anything else from that point to put us in. One of the German guards came up and sat down beside me. He said, "How're the shack jobs in Pittsburgh?" That was the first time I knew he could speak English. I turned and said, "You can speak English as well as I can." He had lived in Pittsburgh for thirteen years and then went back to Germany. He told me how they were going to win the war.

We finally got to a camp near the Polish border, and they found out we had been captured in France. The Germans didn't want us there because many of the prisoners in the camp had been captured in Italy. The prisoners didn't know what was going on in the war, and many didn't even know that D-day had occurred. They stayed up with us all night and could not believe that the Allies were almost at the German borders. It really lifted their morale.

The next morning the Germans shipped us out by train. I went to Stalag IIA, about forty-five miles north of Berlin. It was about the middle of September. The commandant of the camp took all of the medics and officers into one of the barracks to talk with us. He told us that by the Geneva Convention rules we didn't have to work, but he wanted us to volunteer to work. Some did volunteer, but most of us didn't. They put us in a barrack together and cut what rations we got in half. They did it for three weeks, and I would have to say that I got so hungry that I would have worked if they had asked me again, but they didn't. I was proud that I had refused.

We did have to hold sick call each day, and we had about 150 men a day on the sick list. We didn't have a hundred men that were sick all the time, but I put down they were sick to keep them from working for the Germans.

We didn't have too many Americans in this camp until the Battle of the Bulge. That's when things got bad. We went down day and night carrying the wounded to the hospital. These guys were in bad shape. Besides the wounded we had men with diarrhea and vomiting. They were really in bad shape. We jumped from about fifty or sixty Americans in that camp to about five hundred after the Battle of the Bulge. I had one soldier that had pneumonia, and he was really bad. All I had was a little aspirin to give him. I stayed up with him for seven days making him talk with me and trying to get him to fight for his life. The other medics finally made me go to bed. When I woke up, he was dead. I accused them of letting him die, but they hadn't. They cared for him just as I had. We just didn't have the medicine to take care of him.

That winter we lost forty-two men. Most of them died from pneumonia. We had a burial site, and we had to take them out wrapped in blankets, dig their graves, and bury them. We weren't allowed to have any services, but we prayed for them silently. The Germans couldn't stop us from doing that.

One incident really bothered me. We had a soldier who had syphilis. We got very little penicillin, and what we did get we gave to soldiers with pneumonia. The Germans gave us a supply that would be enough for three doses. I knew that if the black soldier didn't get treatment he would die. At the time there were no prisoners with pneumonia so all of the medics got together and discussed if we should give the medicine to the black soldier or keep it in case someone came down with pneumonia. We decided to vote on it. There was a tie vote, and it was up to me to break the tie. I voted on giving it to him. Later a couple of soldiers came down with pneumonia, and we didn't have penicillin to give them. They died, and I have lived with that decision for forty years. I wanted to do the right thing; I just wanted to save a life.

Another time I caught one of the soldiers stealing food from the sick, and I threw him out of the sick bay. He was sick himself but had to go back to work. That was something that you just didn't do. I have always carried that guilt, too. I don't know what happened to the soldier, but I always wondered if he made it.

I never done a day's work for the Germans. One day the Americans bombed the airfield. The commandant lost his mind. He said the officers, the medics, everyone, would go out and fill the holes up. They came in the barrack to get us. I wanted to be able to go home and say that I had never done a day's work for the Germans, so as we were filing out I slipped behind the door. Everyone went out, and I was the only one left in the compound. For four hours I stood there, and for four hours I wished I had gone with them. That was the most miserable four hours in my life. I knew that if I got caught that I would be killed. Finally the boys came back to camp. Only one of them had missed me, and he came up and asked me where I went. He looked at me and said, "You're about stupid. Do you know what they would have done to you if you were caught?" I told him I did, but I wanted to be able to go home and say that I hadn't done a day's work for the Germans.

Another thing about a prison camp is that you have your ups and downs. You learn who is really your friend. I had a friend, Harry Mash. We were looking out the window, and a plane was shot down. I said it was a B-24, and he said it was a B-26. He was in parachutes and he thought he knew more than medics, and we got into an argument over what kind of plane it was. I told him that he got on my nerves, and here he comes with a haymaker. We cleaned the room up. When we finished, I had two black eyes and a scratch across my face. He had a bunch of marks. When we fell out for inspection, the German guard walked up to us and said, "You can't even get along amongst yourselves, can you?" He said, "That's why we are going to win the war."

The camp was cold. We had no heat except a fire that we built for about two or three hours a day. We slept with a partner at night to keep from freezing to death.

Red Cross parcels is what kept us alive. There were two men to a box, although we were supposed to get one apiece. The Germans mostly gave us grass soup and cold coffee made from acorns.

Morale would get really low. We had one soldier that was a little older than us. His name was Dave Miller, or so I thought. He used to come around and was really good at talking with some of us who were younger and helping us keep our morale up. I learned right before we were liberated that his name wasn't really Dave Miller. He had used the German-like name to hide the fact that he was a Jew. He never told me his real name, but said that he would tell me after we were liberated and he was safe from the Germans. I never found out, though, because after we were liberated we ended up separated and I never saw him again.

We were liberated by the Russians on May 15, 1945. Several of us decided we were going to walk out of Germany. It was strictly against orders because orders had come down that we were to stay in the camp until the Americans came after us. It was too dangerous to leave because there were still some Germans fighting, even though the war had ended. We waited for eleven days. We had a lieutenant who had been in the camp for three weeks, and he decided that we were going to play army. He was going to have drills and the works. We refused. We told him that when we got some clean clothes, a bath, and some hot food, then we would play army. One day I had had enough of the lieutenant, and I told one of the guys that I was walking out of Germany. Eight of us started out. When we walked out, it took us three hours to walk through dead children and old people. Some of the kids' bodies were stacked six high.

Harry Mash was with me, and that's when he saved my life. A group of Russian soldiers thought we were German soldiers. Everyone else in the group froze, but he jumped up and let them know who we were before they started to shoot. They let us ride on the tanks with them for awhile.

That's when I wished that I had stayed in the camp. They were going through the towns shooting up houses with .30 caliber machine guns, killing any civilians in sight. It was horrible. We finally got away from the Russians and continued on our way—but we had some of our own soldiers who were angry. I had been. Once while in camp a German soldier had grabbed me and slammed my head into the door. I was mad, and I said to myself that when the war was over I was going to get a knife and kill every German I saw and rape every German woman I saw, but I was mad at the time. Twice on our way out of Germany, soldiers came upon German women and were going to rape them. Once a woman in her forties was walking down a street in one of the villages, and this boy grabbed her. I stepped between them and told him to leave her alone. I said that he wasn't going to rape this old lady. I was nineteen at the time, so I thought she was old. Another time a lady was giving us water, and this same boy started after her. Again I stopped him. Then when we got close to the American lines, I saw a German soldier that had been captured sitting in a ditch. I threw a knapsack of food to him. One of the soldiers asked me what I thought I was doing, and I told him that we were at the American lines and that we didn't need the food. He said, "I hate all Nazis, and I am going to take the food." I told him to leave it alone, and he called me a Nazi lover. I wasn't. The war was over, and it was time to go home.

When we got back to New York, we had a court-marshal waiting on us, but the commanding officer threw it out. He said that we weren't doing anything but trying to come home.

I was sent home for sixty days and then went to Texas, where I was discharged from the army.

You know, for forty years I have felt guilty about surrendering. Especially with a little battle like this that only lasted one day. I found a book on Patton, and as I was thumbing through it I found a chapter on the siege of Troyes, France. That was the first that I knew they had fought for nearly a week there. The Germans had ran over our medical battalion and killed all the doctors in the aid station. The French took care of our wounded soldiers until our battalion could replenish. After that I realized that I was in a situation that I really couldn't do anything about. I also realized that I was lucky, because if I had stayed at the aid station I wouldn't be here today.

Private First Class
Melvin W. Zerkel

U.S. Army
45th Infantry
Captured During A Counterattack
in A Village Near Strasbourg, France
Prisoner of War
December 1, 1944–May 7, 1945
Stalag IVB

In the early days of the war, Melvin Zerkel worked in Chicago, Illinois, making bomb-loading equipment. Because his work contributed to the war effort, he was deferred for fifteen months. He was finally inducted into the U.S. Army on January 20, 1944, just after his twenty-second birthday.

He was trained at Camp Blanding, Florida, for seventeen weeks. After receiving his training he spent a ten-day furlough at home with his younger brother, Herbert, who was also home on leave. Little did Melvin know that it would be the last time he would see his brother alive. Herbert was wounded by artillery on January 19, 1945, in Luxembourg, Germany, and died the next day.

After his furlough, Melvin was sent to Fort Meade, Maryland, and prepared with his unit for the embarkation to Europe. For some reason, as he explains, "the only thing I remember about the week or so I spent there was purchasing a watermelon from a peddler outside the gate."

We were loaded onto a troopship that was part of a large convoy being assembled for shipment to Italy. I recall going through the Strait of Gibraltar on our way to Naples. We landed in Italy the first week of July 1944. The port of Naples was crammed with ships preparing for the invasion of southern France. While we were marching through Naples, which had been heavily damaged by Allied bombers, the Italian orphan children broke into our ranks and started to tear our packs apart looking for food. Later, we marched down to the railroad yards and were put onto small Italian railcars, which

155

carried us north to the Volturno River Valley. The trip through Italy was interesting, with picturesque country like I'd never seen before.

We traveled to a large replacement depot which had been set up on a dairy farm owned by Count Ciano, the son-in-law of Mussolini. The first thing we were told to do upon arrival at the replacement depot was to take all our extra clothing and throw it into a huge pile being assembled there. This was the clothing we had so carefully marked and folded back in Maryland. We were told this was to lighten us up for fast travel. Only the army could put together such an efficient system. On the far side of the pile of clothing, we could see Italian civilians picking out the things they wanted.

We were at this camp for about two months and went through some additional infantry training. I recall the sticky "gumbo" mud that would build up on our boots after a rain. I was not fond of the food at this camp. It was canned corned beef and dehydrated potatoes out of five-gallon cans. I suppose I dumped over half my rations because of the horrible taste. The Italians rummaged through our garbage. Little did I know that in a few months, I would long for something so good and plentiful to eat.

During the time I was at this camp, I had one pass. I went by army bus to visit Naples and Pompeii. Expecting to enjoy my time off, I was very disappointed to find both cities very immoral. Unfortunately, immorality came even into our camp. At night, some of the local Italian women would come to camp. They found some willing customers as they plied the world's oldest profession. Leaving this camp, we traveled to Marseilles. En route, we got into a fierce storm, and I was reminded of the apostle Paul's experiences at sea. At Marseilles, we pitched out tents in a muddy field and slept a few nights on the cold wet ground. One day, we got a pass and went into the city. What struck me most were the outdoor toilets on nearly every street corner. Seeing people use them in the open was a bit embarrassing to me.

Private First Class Melvin W. Zerkel. (Courtesy of Melvin W. Zerkel.)

We left Marseilles by train and traveled through France up to the Alsace region, where our forces were battling the Germans. We traveled in old European boxcars called "forty and eights"; they were designed to carry forty men or eight horses.

At one point we passed by a supply train that was stopped on a siding, and some of our men broke into a couple of cars and stole some things. Mostly, they were looking for cigarettes. I didn't get into the freight cars, but one of the guys who did threw me a can of peaches. I remember they really tasted good.

Around October 15, 1944, we arrived near the front. Two other soldiers and I were assigned to a company in the 45th Infantry Division. This division was part of General Patch's army. We were replacements for men who had been killed or wounded. The 45th had been in action for several months. The front was in a hilly region that reminded me of the Missouri Ozarks. It was filled with small villages, each of which had a large Catholic church.

My first action was in one of these small villages, at the edge of a forest. The Germans were dug in inside the forest and were shelling the village. We went into one house, and the floor was covered with German army packs. We were puzzled by this at first, so one of our men threw a grenade into the cellar of the house. Twenty-eight German soldiers, one being wounded, came out with their hands up. Frequently, we would find dead Germans in the barns and outbuildings we passed.

We spent that night in an old stone house, and the fighting went on all night. The next day, we were ordered to advance through the forest. As we were going up a hill, I spotted a German machine-gun nest right in front of us. I yelled a warning and dove into a shallow depression near me. Another GI dove right beside me. Our bodies were fairly well protected, but our legs and feet were sticking out. The Germans opened fire on us, and one bullet hit the canteen that hung on my belt. Dirt was falling in on us, and I was praying: "Lord, if there is anything to the ninety-first Psalm, this is an excellent opportunity to prove it." Almost immediately, American mortar shells started falling in front of us and silenced the German gun.

My company was then relieved by other troops. We pulled back for a four- or five-day rest as most of the company had been on the front for some time. Like all soldiers in wartime, every time we stopped we were ordered "to dig in." A few times, we were able to sleep in hay in barns along the way. We sometimes had to set up our pup tents on snow-covered ground. One night, a buddy and I "dug in" to sleep, but our rest was interrupted when we were flooded out as water ran in on us. Another time, I remember we were in the basement of a house. While in the basement, I remember walking on dishes that had probably been stored there for protection from the war. Also, most of the basements contained barrels of wine, which the men who drank sampled.

After this, we were put on trucks and moved to another sector near Strasbourg. We moved again, a few miles further, near to the French-German border. We left an American-occupied village early in the morning. We moved towards the next village, which was occupied by the Germans. My platoon was able to get inside the village. When the Germans counterattacked, we were able to get into some of the houses for protection. The Germans were firing on us heavily. I remember our platoon sergeant saying, "If any of you guys can pray, you'd better get at it."

The Germans attacked with infantry and tanks. Two or three American tanks had arrived at the edge of the village an hour or so after our troops. These tanks were supposed to be used in a counterattack; however, they did not help us because we were outnumbered and outgunned. Another soldier and I were in a house with a German soldier we had captured. When the German tanks came up, they spotted us and opened fire with their machine guns. I hit the floor, and the German fire sprayed just above me. When the fire eased up a bit, I got up and started firing out the window at the advancing German troops. I don't know if I killed any Germans, but they were in my sights when I fired.

The Germans were overwhelming us, and our lieutenant, who had been wounded, yelled for us to give up. We sent the German out first. He grabbed a dish towel and began waving it. My buddy followed the German out, but he was shot. I never knew how badly he was wounded, but I don't think he was killed. When I exited the house, a German tank was only twenty-five feet away. Twenty-seven of us were captured in this village. Those of us who were able marched out of the village. I never learned what happened to the wounded prisoners. When we were marched out, I remember seeing many dead and wounded Germans lying on the street where we had been firing. I was captured on December 1, 1944.

The Germans moved us to the next village, where we were searched. They relieved us of anything they wanted. I lost a watch and a little money. We were marched to another town where they were assembling and interrogating prisoners. A German officer, who spoke English well, asked us about our tanks and so forth. I remember him bawling me out for being a German and fighting against the Germans. I didn't tell him that my ancestors had left Germany many generations before (later in life I learned they had left in the 1730s).

When we left there, I recall marching through the old Siegfried Line, where the wall and the concrete tanktraps still stood. Just inside the German border, there was a village that had been heavily bombed by the Allies. The townspeople tried to attack us with pitchforks and clubs. The German guards protected us from their own people.

We were put on a little train—electric, I believe—and traveled to Frankfurt. The train stopped before entering the railyard. We were unloaded and walked through the station area. Allied bombings had heavily damaged the railyard. On the other side of the railyard, we were loaded onto another train and continued our journey. We were moved to Limburg, a large prisoner collection point in central Germany near Frankfurt. We were put in large, old barracks with no heat, and it was really cold. We broke up some bunk beds and made a fire with them in a big fireplace. Later, we were moved to large buildings, where we slept on the floor on straw.

We went two or three days without any food at all. Finally, we were given a little greasy canned sausage and some thin soup made from what I call "cowbeets," somewhat like kohlrabi. Occasionally we would get a little bread. In this camp there were also some Russian prisoners who were on work gangs. They got paid in bread, which they traded for the chocolate and cigarettes that we still had. At this time in Europe, cigarettes were far more valuable than money.

I was at Limburg about three weeks, and then we were loaded onto a boxcar to be moved to another location. As we were leaving Limburg, we were each given a small handful of raw hamburger; our only food for the next seventy-two hours. The temperature got down to fourteen degrees below zero, and it was a miserable trip.

One evening, we stopped on a grade, and U.S. planes began buzzing us. The German guards opened the car doors to give us an opportunity for escape if the U.S. planes attacked. The planes didn't bomb or strafe us, but they made the Germans very nervous. There's no doubt that if the planes had attacked the train many of us would have been killed.

We arrived at a large POW camp at Mühlberg, which is southeast of Berlin. I was there over Christmas. It was cold and snowing, and we were given very little food. We got word from new, incoming prisoners of the German advances in Luxembourg and Belgium. This news was depressing.

From Mühlberg (Stalag IVB) about 125 of us, all American enlisted men, were sent south to the Sudetenland, the area stolen by Germany from Czechoslovakia in 1938. We were sent to a camp at Bomish Leipa to work on the railroads. Bomish Leipa is now Ceská Lípa, about fifty miles from Dresden. We arrived on January 3, 1945. The barracks were right next to a railyard.

When we arrived, a German officer ordered us to begin work unloading an ammunition train. One of our guys stepped up and said, "Hey, according to the Geneva Convention, you can't use POWs to handle munitions." Surprisingly, the officer backed down and sent us on to the barracks.

The buildings were divided into rooms, and about twenty-five men were assigned to each room. The mattresses on the bunk beds were burlap bags filled with wood excelsior, usually used for packing material. They were also full of "little critters"—lice, bedbugs, etc. At night, our clothes were taken from us and put into a separate room, probably to prevent any escape attempts. We each had one thin blanket and one small bar of soap. There was one razor that several of us shared. The Germans gave us two large, five-gallon cans to urinate into at night.

The youngest man in our group was only eighteen years old. He was very upset and distraught at being a prisoner in a work camp. As a result, each night he wet his bed. It sure was a mess.

We worked on a section gang, maintaining the railroad, shoveling snow, clearing switches, etc. It was very cold, and we had meager clothing. My feet were badly frostbitten and bothered me a great deal for several years thereafter. We would wrap shop towels around our hands for gloves, and I cut the sleeves out of my T-shirt to use as socks. I had a Russian overcoat given to me by the Germans.

Breakfast was a dark, coarse bread (which probably contained some sawdust), a little oleo, and coffee made from grain (probably barley). Each of us carried a small pail and a spoon to the work sites to use at lunch. Some of the prisoners also carried a large bucket with beet soup for our lunch. After we ate the soup at noon, we would pick up and put into our pails and soup buckets anything we could find to take back to camp. Occasionally we might find an apple core or a scrap of food thrown away by a civilian that we would take and eat. The smokers would look for cigarette butts, which they would try to smoke. Sometimes, small pieces of coal would fall from passing trains, and we were able to find them at the work sites. We used the coal we picked up, in addition to the coal given to us by the Germans, to try and heat the barracks at night.

At night, we would get more cowbeet soup. Once in a while, red beets were in the soup. We also got three or four small, boiled potatoes each night. A few small bites of meat (probably horse) was in the soup one time a week on weeks one and three of the month. During weeks two and four, a little barley was in the soup. Occasionally, they gave us Limburger cheese, which at the time seemed good. We constantly craved salt.

All we talked about was food. I remember thinking, "If I get out of this place I'll never go hungry again." The smokers traded food for cigarettes, which we got from the Red Cross boxes or occasionally from the Germans.

We were not able to wash our clothes. About once a month, the guards took us downtown to be deloused. They took our clothes and put them through some type of gas chamber to kill the lice. We never got any mail, but approximately three times we received Red Cross boxes to split between every two men. These contained cigarettes, a small amount of chocolate, canned meat, crackers, honey, jelly, something to drink (coffee, tea, or powdered milk) and toilet paper.

We were not really mistreated by the guards, who were mostly old men, but we were always cold and hungry. We were also always short of toilet paper, so one time we tore the shipping documents off the side of the boxcars in the railyard to use for this purpose. The Germans became very angry over this.

As spring came, we began to replace the ties and rails and make any other needed repairs on the railroad. We were transported to the work sites by train each morning. There was a rail junction at Bomish Leipa, with rail lines going in different directions. We were taken out in different directions to work near villages. We rode in passenger cars. Sometimes they used small antique engines to pull the cars. The locomotive had a very high-pitched whistle. Upon arrival we were divided into groups of twenty-five prisoners, one group per work site. At night we returned to the camp by train.

One day we had the rails jacked up for tie replacement at a work site. Suddenly the guards started excitedly yelling at us to get the jacks out. We worked as quickly as possible and just barely had them out of the way when a high-speed military train sped by.

Another day a group of Russian POWs were working near us on the railroad. A train was parked at the site. The Russians, hungry and desperate, stole some industrial alcohol from a rail car to drink. They also took some greens (like spinach) from a freight car. They were caught, and the guards beat them with wooden timbers.

One spring day we saw some German farmers planting potatoes in a field near the tracks. We told the guards we needed a nature call and slipped into the field, where we dug up the potato sets and ate them. Another time, we were sent to a nearby castle to clean it out before the Russian army arrived. We took out the furniture and the paintings and were then sent into the cellar. While in the cellar, we filled our pant legs and coats with potatoes we found.

One night, I remember the guards unlocked the doors of the barracks. We had to get dressed and leave the prison area. We could hear bombing in the distance, which sounded like a distant thunderstorm. We waited about thirty minutes and then were able to return to the barracks.

We saw the Germans move a lot of prisoners from the east as the Russian army approached. Once I saw a couple of prisoners break out of line to try to get a drink from the ditch along the road. The German guards bayoneted both of them.

The German civilians gave us news about how the war was going. We learned of the president's death from the civilians. I remember them saying, "Roosevelt kaput," meaning President Roosevelt had died.

Around the middle of April, the war was winding down. One day the Germans brought a keg of beer in for the prisoners. I didn't drink any. However, I was so hungry that I sure was tempted, thinking that it might have some nutritional value.

One day near the end of the war, a train of tank cars full of diesel fuel was moving through Bomish Leipa. The railroad tracks were next to the barracks. While we were out at a work site, away from the barracks, Russian planes strafed the train. The train burned and was so close to part of the barracks that a portion of one barrack also burned. The fire was so hot that the rails melted. The Germans then used the American POWs and slave labor to rebuild the tracks.

While I was a prisoner, I was able to keep my New Testament and Psalms with me. I read from it for devotions. The comfort and encouragement I received from reading the Psalms was especially helpful to me.

The German guards told us on May 7 that the war was ending. They just opened the doors and told us we were free to leave or to wait for the liberating forces to arrive. The guards then took off.

Most of us decided to set off on foot for the American lines. The camp was in an area that was not occupied by German forces. Due to this fact, the American and Russian armies were some distance from us. The German guards told us that they had heard rumors that the American line was forty miles away; however, the American line actually proved to be much further than that.

As we made our way towards the American lines, we met a column of retreating German troops. Unfortunately, some Russian planes spotted the Germans at the same time and began firing on them. We had to jump into the nearby ditches to avoid being hit by gunfire.

We spent the first night after our release upstairs in a German guesthouse. The only directions we could get were from the German civilians. We tried to scrounge food from the farms along the way. One farm woman gave me some sour milk, like my dad fed to the hogs back home. It tasted pretty good.

On the second or third day, we were near Roudnice, Czechoslovakia. We were forced to hide in a village because the Americans were bombing the Germans at Roudnice. While we were in this village, two truckloads of really rough-looking men with automatic weapons rolled into town. They were members of the Czech underground who had come to pick up and transport American POWs. At this time, we broke up into groups of four or five men.

After the bombings, the Czechs captured about thirty members of the SS and Gestapo, plus a large number of German soldiers in Roudnice. Two or three days later, the Russians came into Roudnice. After their arrival, the SS and Gestapo who had been captured were hung in the middle of town. The Czechs hung them from tree limbs and light poles. A few fell down, and the Czechs simply strung them back up. The next day, the captured German soldiers were marched by their captors past the still-hanging bodies of the dead SS and Gestapo.

We waited a few more days in Roudnice until the rail lines were cleared to Prague. While we were in Roudnice, the Russian army arrived—and it was a sight. They had horses and wagons, old army trucks that looked like Model As, and a lot of Studebaker trucks acquired through lend-lease. Many wounded Germans were on a train parked in Roudnice. Also, many of the defeated German army and their dependents came through the town. They traveled in wagons with horses so worn out that they couldn't pull the wagons, so the people pushed. They were not allowed to stop in the city but were forced to keep moving. One of the wounded Germans was an American from

Los Angeles. He had fought on the German side. He talked to some of us and told us his "sad" story.

We left Roudnice and went by train to Prague and then on to Pilsen, which was in the American sector. We left Pilsen by truck and traveled to Regensburg, Germany, where the Americans had an airfield. They flew us from there on DC-3s to Paris and then on to Camp Ramp on the French coast.

When you begin to eat after starving, you can overeat and die. This happened to a few men, but most of us only suffered from diarrhea. While at Camp Ramp, I found a way to go through the chow line twice at each meal. Between meals, I went to the Red Cross tent, where they had eggnog and sandwiches. My weight had dropped to about 110 pounds during my imprisonment. I was very emaciated, but rapidly started gaining weight back.

We were given the opportunity to go to England, but I declined, fearing that I might lose some of my sixty day ex–POW leave. Since we were still at war with Japan, I didn't want to shorten my leave time with travel to England. We could send mail out, but didn't receive any. I had not received any mail since before my capture.

We boarded a ship, the *Admiral Butler,* at Le Havre, France. They only gave us two meals a day on the voyage, and that sure didn't sit well with me. We arrived at Camp Patrick Henry. The chow line there was tended by captured German troops, which was like rubbing salt in a wound. From Camp Patrick Henry, I was sent to Fort Sheridan in Chicago. Once there, I took a bus home.

Between the bus station and home, I met a neighbor lady. I asked her about my brother, Herbert, who had also been in Europe. She stammered and stuttered a little and finally said that he was dead. That was the first news I had of my brother's death. He had been a gunner in the field artillery of the 87th Division. Herbert had been wounded by German artillery in Luxembourg on January 19, 1945, and had died the next day. It was a bittersweet homecoming.

I spent the next sixty days at home. While I was there, the war in the Pacific ended. The first week of September 1945, I reported to Miami Beach, Florida, to complete my required time in the service, as I didn't have enough points for discharge. I was sent to Camp Stoneman, California, where I spent about six weeks. During this time, the government came out with an order that all ex–POWs with sixty days or more as a prisoner could be discharged, regardless of their length of service. I was then sent to Camp Beale, California, where I was discharged on November 21, 1945.

Private First Class
Arnold F. Franke

U.S. Army
Troop B, 87th Reconnaisance Battalion,
7th Armored Division
Captured During the Battle of the Bulge
Prisoner of War
December 22, 1944–April 7, 1945
Stalag IIA, Stalag IIB, and Camp Leipzig

Arnold was inducted in March 1944 at Fort Sheridan, Illinois, and received his basic training at Camp Fannin, Texas. He left New York in August 1944 on the Queen Mary and went via England, Normandy Beach, and France to join the 7th Armored Division 87th Recon B, as a replacement scout near Overloon, Holland. He was in active combat from Holland, through France, and to the Rhine River.

His unit was ordered to Belgium, and he became involved in combat in the Battle of the Bulge. He was taken prisoner on December 22, 1944, when the Germans broke through the newly arrived 106th Infantry and surrounded the remaining survivors.

We were sent to Belgium to fight because the Germans were making a breakthrough in the front. We fought four or five days back and forth. We would take them for awhile, and then they would take us. We had so many people that had to be replaced because there were so many casualties. It was tough fighting. One platoon would go in and hold for a while and then come out, and another would go in.

I was a machine gunner, and we had gotten into a heck of a battle the second we got there. My buddy, his name was Johnson, was the other machine gunner. We dug a shallow foxhole, because that is all we had time for. It helped give us some cover. He was feeding the gun, and we were really firing. The Germans were coming at us hard. They were camouflaged in snow suits, and it was hard to see them. We had a crossfire, but they were right on top of us before we could get them. After a while they slacked off, but Johnson had been badly wounded. I pulled him out and dragged him back to the

164

medics to try to save him. About the time I got him back to the medics, the Germans started their attack again. I ran back and tried to hold the position.

After we held for a while, the Germans retreated again. I was really nervous, and one of the guys had a bazooka. I had been trained with one, and I asked him if I could shoot it. I shouldn't have done it, but I aimed in on a barn about eighty yards in front of us and shot. I blew a big hole in the side of the barn. I was so nervous, I had to do something.

Then the 106th came in—a brand-new outfit. They didn't have enough ammunition and didn't know how to fight. The Germans found out that they were a new, green outfit, and they just walked right over them. The 106th ran out of ammo and couldn't hold their

Private First Class Arnold F. Franke. (Courtesy of Arnold F. Franke.)

position. The Germans went through them and got behind us. We didn't know they were behind us until the captain got on the radio and told us we were surrounded by the Germans and we would have to fight our way out. So they threw the artillery in on us. We were thirty in a platoon, and the artillery killed all but six of us. The captain told us to fight our way out, it was impossible with only six of us. So we decided to walk at night and hide during the day until we could find an opening in the line. Then we would sneak through the opening during the night. We would walk all night and then hide out in timbers or brush during the day. We were in there for three nights and days. The Germans had spotted us somewhere along the way and set up a trap for us. We had no idea they were anywhere around and we walked right into them.

They never killed anyone, but they did fire machine guns over our heads and told us to get our hands up. They took our guns, and then they took us down into this valley. They took all of our clothes, boots and all. They had a bunch of kids there, and the kids were taking our clothes and putting on what would fit them. In return they were giving us their worn-out shoes and clothes to wear.

I learned after the war that I was lucky I was captured when I was. I was captured very near a massacre site where the Gestapo killed eighty-four American prisoners of war with machine guns. Had I been captured later, I could have very easily been in the group of men killed in that massacre.

They marched us down this road for two days in zero-degree weather, with twenty feet of snow on the ground. We were freezing, with hardly any clothes on. Each night they would put us in a barn or empty building. We got no food or water for the entire trip.

Finally, on the third night, we arrived at a prison camp. They gave us a loaf of black bread that we all had to share. I got a piece—about a two-inch square—each day, and that was all I got.

We stayed there for three days, and then they moved us to a rail station and put about sixty of us in each boxcar. Again they gave us only one loaf of bread, and I got my two-inch square piece. Again we got no water. They had put a box in the middle of the boxcar for waste. They spiked the door shut.

We traveled for days and finally stopped at Stalag IIA for a few days. Then we went on to Stalag IIB. Prisoners were starving to death in those camps. All of them were sick with something. We were there for about a week and then back aboard the boxcars again. Again they spiked the door shut. The only opening we had in the car was a small coal chute. It was covered with barbed wire. The wire strands were about a half-inch apart and spiked into the boxcar.

There were three guys who decided they were going to die in the boxcars if they didn't get out. So they worked on the barbed wire and finally broke it. They were going to get in this coal chute and have us to push them out. We told them we would, but we were going to have to wait till the train had almost come to a stop. When the train was almost stopped, we pushed all three of the guys out.

We went on, and the third day we got to a rail station next to Zittau, Germany, near the Czech border. I could speak German, but I didn't let the guards know I could because I was afraid that they would kill me. We unloaded, and the Germans realized that they were short the three men. They fixed bayonets and stuck them in our bellies. They were yelling that they were going to kill us if we didn't tell them what happened to the three prisoners. The problem for the other prisoners was that the guards were speaking in German. I had told the other prisoners that I would get with them and let them know what was going on when I had a chance. They told us again that they were going to kill us all. One of the Nazi officers could speak English, and I asked him if maybe they had not just miscounted the prisoners. They finally decided that is what must have happened.

They took us to the barrack and locked us up. We were just starving to death. Then they put us to work in a rubber plant near the camp. We had to walk there every day, work till dark, and then walk back. It was about a nine mile walk each day.

Four or five of us got so weak from the lack of food that we couldn't walk anymore. We were about dead. The Nazi guards got a cart and horse, loaded us on it, and took off down the road. We didn't know where we were going, but we figured they were going to take us down the road and shoot us. They took us to the river. All the bridges had been knocked out by our planes, so they couldn't take the cart any further. The river wasn't deep, but it was wide. We walked across it. We got across the river and to Hohenstein, Germany. We were going to stay in an empty building overnight. Two of the guys had got so bad they could not walk at all. We helped them in the building, but later that night the Germans come and got them. We never seen them anymore. I asked the Nazi guard what happened to them, and he said they were dead.

A French doctor who was also a prisoner looked at my shoulder that night. I had been wounded by shrapnel, and he did the best he could, considering we had no medicine.

The next day they put us in a small jail. We were in a cell for a while, and there was one across from us. We looked over, and the three guys that had escaped off of the train were in the cell. They were in bad shape. They looked like dead people.

We stayed overnight, and the next morning they were moving us out. Two of the three prisoners that had escaped were dead. They carried them

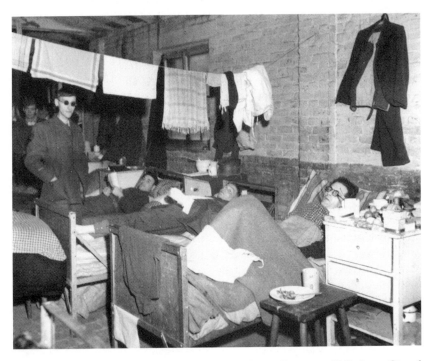

Former prisoners of war in the hospital at Limburg, Germany. U.S. Army Signal Corps photo by TEC/5 Billy Newhouse. (Courtesy of the National Archives.)

out, and then they took us out and put us on a train. We no more than took off and some of our own planes strafed us. The Germans would jump off and hide in the ditches, but they made us stay on the train. We were lucky none of us were killed.

They took us into Leipzig, Germany, and took us to a big motel. There were hundreds of prisoners in the motel. They took us on a work detail to pick up garbage in the town. There was a horse and cart, and we would walk behind it and throw the garbage on it and take it out to a dump. There were two horses, and one of them got sick and laid down. The Nazi guard unhitched it and made two of us take the horse's place. We would pick up garbage and then help pull the cart along with the other horse.

A couple nights later, the Allies bombed the motel. We got into the basement during the bombing, and we lost only about four prisoners. The bombs knocked out our water, so we didn't have any water to drink or no toilet usage.

We went out on work details the next day, and we tried to gather up water in tin cans or anything we could carry it in to bring some back for the other prisoners. We asked some of the civilians for water, but they wouldn't give it to us. Then, finally, one German woman called out to me in German. Of course I could understand her, but I let on like I couldn't. I walked over to her, and she told me they would give us water. She said for us not to get too close to her, because if the SS troops spotted her helping us they would kill both her and her family. We set our containers down by her and stayed back while she filled them, then we picked them up and left the area.

When we got back, one of the guards wanted to move some of us because it was getting too crowded. I was always wanting to move and get away from the crowded conditions when I could, so I volunteered. Eight of us got to go to this area out in the country.

On our way we passed a rail station. There was a train pulling in as we passed. It had railroad cars full of dead Jews. There were hundreds of them thrown in big piles. The smell was awful. I looked at the German guard as we passed. He looked straight ahead as if the trainload of dead bodies wasn't there. He never said a word. Neither did we.

We were getting real weak. All we had to eat was rutabaga soup. I got so weak that I had to crawl everywhere I went. We were in the country for quite some time. They had a guard on a tower with a machine gun guarding us; in the yard they had dogs guarding us. If one of us got close to the fence, those dogs would come after us.

I was in the yard, and some chickens got close to the outside of the fence. There were some kids nearby, and I told my buddies that I was going to try and talk the kids into catching one of the chickens for us. The guard was far enough away that he couldn't hear me, and I told the kids in German to catch one of the chickens and push it through the fence. I couldn't believe it, but they chased those chickens all over, caught one, and put it through the fence. There were a lot of us in the yard so I had a lot of help, and we caught the chicken and got it into the barrack. We had it plucked and was just getting ready to boil it when one of the Nazi guards came in. He went nuts. He took the chicken from us and threw it into the garbage.

We had one guard who was halfway decent to us. He had some seeds for lettuce and radishes that could be planted in the spring. He gave me some of them, and I planted them. The problem was that everyone was so hungry that as soon as a blade would come up someone would pull it and eat it. Everyone was so hungry that they would eat anything. So we never could get any vegetables out of it because no one could wait long enough.

One day some of our planes came over, and the Germans shot them down. Two of them crashed near our camp, and the pilots made it out. The Germans couldn't find them. We didn't know that our troops were that close, but the next day we started hearing artillery.

The day after that, we got up and crawled out into the yard. The place was empty except for those of us that could crawl. All the prisoners were gone, and the Germans, too. About that time the artillery started, and a shell hit the back of the barrack we had been in. It blew the back out of the barrack. Pretty soon another one hit. We crawled to the bomb shelter that the Germans had used and stayed in there. They were really zeroed in by now, and we were starting to get worried.

About that time the two pilots who had been shot down came in. They were in good shape and knew that our troops weren't too far down the road from us. We begged them to go down the road and ask them to stop the artillery. They took off, and when they got close enough they used their shirts to wave at the Americans. The pilots told them the situation. They came back and told us that we had fifteen minutes to get out of there. We crawled, walked, pulled on each other until all of us were out of the camp. They leveled the place.

After the bombing, our troops picked us up and took us by trucks to the rear echelon. They gave us some food and then deloused us. My clothes were greasy. They were so dirty they would almost stand up by themselves. They gave us new clothes. None of us had gotten any medical attention, and we all got physical exams. We were all suffering from malnutrition. The doctor told us that we were in worse condition than any soldiers he had examined.

They flew us to Camp Lucky Strike, where we could eat all we wanted. But it was a big mistake. We were starved, and we didn't know when to quit eating. Two men died after they ate too many doughnuts. Their system just wasn't used to it, and they went into convulsions. I was craving eggs. The kitchen had a big barrel of boiled eggs they had made, and we could have all we wanted. I ate eggs all night long; I was so sick the next morning I could hardly move. We took it easy on the food after that.

I was at the camp for about a month and then boarded the U.S.S. *George Washington* for home. I had to have more points to get my discharge, so they assigned me to guard duty at a German POW camp in Seattle, Washington. It was hard to take. These prisoners were treated so much better than we were.

In 1974 we returned with the 7th Armored back to Europe for a visit. There were several of us that rented a car and went back to the old battle area. I told this colonel that I bet I could find my foxhole. He said there was no way, but we went up this road and as we topped a hill I saw the barn I had hit with the bazooka back in 1944. I told him this was the place. We stopped, and I started walking through the woods. I knew the position we were in from the direction of the barn. The colonel told me I wouldn't find it, but I did. I walked right to it, and there was still an indentation in the ground where we had dug. "Well, how do you know?" the colonel asked. I told him I knew from the position of the barn.

We went down to the brick barn I had hit and found a young man working in the barnyard. We asked him if his grandpa was there. The older man came out, and we asked him how his barn was when he came back into the area after the war. He took us and showed us where he had patched the hole in the side of the barn with new bricks. We never told him what had happened, but when we got back in the car the colonel looked over at me and said, "You really did find your foxhole. Damn, thirty years later."

Corporal Donovan C. Evers

U.S. Army
Company L, 47th Infantry
Regiment, 9th Division
Captured in the Black Forest in Germany
Prisoner of War
March 16, 1945–April 29, 1945
Stalag XIIA

Donovan entered the army on September 23, 1943. He received his training at Camp Walters, Texas. After a short furlough he went to Fort Meade, Maryland, and then to Fort Shanks, New York. Trained as an infantryman, Don was told that he would be a replacement in whichever unit suffered the most casualties during the European invasion. Don landed at Utah Beach in France on June 7, 1944, his birthday. He was assigned to the 9th Infantry Division, a seasoned combat unit from Pennsylvania.

We landed at Utah Beach and headed across country. The first thing I saw when we landed was the dead glider pilots. The undertaker division had not been able to get to them yet. There were hundreds of them. They were still in their gliders, where they had hit the hedgerows or where they had crashed in the fields or where they had been shot down. It made me sick inside and made me realize how terrible war can be.

It took from June 7 until June 26 to surround and capture Cherbourg. The Germans had what we called "Potato mashers." This was the German hand grenade, and the Germans were good at throwing them. We attacked the German gun emplacements where they had 16-inch guns overlooking the harbor. We had to take them out so that Allied ships could come into the harbor. We fought our way to the gun emplacements; while I was throwing hand grenades into the opening where the 16-inch guns were, they were throwing their grenades out. I got hit in the leg, but we took the German guns. It was the first harbor that was taken from the Germans.

I was out with the leg wound for about seven days, and then they sent me back to the same division. We started across the Cherbourg Peninsula and cut the Germans off. It was like shooting fish in a barrel. They had no

Private First Class Donovan C. Evers. (Courtesy Donovan C. Evers.)

place to go. After we took the whole peninsula, we started across country, fighting hedgerow to hedgerow for months. A hedgerow is about twenty feet across and about eight feet tall. It's what the Europeans use to keep pastures and cattle separated. Every once in a while there would be an opening where the farmers could get their wagons through, but that was it. We would take four or five hedgerows each day, if we were lucky. On a couple of occasions, communications got messed up and some of our units ended up fighting each other for a few hours. There was a lot of firepower, but luckily there was no one killed.

We came into the city of Cherbourg on June 26, and we stayed there for about four days. Then they loaded us on trucks and took us almost to St. Lô, because the British and the other Allied forces had advanced that far. We were in open country now. We got on the backs of Patton's tank division and rode across Germany for a few days. The Germans were in full retreat, until they reestablished themselves on a front a little ways into Germany.

I was in a tank parked in a small brick building when an A.P. [Armor piercing] shell went through one side of the tank and out the other. I didn't get a scratch, but I couldn't hear anything for a day and a half. They sent me back to an aid station, but two days later I was back on the front.

Sometime in September 1944, we were crossing a river on rubber boats. The banks were steep, and as we climbed the bank we literally caught hundreds of Germans coming across an open field. We just slaughtered them. They were out there moaning and groaning, and we just kept firing. After about five minutes a German officer with a white flag came out from the trees at the far end of the field. We thought they were going to surrender. Our lieutenant met with the German officer, and they decided that we would let the Germans pick up their wounded and retreat. We sat with a cease-fire for about thirty minutes. Our lieutenant said that it was a good deal because we wouldn't have to take care of their wounded.

I got assigned along with a friend of mine, James C. Dressel, to take some German prisoners to the rear. After we delivered them, we were returning to our unit. It was dark, and we took a wrong turn. We ended up in Belgium just minutes after the Germans had left. The Belgians thought we were Germans because of the sound of our boots on the cobblestone streets. They stayed in their homes. The next morning our unit came into the town. Although the history books give credit to the 47th Division for the liberation, myself and Dressel did it the night before.

We continued to fight one town at a time, and finally we reached the Maginot Line. We went through Hitler's line without a shot being fired. We walked into Sangerhausen, Germany. We were there at least fourteen or fifteen days, waiting for the troops from the 1st and 29th divisions to come up on our right and left flanks. That was probably the best duty I had, because we stayed in a house. It had a screen porch, and I didn't have to sleep on the ground, and I would go out every day and pick pears. I must have ate a dozen a day. I didn't care for the C rations—ham or stew.

We had the run of the town. One evening me and a couple of other GIs were walking along the cobblestone streets, and we heard tank treads. We didn't pay much attention. The tank stopped, and a soldier popped his head out and said something in German. I never saw so many people move in my life. We ran for cover, and the soldier ducked back into the tank and took off. I don't think the Germans even knew we were in the town until that time. Two days later we had a counterattack, which we stopped.

We stayed in the town until November 16, 1944. That's when we had the breakout by the Germans, and I was shot through the shoulder the first day. It was a clean shot, all the way through. It felt like someone had stuck a hot poker through my shoulder. It knocked me down, but I got up, and I could see where I was hit. I wasn't too bad, but I had to go back to the rear. One of the officers told me to take some of the German prisoners we had captured with me. I could still use my left arm to hold a rifle, so I was able to get them back to the rear without a problem.

I'll never forget what the doctor told me when he saw me. He looked at my shoulder and said, "Hawk and spit for me." I did, and he said, "Huh, no blood in your lungs. Sit down and we will get to you later."

On Thanksgiving Day 1944, I was in a hospital in Leuze, Belgium. The opposite side of the hospital was hit by a buzz bomb. The next day they put me on a train and shipped me to a hospital in Paris. I had a view of the Eiffel Tower from my hospital room. I was there for about a month and then I was sent to England. I was there through February and missed the Battle of the Bulge.

I rejoined the 9th Division somewhere in Germany about the first of

March. We were picked up by the Red Ball Express [truck unit of black soldiers], who moved our units farther north into Germany. We crossed a bridge on March 7, and as we crossed the bridge soldiers were falling all around me. I couldn't hear anything. Then suddenly we heard the sounds. We were being attacked by jets.

The next day or so we captured an airfield, and we found thirty jet planes sitting on the runway. They had no fuel. If they had had fuel for those jets, I believe the war would have lasted a lot longer. They could have pushed us back with that weapon.

The fighting was fierce in the town. We went for a day or so and were pinned down the entire time. Our lieutenant decided that we were going on a recon patrol. There were six of us, and we went down the river and crossed the river on a pontoon boat. We got lost, although the lieutenant said we weren't, and ended up in a little town near Hamburg. It had about one hundred and fifty people in it. We fooled around and captured a few prisoners. One of the German soldiers had lived in Chicago and worked as a waiter in a restaurant. We talked and talked, and then we heard that sound again. Tank treads coming up the street. We hid in the basement. It didn't do any good because the Germans had spotted us as we were going into the house. After a while some straw that had been placed at the basement window was pulled back by a German soldier. They yelled in German for us to come out. We didn't move, so they aimed the barrel of the tank at the window. We knew that one shell would kill us all. We started up the steps to surrender. I had a lot of thoughts walking up those steps about all the atrocities that we had committed on the German soldiers. We didn't know what to expect from the Germans.

When I walked out the door of the house with my hands up, a young German soldier about sixteen years old stuck an automatic pistol in my stomach and said, "For you the war is over." I thought that was it, that he was going to shoot me. But he meant that I was going to be a prisoner of war.

We were marched out of town at gunpoint and into the woods. I've seen several movies since the war with SS soldiers—but this was for real. Standing in the woods was an SS soldier, dressed in a black uniform. He was tall, muscular, and had blond hair. He interviewed us one at a time, standing in the woods. Then we were taken back to an old schoolhouse.

When we got to the schoolhouse, the Germans separated the enlisted men from the officers. We were taken into the coatroom, and we could hear laughter in another room. We looked through the cracks in the wall and could see a stage show going on in the classroom. We couldn't believe they had such a show going that close to the front. We watched the show through the cracks of the wall. Later that night we were interrogated again.

The next morning they moved us again. We ended up in Limburg. While we were there, we worked on railroad tracks. The tracks went right through the middle of town, and every day the Allied planes would come through and bomb those tracks. Every day the prisoners of war would go out and repair the tracks.

They gave us potato soup, one piece of barley bread, and a small piece of cheese. The cheese was about the size of a silver dollar—about one-inch thick—and it was jellied. It looked like grease around meat. I didn't care much for it, but I ate it.

I was taken to Stalag XIIA for a few days and the treatment was pretty good. The Germans respected the air force and the camp had a lot of officers. There were several British Generals there and they sat around and netted. They had been there for a long time and they were not allowed to work. Of the 1500 prisoners in this camp there was a group of Mongolians. I don't know where they came from, but they had a group separated from the rest.

I was moved from this camp and stayed in barns, schools, and sheds as we moved. They had to give us breaks because we had dysentery and everything imaginable. One day we were relieving ourselves and were able to slip away from the Germans and hide. We got by with it for about a day and then were recaptured. They took us to a train and loaded us into boxcars with another group of prisoners of war.

When we got to the train, the other prisoners were already loaded. The Germans made us jump up to the window of the train and pull ourselves in while they beat us on the back and buttocks with cane poles. We were being punished for trying to escape. I could hardly move after the beating.

The next morning we were still sitting on the tracks, and we were spotted by French planes. The Germans had put red cross markings on the boxcars, but they had an antiaircraft gun mounted in a middle car and one at the end of the train. Evidently the French didn't believe it was a Red Cross train because they strafed us from one end to the other. The fellow next to me was reading a Bible and was hit in the head.

The Germans opened the boxcars and let us out. Some of the five hundred prisoners had a good idea. They ran over to the bank of the track and wrote "POW" in the dirt. The planes stopped their attack. Then the Germans put us back on the train, and we started off for another camp.

The Germans didn't have anything to feed us during the trip. We had a little water, but that was it. By the time we arrived at the next camp, we had slept in hog barns, straw, and sheds. We had cooties, fleas, lice, crabs, and dysentery.

This camp was a little different than the others. There were several Americans that had been POWs for a long time. There were collaborators in this camp. They would get the food and take it into another room for themselves before anyone else got food. The second night we were in the camp, one of them was killed. The next day the Germans moved us out and would not allow any prisoner to stay with another prisoner for more than three days at a time.

1st Army troops at the entrance to Stalag XIIA, March 27, 1945.

By now we had no more transportation. We walked day and night, going deeper into Germany all the time. My clothes stunk. I hadn't shaved or been able to wash or take a bath. I had lost a lot of weight. Sometime during the two-week march, F.D.R. died. The Germans told us that the war would end quickly now, because they would soon have only the Russians to deal with. But as we walked deeper into Germany, we could also hear the artillery every night. It was getting closer and closer, and the German guards were getting nervous.

Our group of about twenty-five POWs was hoping to get liberated that night. We slept in a ditch because it was the best place to be when the artillery hit. While the shelling was going on, half of the German guards left. All that was left to guard us was the old guards. After the shelling stopped, myself and one of the other prisoners slipped off and hid in the woods. The next morning the column left without us.

We hid all day in the woods. When night came, we walked toward the gunfire. We seen a small village and went into it. No one would answer their doors, and we were afraid to go into any empty houses because of booby traps. So we slept on the ground that night.

I should say that the people in Germany during March and April 1945 were defeated people, and they honored us in their retreat. They wanted to surrender to anyone except the Russians. The only ones that refused to believe that they were defeated were the SS troops. They never accepted the defeat.

The next morning we heard troops, and we assumed that they were our troops, but they were British. We walked toward them holding our hands up and telling them that we were American POWs. They took us and fed us and then sent us to their rear echelon. They didn't have the facilities to take care of our bug problem, so they shaved our entire body. Every hair on my body was shaved. I mean every hair. It was pitiful. Then they ran us through some kind of spray and gave us some new clothes. Then they shipped us to an American unit.

Two days later a medical team examined us. I had lost thirty-eight pounds in the last forty-five days. After the exam was completed, they shipped us to the French Riviera. It wasn't as nice then because of the war, but we stayed there until a ship picked us up to take us home.

In the latter part of April, we boarded the USS *George Washington,* which had a strange cargo. On the bottom deck was a group of American prisoners who had murdered, raped, or done other crimes. They were being sent back for trial. On the middle deck was us—the POWs. On the top deck was pregnant WACs.

It took us five days to get home. We arrived at Newport News, Virginia. We landed about three o'clock in the morning. We couldn't believe it. They had a band playing for us. They interviewed us, gave us medical checks, and then the next day put us on a train. I was going to Florida, but I got a seven-day pass, which I spent at home.

After the seven days I went to the Sands Beach in Miami, Florida, for rest and recuperation. And then I was sent to Fort Sheridan.

At Fort Sheridan we had the run of the camp. On one weekend I went home. When I came back I was up for a summary court-martial. Come to find out that two of my buddies had signed my name to a letter that they had written about the treatment of the German POWs at the camp. The Germans were being treated better than we had ever been as prisoners—or for that matter as soldiers. They had good food, they were invited to the dances we had on base and all that. My buddies complained in a letter to the newspaper and signed my name to it also. The commanding officer of the base court-martialed them for it, but they dropped charges against me when they found out that I had been gone and that someone else had signed my name.

I stayed there for a few more weeks, and I was discharged on November 2, 1945.

Appendix A: Approximate Locations of Prison Camps

The list below is of Nazi prison camps, hospitals, work camps, and their approximate locations. Allied prisoners of war were held in these camps throughout the duration of the war. The information about these camps and their locations came from the International Red Cross, from prisoners of war, and from Allied intelligence.

Stalag (Main Camp) Approximate Locations

STALAG IIA	Neubrandenburg, Mecklenburg, Germany	STALAG XB	Hannover
		STALAG XC	Nienburg
		STALAG XIA	Saxony
STALAG IIB	Hammerstein	STALAG XIB	Fallingbostel
STALAG IIE	Mecklenburg	STALAG XIIA	Limburg
STALAG IIIA	Luckenwalde	STALAG XIID	Waldbreitbach, Bavaria
STALAG IIIB	Fürstenburg		
STALAG IIIC	Altdrewitz	STALAG XIIF	Freinsheim, Bavaria
STALAG IVA	Hohnstein	STALAG XIIIB	Weiden, Bavaria
STALAG IVB	Mühlberg	STALAG XIIIC	Hammelburg, Bavaria
STALAG IVC	Wistritz, Czechoslovakia		
		STALAG XIIID	Nürnberg, Bavaria
STALAG IVD	Saxony	STALAG XVIIA	Kaisersteinbruch, Austria
STALAG IVD/2	Saxony		
STALAG VA	Ludwigsburg	STALAG XVIIB	Gneixendorf, Austria
STALAG VB	Villingen	STALAG XVIIIA	Wolfsberg, Austria
STALAG VC	Offenburg, Bavaria	STALAG XVIIIC	Markt Pongau, Austria
STALAG VIC	Osnabrück, Bavaria		
STALAG VIG	Bonn	STALAG XXA	Toruń, Poland
STALAG VIIA	Moosburg	STALAG XXB	Marienburg, East Prussia
STALAG VIIB	Memmingen, Germany		
		STALAG XXIA	Posen, Poland
STALAG VIIIA	Görlitz	STALAG 344	Lamsdorf
STALAG VIIIB	Teschen, Poland	STALAG 357	Kopernikus, Poland
STALAG VIIIC	Sagan	STALAG 383	Hohenfels, Bavaria
STALAG IXB	Hessen-Nassau	STALAG 398	Pupping, Austria
STALAG IXC	Thuringia	Work Camp 21	Blechhammer

179

Marine Camp and Oflag (Officers Camp) Approximate Locations

MILAG- MARLAG	Tarmstedt, Hannover	IX A/Z XB	Rotenburg Westphalia
IVC	Colditz	XIIIB	Hammelburg, Bavaria
VIIB	Eichstätt, Bavaria	XIIIC	Ebelsbach, Bavaria
VIIIF	Brunswick	XXI B	Alburgund, Poland
IX	Hessen-Nassau		

Luft (Airmen) Camp Approximate Locations

LUFT I	Barth, Pomerania	LUFT IV	Pomerania
LUFT III	Sagan	LUFT VI	Heydekrug, East Prussia
LUFT VII	Bankau		

Dulag (Transit Camp) Approximate Locations

DULAG IVA	Saxony	DULAG VIJ	Düsseldorf, Rhineland
DULAG IVG	Leipzig	DULAG VIIA	Freising, Bavaria
DULAG VB	Rottenmunster	DULAG IXB	Hessen-Nassau
DULAG VIC	Hannover		
DULAG VIG	Gerresheim, Rhineland		

Lazarett (Hospital) Approximate Locations

LAZ IXC(a)	Thuringia	LAZ XB	Hannover
LAZ IXC(b)	Meiningen	LAZ XIIID	Nürnberg
LAZ IXC(c)	Hildburghausen	Marine LAZ	Cuxhaven, Hannover
LAZ XA	Schleswig	Luftwaffen LAZ	Wismar

Appendix B: German Regulations Concerning Prisoners of War

The German prisoner of war regulations presented here constitute excerpts from documents of the Nazi regime. These documents were captured by the U.S. Army's Provost Marshal General's Office shortly after the war ended in Europe. The regulations were translated by the Liaison and Research Branch of the American Prisoners of War Information Bureau. The list of abbreviations and translations is also provided by the Liaison and Research Branch.

Abbreviations of German Military Terms

Abbreviations	*Translation*
Abw	Counter Intelligence
Ag.E.H.	Section for Replacement Training and Army Matters
AHA	General Army Office
Arb.Ndo.	Work detail
AWA	Section for General Armed Forces Matters
B.d.E.	Commander of the Replacement Training Army
Bkl.	Clothing
Ch.H.Ruest	Chief of Army Equipment
Dulag	Transit camp for prisoners of war
Gen.D.Pi.	General of the engineers
Gen.Qu.	Quartermaster General
Genst.D.H.	Army General Staff
GVF	Fit for garrison duty in the field
GVH	Fit for garrison duty in the interior
H.D.St.O.	Army disciplinary regulations
H.Dv.	Army service regulations
H.P.A.	Army Personnel Office
HV	Army administration
H.V.Bl.	Army bulletin
In.Fest.	Inspectorate of Fortresses
Kriegsgef.	Prisoner of War Department
Kv.	Fit for war service

Abbreviations	*Translation*
Oflag	Officers' prisoner of war camp
Ob.d.L.	Commander-in-Chief of the Air Force
O.K.H.	Army Supreme Command
O.K.M.	Navy Supreme Command
O.K.W.	Supreme Command of the Wehrmacht [Armed Forces]
P.A.	Personnel Office
P.U.	Mail censorship
R.d.L.	Reich Minister of Aviation
S.D.	Security service
S.S.	Elite guard of the National Socialist Party
Stalag	POW camp for enlisted men
VA	Army Administration Office
VO	Decree
Wam.	Guard detail
W.A.St.	Information Bureau of the Wehrmacht
W.F.St.	Armed Forces Operation Staff
W.Pr.	Wehrmacht Propaganda
W.V.	Army administration

SUPREME COMMAND OF THE WEHRMACHT
Berlin-Schoeneber, 16 June 1941

I. Chief group.

1. *Prisoners of war of alien nationalities in enemy armies.*

Frequently recurring doubts in determining the nationality of alien prisoners of war are now definitely resolved in that the *uniform* is the determining outward factor in establishing the fact of the prisoner's belonging to the respective armed forces.

Accordingly, Polish prisoners of war captured in French uniforms will be considered *Frenchmen*, while Poles captured in *Polish* uniforms will be considered *Poles*.

2. *The title "camp officer" instead of "camp leader."*

The title "camp leader" is not accepted in any of the regulations. It is therefore no longer to be used, and is to be replaced by: "first camp officer" and "second camp officer."

3. *Reward for the recapture of escaped prisoners of war.*

The OKW has requested the German newspapers to publish the following:

In view of the increase in the number of escape attempts by prisoners of war commonly occurring in the spring, the military and police services will welcome the cooperation of the general public. Persons offering effective aid in apprehending escaped prisoners of war may be granted financial awards, applications for which must be directed to the respective prisoner of war camp.

The reward herewith provided for are to be paid out of Reich funds…. The reward of one individual shall not exceed 30 marks even when several prisoners of war are apprehended. The amount is fixed by the commander of prisoners of war having jurisdiction in the respective prisoner of war camps.

II. Group I.

. . . .

4. *Personal contact of prisoners of war with women.*

Certain inquiries addressed to the OKW make it necessary to point out the following:

The prohibition of 10 Jan 1940 applies only to association of prisoners of war with *German* women.

It is therefore not necessary to submit a detailed report in cases of illicit traffic of prisoners with women of foreign nationality, unless certain circumstances make it a penal offense (rape, intercourse with minors, etc.).

The question as to the prisoner's liability to disciplinary punishment is left to the discretion of the disciplinary superior officer. The inquiry of the Army District Command V of 29 April 1941 I 3330 is thereby settled.

5. *Questionnaires for French officers.*

The French Armistice Commission had some time ago requested, in connection with the reconstitution of the French army, that newly arrived French prisoner-of-war officers in all the camps fill out questionnaires. Since the work is now finished, the questionnaires need not be filled out any longer.

6. *Transfers to officers' camp IV C Colditz.*

Several officers' camps frequently transfer to officers' camp IV C prisoner-of-war officers who have not yet completed disciplinary sentences pending against them.

As the few guardhouse cells in officers' camp IV C are currently occupied by prisoner-of-war officers serving sentences imposed by the headquarters of the camp, the transfer of officers to officer's camp IV C may be undertaken only after they have completed their previously imposed disciplinary sentences.

7. *Jews in the French Army.*

A transfer of the Jews to special camps is not intended; *they must, however, be separated from the other prisoners of war* and, in case of enlisted men, must be assigned to work in closed groups outside the camp.

Jews are not to be specially marked.

8. *Punishment of prisoners of war by the suspension of mail service.*

Several cases have been recently reported where camp commandants have suspended prisoner of war mail service as a disciplinary measure.

Attention is called to Art. 36, sec. 1, of the Geneva Convention of 1929 prohibiting the stoppage or confiscation of incoming or outgoing mail of prisoners of war.

Article 57, sec. 2, merely provides that packages and money orders addressed to prisoners of war undergoing disciplinary punishment may be handed to them only after the completion of their sentence.

The decision as to whether mail is to be handed out to prisoners of war under a court sentence rests with the competent penal authorities....

SUPREME COMMAND OF THE WEHRMACHT
Berlin-Schoeneberg, 23 July 1941
. . . .

3. *English books for training in radio broadcasting to foreign lands. (Talk work).*

In camps occupied by British prisoners of war several copies of the books named below will probably be found in possession of the prisoners:

Field Service Regulations, vols. 1 & 2
Manual of Organization and Administration
Field Service Pocket Book
Infantry Training, vols. 1 & 2
Cavalry Training
Artillery Training
Infantry Section Training
Engineer Training

It is requested that one copy of these books be procured & forwarded *directly* to the OKW/W Pr (IV h i) Berlin W 35, Bendlerstr. 10.

Should other books of similar nature not mentioned above be found it is requested that one copy of these too, be forwarded.

No statement as to where the books are being sent is to be made to the prisoners of war....

14. *Questionnaires on cases of death of prisoners of war.*

In case of death of a prisoner of war, in addition to the report to the Information Bureau of the Wehrmacht, a special questionnaire must be *immediately* filled out and submitted to the German Red Cross, Berlin SW 61 Bluecherplatz 2, so that the relatives of the deceased can be notified without delay (OKW file 2 F 24. 62a. Kriegsgef. Vi No. 135/11 dated 7 Jan 1941). *Direct* notification of the next of kin of the deceased is not permitted. *Double reports* are to be avoided. Should the prisoner of war die while in a hospital, the camp is to be informed of the date on which the questionnaire has been forwarded to the German Red Cross. *No* questionnaires are to be filled out in cases of death of *Russian* prisoners of war....

SUPREME COMMAND OF THE WEHRMACHT
Berlin-Schoeneberg, 1 Sep 1941

. . . .

4. *Religious functions at prisoner of war camps.*

In view of the general lack of interpreters, it will be sufficient for a specially selected, qualified guard to be present at divine services in which only the *Sacrifice of the Mass is performed and Communion is given,* in order to see to it that the minister does not add anything in the way of a special sermon....

11. *Guard personnel in officers' camps.*

Complaints have been repeatedly made that guards, who are entirely unfit for their task by reason of physical disabilities (club-foot, impaired hearing, marked near-sightedness, etc.) or low intelligence, are being used for the surveillance of prisoner-of-war officers.

For the sake of the prestige of the German Wehrmacht, officers' camps are to use only such personnel as are physically and mentally unobjectionable and who are thus not liable to produce an unfavorable impression on the prisoner-of-war officers. An appropriate exchange of personnel within the guard battalions is to be undertaken immediately....

SUPREME COMMAND OF THE WEHRMACHT
Berlin-Schoeneberg, 8 Dec 1941

. . . .

14. *Supplying camp canteens with rubber collars for Yugoslav prisoner-of-war officers.*

The firm "Rheinische Gummi & Celluloid Fabrick," Mannheim, was exporting before the war considerable quantities of rubber collars to Yugoslavia, for use by officers of the Yugoslav army. The firm still has on hand about 700 dozen collars, left from an order which could no longer be delivered and otherwise disposed of.

The Chamber of Industry & Commerce in Mannheim has approached the OKW with the request to be permitted to sell the collars to canteens of those camps where Yugoslav prisoner-of-war officers are interned.

Since the disposal of these collars, usable only by Yugoslav officers, is in the interest of our national economy, the prisoner of war camps in question are being informed of the opportunity to purchase rubber collars from the firm, Rheinische Gummi & Cellulois Fabrik Mannheim....

SUPREME COMMAND OF THE WEHRMACHT
Prisoner of War Department
Berlin-Schoeneberg, 31 December 1941 Badenschestr 51

· ·

7. Re: *Tin boxes of British fliers.*

British fliers brought down have been found to carry with them tin cans containing a small saw made of steel, a map of Northern France and of the North-German coast, chocolate, and concentrated food tablets. These tin cans presumably are to help the Britishers to avoid capture or to escape from imprisonment after capture. Such special equipment has been repeatedly found on British fliers. It apparently belongs to the "iron rations" (emergency kits) of the British air force.

Special attention is to be paid to this when capturing British fliers shot down or delivering them to a prisoner of war camp.

8. Re: *Informing newly arrived prisoners of war of camp regulations.*

There are cases on record where prisoners of war, newly arrived in a collecting camp *to be released,* and unfamiliar with the regulations of the new camp, were severely wounded or killed by warning shots or by deliberate fire.

Since the same regulations governing order & discipline in camps do not apply in all camps, care must be taken that newly arrived prisoners of war be immediately made familiar with the new regulations, even if their stay at the camp is to be temporary.

Posting alone on blackboards and in the halls is not sufficient.

A reliable prisoner-of-war noncommissioned officer or the camp spokesman may be entrusted with this task....

SUPREME COMMAND OF THE WEHRMACHT
Chief of the Prisoner of War Department
Berlin-Schoeneberg, 11 March 1942 Badenschestr.51

· ·

5. Re: *Marking of Jews*

The Jews in Germany are specially marked with a star, as a measure of the German government to identify them in the street, stores, etc. Jewish prisoners of war are *not* marked with a star, yet they have to be kept apart from the other prisoners of war as far as possible....

23. Re: *Cases of death of prisoners of war.*

Reports to the Information Bureau of the Wehrmacht on deaths of prisoners of war and the corresponding notices to the German Red Cross through questionnaires are to be drawn up in such a way as to obviate the necessity of further time-consuming inquiries.

The following is therefore to be observed:

1. The report of the death of a prisoner of war to the Information Bureau of the Wehrmacht must indicate the *cause* of death in exact accordance with the facts, and also give the *place* of death in a way to make the competent registrar's office easily identifiable. It is not enough, for instance, to state: "Shot." Rather must it be worded: "Shot while trying to escape," or "Shot in execution of sentence pronounced by … division on…" It is likewise not enough to give as place of death merely "Camp Erlensbusch," but rather "Camp Erlensbusch near Village X. The exact location of a work detail in a death report is essential, even when such detail is located near a stalag, as it cannot be automatically assumed that the 2 places belong to the same registrar district.

2. The report on the death of a prisoner of war to the presidency of the German Red Cross constitutes the basis for the notification of the family of the deceased. The death notice is prepared by the German Red Cross and is transmitted to the next of kin through the local Red Cross office of the latter. *The questionnaire proper* is then forwarded by the German Red Cross to the International Red Cross in Geneva.

   In preparing the "death-notice questionnaire" the following is to be observed:

   a. The questionnaire must be speedily & fully filled out and promptly forwarded to the presidency of the German Red Cross, Berlin S W 61 Bluecherplatz 2. Only this agency is competent to receive such questionnaires. Sending same to any other agency is not permitted, even though the questionnaire was made up by the International Red Cross in Geneva.

   b. *Careful formulation of the cause of death* in case of unnatural death, as the questionnaire is to be sent abroad (International Red Cross).

   c. The nationality of the deceased must be given right after the name, and the name of the country after the address of his next of kin.

   d. The last question must be answered in the greatest detail, insofar as there are no objections to the answer becoming known abroad.

3. For the time being no questionnaire is to be filled out for deceased *Soviet prisoners of war.*

4. Deaths of prisoners of war are not to be reported to the Protecting Powers either by camp commandants, or by the spokesmen.…

46. Re: *Poaching by prisoners of war.*

The Reich master of hunting reports a recent increase in cases of poaching by prisoners of war doing farm labor—particularly French.

Prisoners of war are to be told that violations of German laws are severely punished....

56. Re: *Polish soldiers belonging to the French Army.*

The nationality of a soldier is determined by the uniform he is wearing at the time of capture.

In doubtful cases, the place of residence of the prisoner of war before the war and the present residence of his next of kin will determine his nationality....

59. Re: *Engagements for work by British noncommissioned prisoner-of-war officers.*

British noncommissioned officers who signed a pledge to work but are no longer willing to do so are to be returned to the camp. Their unwillingness is not to be considered as a refusal to work. The employment of British noncommissioned officers has resulted in so many difficulties that the latter have by far outweighed the advantages. The danger of sabotage, too, has been considerably increased thereby....

75. Re: *Contact between French & Soviet prisoners of war.*

Soviet prisoners of war must be strictly kept apart from prisoners of other nationalities, particularly Frenchmen. They should also be permitted no opportunity for establishing such contacts at their place of work.

Strictest measures are to be taken against contractors who fail to comply with the above security requirements....

79. Re: *Position of prisoner-of-war officers with respect to German personnel.*

A particular incident has moved the Fuehrer to emphasize anew that, when considering the relationship between prisoner-of-war officers and German camp personnel, the most humble German national is deemed more important than the highest ranking subject of an enemy power....

81. Re: *Smoking by prisoners of war.*

Complaints are voiced by the Reich conservator of forests that prisoners of war smoke in the forests and thereby increase the danger of forest fires.

Reference is made to sec. 15 of the Compilation of Orders No. 5, dated 10 Oct 1941. Attention of the prisoners of war is to be particularly called to the fact that smoking in forests is forbidden and that any infringement will be severely punished under German law....

85. Re: *Beards of prisoners of war.*

Prisoners of war wearing beards for religious reasons, e.g., Indians & orthodox clergymen, may continue to do so. Individuals enjoying a nonprisoner status, such as medical officers, army chaplains, and medical corps personnel may also keep their beards, if any....

109. Re: *Subjecting enemy prisoners of war to the operation of the Military Penal Code.*

The order of 10 Jan 1940 forbidding association with German women and girls is to be made known also to French medical corps personnel taking the place of, or about to take the place of, the former medical personnel by way of exchange....

110. Re: *Handling of medicines.*

The provision contained in section 22 of the Compilation of Orders No. 5 concerning the handling of medicines sent in packages to prisoners of war is hereby canceled.

The order *OKW 2 f 24, 82 u Kriegsgef. Allg. (A) AbW III (Kgf.)* remains in force. The latter provides that packages found to contain medicines, restoratives, etc., are to be confiscated and their contents disposed of in accordance with section 3 of the order. Medicines, etc., are to be destroyed.

111. Re: *Prisoners of war as blood donors.*

"For reasons of race hygiene, prisoners of war are not acceptable as blood donors for members of the German community, since the possibility of a prisoner of war of Jewish origin being used as a donor cannot be excluded with certainty."...

114. Re: *Killing & severe wounding of British prisoners of war or civilian internees.*

Every case of the killing and the severe wounding of a British prisoner of war or civilian internee must be reported immediately.

An investigation is to be initiated by a judicial officer or an otherwise qualified officer. Where comrades of the prisoner of war or the civilian internee were witnesses to the incident, they, too, must be heard.

The result of the investigation and the minutes of the depositions are to be forwarded to the IKW/Kriegsgef. Allg. for notification of the Protecting Power....

167. Re: *Poison in possession of prisoners or war.*

Narcotic poisons such as "Kif," "Takrouri," & "Souffi," have frequently been found in parcels addressed to Arabian prisoners of war under the guise of tobacco packages.

These poisons are extremely harmful to health and are therefore forbidden in the French army. When searching parcels, particular attention is to be paid to these substances. They are neither to be delivered to the prisoners of war, nor to be kept by the guards. The packages are to be immediately destroyed....

171. Re: *Display of flags in prisoner of war quarters.*

Since the British government has forbidden the display of German flags in prisoner of war quarters, *British* flags are to be immediately withdrawn in all German camps. The prisoners are to be notified of the above reason during the roll call....

176. Re: *Reparation for willful destruction.*

Prisoners of war proved guilty of willfully destroying or damaging state or other property as, for instance, in connection with tunnel construction, are to be punished and, in addition, made liable for damages. Should the actual perpetrators not be discovered, and should the prisoners of war involved be British, the whole camp community may be collectively held responsible for damages—which is the customary practice in England & Canada (canteen funds)....

179. Re: *"Warning" wire: testing of wire enclosures in prisoner of war camps.*

Experience has shown that weeds growing within the stockade seriously obstruct the view of the enclosure. Several escapes in *day time* may be attributed to this fact.

Since the removal of the weed is in most cases not feasible, a "warning" wire is to be strung within the camp—if this has not been done already—at least 2 meters away. The space between the warning wire and the main stockade is to be kept free of weeds.

Several escapes have recently been made possible by the fact that the wire fences, more than 3 years old in most camps, were damaged and rusted through.

These wire fences must be carefully inspected for reasons of security and existing defects corrected. Reconstruction or repairs should be proceeded with only within the limits of the available supplies of barbed wire. A new supply of barbed wire over and above the fixed quota is not to be reckoned with....

189. Re: *Treatment of Soviet prisoners of war refusing to work.*

Cases have been observed in some places where Soviet prisoners of war did not receive their prescribed food rations or received rations of inferior quality. This was due in part to shortages of supplies in some areas (e.g., potatoes), and in part to faculty organization in delivery of food (dinner at 8 P.M.).

The resulting drop in efficiency was frequently interpreted as a deliberate refusal to work and was punished accordingly.

Commandants are again directed to pay close attention to the feeding of

Soviet prisoners of war and to remove any difficulties of local character. Should the contractor not be able to supply the prescribed food rations, the prisoners of war must be withdrawn to preserve for the Reich this valuable manpower before it has been rendered useless....

190. Re: *Withdrawal of boots and trousers from prisoners of war.*

The commanders of prisoners of war may direct within the military districts that boots & trousers of prisoners of war may be left with the latter for the night:

In large work details to save time;
In work details exposed to air raids;
For working noncommissioned officers.

191. Re: *Money rewards for recapture of escaped prisoners of war.*

Supplementing the reference order:

Rewards may also be paid for successful *prevention* of escape. The decision as to whether the action of a person not qualified to belong to the army, the police, or the frontier guard may be considered as having foiled an escape lies with the camp commandant....

199. Re: *Handling of tin cans for prisoners of war.*

In a few camps it has lately become common practice, when issuing tin cans to prisoners of war, to be satisfied with the opening of the can and a superficial examination of its contents, and then to hand the open can and contents to the prisoner. When underway, even unopened cans are issued as marching rations. It is again pointed out that, for reasons of security, only the *contents* of the tin can may be issued to the prisoner of war. Deviation from this rule may be permitted only in exceptional cases, as when other receptacles are not available. In such cases the tin cans themselves must be examined as a security measure prior to their issuance....

202. Re: *Sports events in prisoner of war camps.*

Since sports contests between prisoners of war of different nationalities have resulted in brawls, such contests are prohibited in the interest of good discipline....

223. Re: *Shooting & severe wounding of prisoners of war & civilian internees (except Poles, Serbs, and Soviet Russians).*

An inquiry by a court officer or any other qualified officer is to be initiated in each case of fatal shooting or wounding of a British, French, Belgian, or American prisoner of war or civilian internee. If comrades of the prisoner of war or civilian internee were witnesses of the incident, they, too, will be heard. The result of the inquiry and a copy of the examination proceedings are to be submitted immediately to the OKW Kriegsgef. Allg. (Ia), reference being made to the file number below. This report is to be designated as "Report on the use of arms by soldier X." A detailed report against soldier X will be necessary *only* when there is a suspicion of the latter having committed a legally punishable act and when an immediate court decision appears desirable....

224. Re: *Casualties of British, French, Belgian, and American prisoners of war resulting from enemy air raids.*

Deaths & injuries of British, French, Belgian, and American prisoners of war resulting from enemy air raids are to be reported in writing immediately after the raid to the OKW/Kriegsgef. Allg. (V), giving the file number below. The following are to be stated in the report:

1. First name and surname
2. Rank
3. Prisoner of war number
4. Date of birth
5. Wounded or dead
6. Address of next of kin.

In addition, the camp headquarters are to send carbon copies of the reports directly to: the Bureau Scapini, Berlin W 35 Standarten strasse 12—when French prisoners of war are involved, and to the Belgian Prisoner of war committee, Berlin W 8, Hotel Adlon, Unter den Linden—when Belgian prisoners are involved.

A report is also to be submitted to the Information Bureau of the Wehrmacht.

The reports concerning special incidents to be submitted in accordance with the order OKW file 2 of 24. 83n Kriegsgef. Allg. (Ia) No. 71/42 of 17 Feb 1942, are not affected hereby....

228. Re: *Prohibition of the so-called "Dartboard Game."*

The so-called "dartboard game" is forbidden, as the darts needed for this game are to be considered as weapons and may be employed in acts of sabotage. The game is to be confiscated....

239. Re: *Transport of recaptured or unreliable prisoners of war.*

A certain case where a guard was murdered by 4 recaptured Soviet prisoners of war during transport after dark makes it appropriate to point out that recaptured prisoners of war or prisoners known to be unreliable should, as far as possible, not be transported *after nightfall*. Should the transport after dark be unavoidable, *at least*, 2 guards must be assigned to the detail.

240. Re: *Association of prisoners of war with German women.*

There are several cases on record where judicial prosecution and punishment of prisoners of war for association with German women was frustrated by the fact of their having been already punished disciplinarily, the matter being apparently considered as but a slight offense.

The camp commandants must apply the most rigid criterion in deciding whether the case is a mild one, as the association of prisoners of war with German women must be prevented at all costs....

243. Re: *Consumption of electricity by prisoners of war.*

In order to assure the most economical consumption of electricity, all lighting installations in the prisoner of war quarters are to be examined again; all superfluous lights are to be eliminated.

Lighting installations are allowed, where necessary, within the limits of the quota of Wm. Verw. V., part II, appendix 14, same as for squad rooms in barracks.

The following are thus allowed in officers' quarters:

In rooms occupied by 1 to 4 men . . . . . .40 watts
In rooms occupied by 5 to 8 men . . . . . .75 . ."
For every additional man . . . . .10 . ."

Quarters of noncommissioned prisoner-of-war officers and men are allowed ½ of this quota.

For the use of electric utensils for cooking gift food, etc., written permission of the camp headquarters in each individual case is necessary....

246. Re: *Securing prisoner of war camps against escape attempts.*

1. *Fencing in of the camp.*
   The wire entanglements between the inner and outer fences must be so concentrated that an escaping prisoner of war will be able neither to climb over them, nor to crawl under them. Anchor posts should be just only slightly out of the ground.

2. The foreground of the stockade, as well as the space between the warning wire and the fence must present an open field of view and of fire. It is therefore to be kept free of brushwood and all other objects impeding vision.

3. *Watch towers.*
   There are no generally applicable detailed instructions for the construction of watchtowers. It depends on the topographic and climatic conditions of the camp and must provide the best possible field of view and of fire.

The functional shape of the watchtower is to be determined by the camp commandant....

252. Re: *Repair of private apparel of prisoners of war.*

Prisoners of war are permitted to repair their private apparel (including shoes) with materials from collective gift shipments. Such repairs are to be made primarily by the prisoners of war themselves. In case they are not able to do so, the repair job may be performed in the camp repair shops....

259. Re: *Supervision of enemy army chaplains and of prisoner of war chaplains.*

1. Enemy army chaplains and prisoner-of-war chaplains have repeatedly abused the permission to minister to the spiritual needs of the prisoners of war by creating unrest among the latter through inflammatory speeches.

   All chaplains are to be advised that they must, in their contacts with prisoners of war, refrain from exercising over them any inciting influence. They must be given emphatic warning and their activity must be strictly supervised.

   Chaplains engaged in inciting prisoners of war are to be denied the right to perform their pastoral functions and are to be called to strict account; the military district is to be notified of the matter simultaneously.

   In critical times visits to several work details by one chaplain (traveling preacher) will be forbidden on short notice and for a limited period.

2. Attention is again called to the reference orders stipulating that *sermons* may not be preached by field chaplains and by prisoner-of-war chaplains except in the *presence* of an *interpreter.*

3. In the event the divine service for a work detail can be held neither in the quarters nor in the open, it is the task of the stalag to provide a suitable room. The contractor may request, but not demand, that such a room be placed at disposal of the prisoners of war....

271. Re: *Raising rabbits in prisoner of war camps.*

In the future, the raising of rabbits in prisoner of war camps will be governed by the provisions of reference order 2 above. The OKW decree— file 2 f 24. 20 Kriegegef. (II) NO. 1261/49 is canceled.

The cost of raising rabbits will henceforth be charged in *all* the camps to the Reich. Angora rabbits, warrens, tools, etc., till now maintained with canteen funds, are to be taken over by the Reich at a price fixed by an agricultural expert of the Military District Administration. The proceeds of the transaction are to be turned over to the prisoner-of-war canteen.

272. Re: *Procuring wrapping paper for Soviet corpses.*

The camp headquarters will henceforth report the amount of oil paper, tar paper, and asphalt paper needed for the burial of dead Soviet prisoners of war directly to the nearest paper wholesaler. The latter will then apply to the competent Army Raw Material Board for an army paper ration certificate. The further procedure is familiar to the wholesalers.

In view of the scarcity of the above kinds of paper, they may be used only for wrapping corpses. Their use is to be held to the barest minimum....

278. Re: *Internment of fallen or deceased members of the enemy armed forces.*

To remove any doubt as to whether prisoners of war shot during flight or in acts of insubordination are entitled to burial with military honors, the following is ordered:

I. As a matter of principle, every honorable fallen enemy is to be buried with military honors.

II. Flight is not dishonorable, unless dishonorable acts were committed during such flight.

III. Cases of insubordination must be individually examined as to whether acts reflecting on the soldier's honor have been committed. Where such violations of the soldier's code of honor have been established without question, military honors during burial are to be excluded.

279. Re: *Accepting bribes by guards.*

A private first class on guard duty in a certain camp has on several occasions accepted bribes of cigarettes and chocolate from prisoners of war and permitted them to escape without interference, instead of reporting them to his superior at their very first suggestion. He was sentenced to death for dereliction of guard duty, for willfully releasing prisoners of war, and for accepting bribes.

All guard personnel entrusted with the custody of prisoners of war are to be informed of the above with the appropriate comments. The announcement is to be repeated at least every 3 months....

307. Re: *British prisoners of war.*

The instructions contained in the OKW memorandum: "The German soldier as prisoner of war custodian" outlining the duties of German guard personnel assume a particular importance with reference to British prisoners of war, whose frequent display of arrogance toward guards & civilians is not in keeping with the discretion expected of a prisoner of war.

The guards are to be instructed to severely repress any attempt of British prisoners of war to evade their full work duty or to associate with civilians beyond the limits set by the circumstances of their employment.

Only British noncommissioned officers who exert a beneficial influence on their British subordinates may be used in supervisory capacities. British noncommissioned officers found unsuitable for this task are to be replaced. Unless they volunteer for a job, they are to be transferred to Stalag 383, Hohenfels....

313. Re: *Death sentence of a prisoner of war guard member of a regional defense unit.*

The private first class Jungmichel, assigned to a guard detail at a officers' prisoner of war camp, entered into personal relations with a Polish officer interned at that camp. He supplied the officer, at the latter's request, with various tools, maps, and other items intended to facilitate the escape of this and other prisoners of war. Jungmichel was sentenced to death by the

Reich court-martial for war treason. The sentence carried out on 5 Marsh 1943.

The above sentence is to be made known to all the members of the administration headquarters and the guard units....

324. Re: *Use of identification tags by prisoners of war.*

To prepare and to conceal escapes, more and more prisoners of war use the device of exchanging identification tags with other prisoners, or of getting rid of them altogether. Such practices are to be prevented by the imposition of heavy penalties, if necessary. When calling the roll, a check of the identification tags must not be neglected.

325. Re: *Prevention of escapes through the gate in officers' camps.*

The entrances and exits in officers' camps—where this has not yet been done—must be shaped like sluices and provided with a double control. At least one of the 2 consecutive gates is to be occupied by a qualified non-commissioned officer, thoroughly trained for the task, from headquarters....

397. Re: *Taking winter clothing away from prisoners of war during summer months.*

No objections may be raised in the practice of leaving overcoats with prisoners of war, even in summer months, in areas subject to air raids—a practice designed to enable the prisoners to take these along to the air raid shelters during an alarm for protection against colds and to lessen the danger of the coats being destroyed by fire. For all other prisoners of war doing outside work and exposed to the inclemencies of the weather, the unit leaders are to decide on their own responsibility whether the overcoats are to be taken along to the place of work or are to remain in storage. The use of overcoats for additional blankets is forbidden....

404. Re: *Preventing escape by taking away trousers and boots.*

When establishing new work details, an appropriate room is to be set aside for the safe storage of trousers and boots taken from the prisoners of war for the night....

409. Re: *Transfer of prisoners of war.*

To reduce the number of escapes, prisoners of war scheduled for transfer to another stalag are to be notified as late as possible of such transfer, and not at all of their new place of internment....

421. Re: *Sale of cellophane envelopes & China ink in prisoner of war camp canteens.*

Effective immediately, the sale of cellophane envelopes and China ink to prisoners of war is forbidden, since these have been misused to prepare and carry out escapes....

422. Re: *Thefts from bomb-wrecked homes.*

When prisoners of war are assigned to wreckage-clearing jobs after air raids, their attention is again to be called to the death penalty as provided by the reference order....

429. Re: *Escape of prisoners of war in civilian clothes.*

Escapes of prisoners of war in civilian clothes are on the increase. Frequently civilian clothes are kept hidden in the barracks. The latter, therefore, as well as all other premises and spots accessible to the prisoners of war (corners under staircases, basements, attics) are to be constantly searched for such hidden articles. The contractors are to be urged to proceed in like manner in places accessible to prisoners of war during working hours....

431. Re: *Malingering by prisoners of war.*

Recent reports indicate that French prisoners of war frequently claim to suffer from stomach ulcers, the effect of which is produced by swallowing small balls of tinfoil showing under X-rays as black spots, similar to those produced by ulcers. The possibility of malingering must be kept in mind by the chief surgeons and camp physicians when prisoners of war are suspected of suffering from stomach ulcers....

462. Re: *Timely use of arms to prevent escapes of prisoners of war.*

In view of the increasing number of individual and mass escapes of prisoners of war, it is hereby again emphasized that guards will be subject to the severest disciplinary punishment or, when a detailed report is at hand, to court-martial, not only for contributing to the escape of prisoners of war through negligence, but also for failure to use their arms in time. The frequently observed hesitancy to make use of firearms must be suppressed by all means. Guard personnel must be instructed in this sense again and again. They must be imbued with the idea that it is better to fire too soon than too late....

504. Re: *Use of firearms against prisoners of war.*

The service regulations for prisoner of war affairs do not provide for any warning shots. Should the occasion for the use of firearms arise, they must be fired with the intent to hit....

513. Re: *U.S. prisoners of war in British uniforms.*

Prisoners of war of U.S. nationality captured as members of the Canadian armed forces are considered British prisoners of war, regardless of whether they joined the Canadian services before or after the entry of the U.S. into the war....

The uniform is the deciding factor....

517. Re: *Fuel*

To stretch the supply of fuel, experiments are to be made in the use of a mixture of coal dust (50%–75%) and clay, formed into egg-shaped bricks, for the heating of prisoner of war quarters wherever local conditions permit.

The result of the above experiments are to be reported by the military district administrations not later than *15 June 1944....*

522. Re: *Pay of American prisoner-of-war noncommissioned officers and enlisted personnel.*

The American authorities pay to all German prisoner-of-war noncommissioned officers and enlisted personnel an allowance of 3 dollars per month, regardless of whether they are employed or not.

As a reciprocity measure, all American prisoner-of-war noncommissioned officers and enlisted personnel are to receive, effective 1 Nov 1943, 7.50 marks per month.

The American prisoner-of-war noncommissioned officers and enlisted personnel are to be notified of the above through their spokesmen....

534. Re: *Transport of prisoners of war in motor buses.*

In accordance with the existing regulations of the German Post Office Department, the transport of prisoners of war in motor buses is not permitted. No motor-bus vouchers may thus be issued for prisoners of war, nor may the latter be allowed to use motor buses accompanied by guards.

In view of the special operating conditions of the motor buses, it is not possible to relax or cancel these regulations....

546. Re: *Enemy leaflets in possession of prisoners of war.*

Prisoners of war must immediately deliver to their military superiors (camp officers, leaders of work details, etc.) all leaflets, weapons, munitions, and other prohibited articles found by them after enemy air raids, or obtained in some other way.

This, together with the punishment to be expected for disobedience in more serious cases, is to be made known to all the prisoners of war....

565. Re: *Reports on British and American prisoners of war.*

For reasons of reciprocity, each capture of a British or American prisoner of war must be reported by the Supreme Command of the Wehrmacht *by telegram* to the respective enemy powers. The camp commandants are responsible for the immediate submission of a *written* report to the OKW/Chief Kriegsgef. Allg. V on all new British or American prisoners of war upon their arrival in the first stalag. Such report must contain the following data: Last & first name, rank, date and place of birth. The report to the Information Bureau of the Wehrmacht is not affected hereby....

572. Re: *Mail for British & American prisoner-of-war airmen.*

All incoming mail for British & American prisoner-of-war airmen is centrally examined in Stalag Luft 3, Sagan. The prisoners are to be instructed to indicate this camp only, under the heading "Sender," on all outgoing mail, so that the incoming mail is forwarded directly to Stalag Luft 3. A further examination of the mail in the individual prisoner of war camps is unnecessary.

573. Re: The prisoner of war camps must do everything within their power to prevent the rifling of gift shipments for prisoners of war, and to have such thefts uncovered immediately. Particular attention is to be paid to the shipment of gifts from camps to work details, carried out on the responsibility of the military services. Pilfering of gift shipments by the prisoners of war themselves is to be reported to the OKW....

576. Re: *British & American parachutists, airborne troops, & antiaircraft personnel.*

Parachutists, airborne troops, and antiaircraft units are constituent parts of the British & American armies. Prisoners of war from these troops categories do not thus belong to the "prisoners of air force proper" in the sense of the "Provisions Concerning Prisoners of War" of 30 May 1943. They are therefore not quartered in the prisoner of war camps of the Luftwaffe but in those of the OKW.

They are put to work in accordance with the rules in force for prisoners of war of the respective nationality. However, paratroopers are to be assigned to work in closed groups and under special guard.

Since the above service branches within the German armed forces are parts of the Luftwaffe, the *questioning* of newly arrived prisoners of war for intelligence purposes is the task of the Luftwaffe.

Newly captured British & American parachutists, airborne troops, and members of air-defense units are therefore to be sent for interrogation to the "evaluation center," West Oberursel/Taunus, where only small units are involved (up to 20 prisoners). Where the number of such prisoners brought in at one time is 20 or more, arrangements are to be made in each case over the telephone as to whether the prisoners shall be taken for interrogation to Oberursel/Taunus, or whether the evaluation center West should send an interrogation detail to the spot.

At the end of the interrogation the respective prisoners of war are sent to the prisoner of war camps of the OKW....

583. Re: *Return of prisoners of war, recovered from illness, to their old place of work.*

Complaints are heard from management quarters about the slow return of prisoners of war from hospitals to their old place of work after recovery. The prisoners of war, again able to work, are kept too long in the camps after their release from the hospital.

It is the duty of the camp commandants to see to it that prisoners of war, released from hospitals as fully able to work, be sent back in the quickest possible way to their former places of work.

584. Re: *"Stepping out" by prisoners of war during work.*

Since the prisoners of war misuse the unauthorized "stepping out" for the purpose of escape or loafing, it may be recommended—as has already been done in some plants—that a fixed time be set for such practice. Exceptions are to be permitted only for reasons of health.

No generally binding rule is possible in view of the varying local conditions, the strength of the work details, etc. However, the stalags are to keep an eye on the problem, since uniformity, wherever possible, is greatly desirable as a means of avoiding the above-stated difficulties. Appropriate rules might be incorporated in the plant regulations applying to prisoners of war.

The stalags are to instruct the leaders of the larger work details to communicate with the plant managers in regard to the above matter....

589. Re: *Gate control of incoming and outgoing vehicles.*

Reports on escapes of prisoners of war indicate that the control of incoming and outgoing vehicles at the gates is not always carried out with the proper care. There are cases on record where prisoners of war have left the camps undisturbed, hidden under loads of sand, linen, etc. Care is to be taken that the vehicles are always closely scrutinized.

590. Re: *Quartering of mentally ill prisoners of war or internees.*

There is occasion to point out that prisoners of war or internees suffering from mental disorders but not requiring confinement in a closed institution must be kept in camps or hospitals in such a way as to avoid, under all circumstances, the possibility of mishaps (such as entering the area outside the warning wire without permission).

591. Re: *Organization of the Bureau Chef Kriegsgef.*

The Bureau Chef Kriegsgef is organized as follows:
  I. Chef Kriegsgef:
    Colonel Westhoff

Staff Group:	Central processing of all basic matters and
Major Baron V. Bothmer	of those affecting in common the divisions Kriegsgef. Allg. and Kriegsgef. Org., with the:

a. Paymaster: Administration, salaried employees, and workmen.
b. Registry.

II. Chef Kriegsgef. Allg.: Col. Dr. V. Reumont	General & political affairs of the prisoner of war set-up.
Group Allg. I: Lt. Col. Krafft	Treatment of prisoners of war and effects of the prisoner of war problem on national policies.
Group Allg. II: Major Roemer	The prisoner of war problem in its foreign-political aspects; escorting of representatives of the protecting powers, of the I.R.C., etc., on their visiting trips.
Group Allg. III: Major Clemens	German prisoners of war in enemy lands and members of the Wehrmacht interned in neutral countries.
Group Allg. IV: Oberstabsintendant Dr. Fuchs	Problems of administration of the prisoner of war set-up.
Group Allg. V: Captain Laaser	Welfare of prisoners of war in Germany, and mail & parcel service. Cooperation with German Red Cross & I.R.C.
Group Allg. VI: Captain Recksiek	Exchange, furloughs, & release of prisoners of war. Problems of minorities.
III. Chef Kriegsgef. Org.: Col. Diemer-Willroda	Organization of the prisoner of war set-up.
Group Org. I: Major Dr. Hausz	The functioning of the German prisoner of war bureaus and custodial forces. Distribution of prisoners of war (planing); statistics.
Group Org. II: Lt. Col. Reinacke	Officer personnel matters (commandeers of prisoners of war, prisoner of war-district commandants, camp commandants and their deputies.
Group Org. III: Col. Lossow	Labor service and transport.
Group IV: Maj. Elickhoff	Camp management, index-files of prisoners of war.

595. Re: *Individual requests for enemy clergymen for prisoner of war camps.*

Individual requests for enemy clergymen are to be submitted no more.

Requests for enemy clergymen are to be collected and presented quarterly at a fixed date by the Military District Commands, as per model I and II contained in order OKW, file 2 f 24.

596. Re: *Spiritual care in army prisons.*

1. In accordance with the reference order, *no* religious services are to be held for prisoners of war in army prisons. Army chaplains, civilian and prisoner-of-war clergymen may render spiritual aid to a prisoner of war only when the latter is gravely ill or under death sentence.
2. The reference order is relaxed in that prisoners of war in military prisons may hold religious services among themselves provided they request it specifically in each case....

619. Re: *Securing of prisoner of war transports against escape.*

The freight cars for the transport of prisoners of war frequently carry boards in the sliding doors, arranged so as to pass in stove pipes. These boards are to be removed before shipping the prisoners of war, since they render the barbwiring of the doors difficult and can easily be forced.

To better secure the sliding doors of these freight cars, not only the bolts, but also the door casters may be wired....

640. Re: *Reward for capture of fugitive prisoners of war.*

The Reichsfuehrer and the Reichsminister of Interior have authorized the Criminal Police, in the decree of 14 Dec 1943—S—V A 1 No. 978/43, to pay a reward of up to 100 marks for assistance in apprehending fugitive prisoners of war or other wanted persons. In case more than one person participated in the capture, the reward is to be divided proportionately. Should the amount of 100 marks not suffice to properly reward all the participants for their cooperation, the matter of increasing the amount is to be submitted for approval to the Reichsfuehrer and the Reichsminister of Interior.

Rewards for capture of fugitive prisoners of war are not to be paid anymore by the prisoner of war camps....

646. Re: *Confiscation of gifts from the American Red Cross bearing propaganda legends.*

Gifts of tobacco supplies have recently arrived from the American Red Cross bearing propaganda legends on the wrappings. Most characteristic are packages of cigarettes with the word "Freedom" printed thereon. These articles were confiscated on several occasions because of this legend. It has been found that smokes with these legends were sent to the prisoner of war camps with no malicious intent, but that it was a form of propaganda for American consumption only commonly used in America. Such articles with propaganda legends should not be confiscated, provided the legends are not of outspoken anti-German character and provided there was no malicious intent on the part of the sending agency. The tobacco articles are to be released upon removal of the wrapping. In case of doubt the OKW is to be consulted.

The American Red Cross has been notified and has promised to make sure that further gifts to prisoners of war are free of all propaganda; it has, however, requested that shipments already packed be accepted.

647. Re: *Handling of prisoner of war mail for American prisoners of war & civilian internees.*

Letters and parcels arriving from U.S.A. for American prisoners of war and civilian internees have in a number of cases not been released by the camps for distribution because the U.S. postmark stamps contained advertising matter. These stamps were placed on the prisoner of war mail for no special purpose; they are the same used in the postal service within the U.S.A. The U.S. government has promised henceforth to refrain from placing on prisoner-of-war mail any legends relating to the present war. Mail is therefore to be released for distribution provided the postmark stamps and other legends are not of an unspoken anti-German character and where no malicious intent is discernible....

677. Re: *Supplying prisoners of war with beer.*

The reference order is hereby modified to the effect that henceforth not more than five liters of beer may be released monthly for prisoners of war and military internees in prisoner of war camps (Polish and Soviet-Russian prisoners included)....

679. Re: *Fixing of bayonets while guarding prisoners of war.*

It is in order to call attention to sec. 475 of the Compilation of Orders 30 of 16 Oct 1943, whereby guards are to stand with their rifles loaded and placed at "safe" and their bayonets fixed, unless the camp commandant, for special reasons, orders a deviation from that rule. This order is extended to provide that guard details accompanying prisoners of war on transports or on their way from and to work have their bayonets fixed. French bayonets, which are too long, can be ground down to the standard size of German bayonets....

685. Re: *Use of sidewalks by prisoners of war.*

It is in order to point out that prisoners of war conducted through cities by guard details, singly or in groups, are not permitted to use the sidewalks but must use the roadway, like the smallest troop unit on the march.

Prisoners of war from broken ranks of work commandos marching alone from and to work are permitted to use the sidewalks, but must, when same are crowded, step off into the roadway....

687. Re: *Private conversation between German soldiers and prisoners of war.*

All conversation between German soldiers and prisoners of war not justified by the needs of the service or the work assignment is forbidden.

It is the primary responsibility of the company commanders to educate their subordinates to the importance of maintaining the proper distance between themselves and the prisoners of war and to put a stop to all attempts of the prisoners to start unauthorized conversations....

692. Re: *Assault on guards.*

Lately several guards have been attacked and killed while transferring prisoners of war after dark.

Prisoners of war are to be moved on foot after dark only in case of utmost necessity, and only under particularly vigilant surveillance.

Attention is to be directed continually to this prohibition and to the danger of attack....

713. Re: *Instructing guard personnel in the guard regulations.*

There is reason to point out that guard personnel engaged in guarding prisoners of war must be given continuous instruction in guard regulations. It does not suffice to hand the guard personnel a copy of the regulations and expect them to study its contents by themselves.

714. Re: *Taking away boots and trousers from prisoners of war in work details.*

In order to render more difficult the escape of prisoners of war assigned to and quartered in work details, their boots and trousers are generally to be taken away for the night and stored in such a manner as to make their recovery by the prisoners impossible.

715. Re: *Air defense measures in the prisoner of war service.*

During an air raid alarm prisoners of war may be assigned to the defense of their own quarters and workshops in exactly the same manner as the German employees.

After the all-clear signal they may also be assigned to damage-control work in other places, but, in this case, must be kept under safe, regular surveillance.

716. Re: *Disposal of tin cans sent to prisoners of war.*

The regulations contained in the above reference, insofar as they concern the handling of tin cans sent to prisoners of war, are summarized, changed as follows:

1. Tin cans of all kinds, with or without their contents (from parcels received from home, from love gifts, from rations supplied by the army or the manager of the plant) may be left in the hands of individual prisoners of war in strictly limited quantities and under strict supervision.

Purpose of this regulation:

a. To prevent the accumulation of larger amounts of food stuffs to facilitate escape.

b. To eliminate empty tin cans as means of escape, such as in the construction of tunnels, the preparation of imitation buckles, etc.

c. To prevent the smuggling of forbidden messages and of objects useful in escape, espionage, and sabotage.

2. The individual prisoner of war may be allowed a maximum of six tin cans for the storage of his food supplies (meat, spread on bread, sugar, tea, etc.), provided no other means of storage are available in sufficient quantities and provided there is no danger of the wrong use of these cans.

Before a filled tin can is issued, it must be examined before and after opening; such examination may be limited to random sampling in the case of tin cans (and tubes) sent by the British and American Red Cross in standard packages.

3. When new tin cans are issued, the old ones must be withdrawn.

Used tin cans must be emptied, cleaned, and stored in a place out of reach of the prisoners of war. They must be sent every three months to the scrap-metal recovery place, together with tin cans used by the German troops.

4. Compliance with regulations 1, 2, and 3 is to be enforced by orders of the camp commandants; these are to reach down to the smallest labor commandos....

718. Re: *Behavior of prisoners of war during air raids.*

1. *Guarding of prisoner of war labor commandos.*

In work shops which, according to the air defense regulations, must be vacated by their crews during air raids, provisions must be made, in agreement with the shop management, that the prisoners of war be kept at all time under surveillance by the guards and latter's assistants while leaving the premises and remaining outside of same, as well as while returning thereto. Alarm plans are to be prepared fixing the place of the air raid shelters and the ways of reaching same.

2. *Marshing prisoners of war seeking protection in public and private air raid shelters.*

No objection may be raised against prisoners of war on march seeking protection in public air raid shelters in a sudden air attack; private shelters, too, may be used by prisoners of war in an emergency, provided the number of the prisoners is small.

It is presumed that the German civilian population will take precedence and that the prisoners of war will be kept close together in one room or one place. Dispersal among the civilian population is forbidden. In case of need, the prisoners of war may be distributed under guard in smaller groups in several parts of the air raid shelter.

Details are to be fixed in agreement with the local air raid authorities....

729. Re: *Civilian clothing confiscated from individual packages sent to prisoners of war.*

Civilian clothes sent to prisoners of war by their next of kin are not to be placed in safekeeping, but must be confiscated. Relatives of prisoners of war well know that civilian clothes are not allowed to be sent to the latter. Confiscated civilian clothes are to be treated like clothes of recaptured escaped prisoners. Civilian clothes must not be sent to receiving camps for safekeeping when prisoners of war are transferred (also when they are delivered at army prisons)....

738. Re: *Air raid shelter trenches.*

In a number of cases prisoners of war have declared through their spokesman their unwillingness to work on air raid shelter trenches. Such a refusal on the part of a group of prisoners of war, in view of the internationally binding provisions of the Convention of 27 July 1929, is to be ignored.

The construction of temporary air raid trenches must therefore be continued without fail.

739. Re: *Use of confiscated gift packages.*

When gift packages of collective shipments are confiscated on the basis of the above order, or for some other compelling reason, the confiscated items are to be disposed of as follows:

1. Confiscated *articles of food* from gift packages are to be used in the preparation of meals in the kitchen; in that case the food rations supplied by the Reich may be correspondingly cut.
2. Confiscated articles of *consumption* like coffee, cocoa, tea, etc., are likewise to be used in the community kitchen in the preparation of breakfast and supper.
3. Confiscated *soap* is to be used in laundries servicing prisoners of war, or to be given to prisoner-of-war hospitals for use in their respective laundries.
4. Confiscated *tobacco supplies* may be distributed as a reward for good work to prisoners of war of all nationalities, including Soviet-Russians. A receipt is to be issued and entered on the records of the respective camps.

   Care must be taken that members of the German armed forces and other German nationals have no share in the confiscated gift packages, and that the assignment of the confiscated items for the sole use of the prisoners of war may be conclusively proved to the representatives of the Protecting Powers or the International Red Cross....

743. Re: *Working together of prisoners of war and concentration camp internees.*

The working together of prisoners of war and concentration camp internees has repeatedly led to difficulties and has unfavorably affected the efficiency of the prisoners of war. Employment of prisoners of war and of concentration camp internees of the same job at the same time is therefore forbidden. They may be employed in the same shop only when complete separation is assured....

745. Re: *Civilian clothes in prisoner of war barracks.*

Attention is again called to the regulation which forbids prisoners of war to have in their possession civilian articles of apparel, except properly marked work clothes. Such articles of apparel arriving in packages for prisoners of war are to be confiscated. Prisoners of war are allowed only pullovers and underwear, insofar as the latter cannot be used as civilian apparel. Sport clothes, especially shorts, are to be handed out only after they had been specially marked as prisoner of war apparel. The way of so marking is left to the discretion of the camps. The prisoner-of-war quarters are to be checked again and again for civilian articles of clothing....

784. Re: *Ecclesiastical services for prisoners of war.*

Ref 1. Order OKW file 31 AWA/J (Ia) No. 2411/41 of 12 May 1941 paragraph IV.

2. Order OKW file 2 f 24. 72 f Kriegsgef. Allg. (Ia) No. 10/44 of 10 Jan 1944, section 3.

In order to clear up certain doubts concerning the use of enemy clergymen in pastoral capacity at prisoner of war reserve hospitals, attention is called to the following:

1. In accordance with reference order 1, surplus prisoner of war clergymen—enlisted men or noncommissioned officers (i.e., members of enemy armed forces who were clergymen in civilian life and were captured as soldiers with arms in the hands) are to be assigned, as far as possible, to prisoner reserve hospitals as medical corps personnel. There they will perform their ecclesiastical duties in accordance with the provisions in sections 7 and 8 of this order.

[The next page has not been received from the archives, so the text will be picked up where it begins again.]

... allowed to perform their pastoral duties in:
stalags for enlisted men,
prisoner of war hospitals,
prisoner of war construction and labor battalions,
provided they assume these duties voluntarily.

b. The same applies to enemy field chaplains, provided they volunteer for service.

c. The use of these clergymen in accordance with 2a and b is contingent upon their steady residence at the place where they are employed....

810. Re: *Prohibition of the use of ink & colored pencils in letter writing by prisoners of war & military & civilian internees.*

Several cases are on record where prisoners of war have dyed their uniforms, blankets, and underwear with ink & colored pencils for the purpose of escape.

Ink & colored pencils in possession of prisoners of war and military and civilian internees are therefore to be confiscated immediately. Ink and colored pencils are no longer to be sold in camp canteens, and the issuance of same in all private shops for prisoners of war is to be prohibited.

Outgoing mail written with ink & colored pencils *before* this order was announced is to be forwarded. Such mail received for delivery *after* the announcement is to be destroyed.

Colored pencils may be acquired from time to time in the open market in limited quantities for drawing and instructional purposes; these are to be taken away every day after use and kept under lock and key. Strict control is necessary to avoid misuse....

812. Re: *Forbidding prisoners of war to produce glider models.*

Prisoners of war are for security reasons forbidden to produce models of gliders....

822. Re: *Working time of prisoners of war: here: on Sunday.*

As a matter of principle, prisoners of war are to work the same number of hours as the German workers on the same job. This principle applies also to Sunday work; it is to be noted, however, that prisoners of war, after three weeks' continuous work, must be given a continuous rest period of 24 hours which is not to fall on Sunday.

When a plant which normally works on Sunday is closed for that day, the right of the prisoners of war to a continuous period of rest is still to be respected. However, no objection can be raised to prisoners of war working beyond the usual working day and on free Sundays on *emergency jobs* when German workers or the German population are required to take part in such emergency projects.

However, the rest period thus lost on the emergency jobs must be made up for—even on a week day—if the last continuous rest period was taken at least three weeks back.

In special emergency cases prisoners of war may be called upon to work for the relief of same even when the services of German workers or the German population are not required. The decision in the matter lies in each individual case with the respective camp commandant, in agreement with the local authorities, the competent Labor Office and the agency in need of assistance....

837. Re: *Verification of personal data supplied by escaped and recaptured prisoners of war.*

Recaptured prisoners of war often falsely give to the camp authorities, to whom they have been delivered, names and identification numbers of other prisoners of war of their former camp and of the same nationality, known to them as having likewise escaped. Now and then they try to hide behind the name and the identification number of prisoners of war whose approximate description and circumstances of whose escape they had learned at the very time of their own escape. Such attempts at camouflage are made particularly by escaped and recaptured prisoners of war having a court suit pending against them at their former camp.

Security officers of prisoner of war camps are to verify in each case the personal data supplied by recaptured prisoners of war from other camps.

838. Re: *Death penalty for prisoners of war for illicit intercourse with German women.*

The Serbian prisoner of war Pvt. Pentalija Kabanica, identification number 104325YB, was sentenced to death by a court-martial for the military offense consisting of illicit traffic with a German woman, combined with rape. He had rendered defenseless the peasant woman in whose farm he was engaged as laborer, and then used her sexually.

The sentence was carried out on 14 Sep 1944.

The sentence is to be made known in this version to all the prisoners of war....

840. Re: *Killings and serious injuries of prisoners of war and civilian internees (except Poles, Serbs, and Russians.)*

The reference order has often not been observed, with the result that the OKW has had again and again to learn of cases of violent deaths of prisoners of war through the Ministry of Foreign Affairs or the Protecting Powers. This situation is unbearable in view of the reciprocity agreements with the enemy governments. The following additional orders are therefore announced herewith:

To 1. Every case of violent death or serious injury is to be promptly reported through channels to the OKW/Kriegsgef. Allg. (IIb) (for exception see 2). In cases involving the use of arms, written depositions of the participants and witnesses, including prisoners of war, are to be attached; action is to be taken by the camp commandant and the prisoner-of-war commander ("Kommandeur").

The name, camp, identification number, and home address of the prisoner of war involved must be given. Should a long search for these be necessary, a preliminary report is to be submitted at once, and the result of the search reported later.

Reports are also necessary, in addition to cases involving the use of arms, in cases of *accidents of all kinds*, of suicides, etc.; written depositions of witnesses will be mostly unnecessary here.

To 2. Losses due to enemy action are to be reported immediately to the OKW/Kriegsgef. Allg. (V) in the form prescribed by reference order to 2....

848. Re: *Rendering prisoner of war camps recognizable.*

Prisoner of war camps in the home war zone are not to be made recognizable for enemy air forces....

851. Re: *Transport of enemy fliers brought down, or prisoner of war officers.*

In view of the present state of transportation, especially in Western and Southwestern Germany, no more railway compartments may be ordered or used in the trains of the public railway system for the transport of enemy fliers brought down or prisoner-of-war officers to and from prisoner of war camps (also camps for interrogation and classification of prisoners of war). In agreement with the competent Transport Command headquarters ("Transport Kommandantur"), freight cars are to be requisitioned instead and attached, as far as possible, to passenger or fast freight trains; in order to economize on rolling stock in small transports, the number of prisoners of war on each trip must be correspondingly increased. In particularly urgent cases troop compartments may be used in EmW, DmW, and SF trains ("Eilzug mit Wehrmachtabteile"; "Durchgangszug mit Wehrmachtabteile"; "Schneller Frontzug")....

853. Re: *Prisoners of war mustered into Waffen SS (volunteer groups).*

Prisoners of war who have voluntarily reported for service in the Waffen SS have had their lives threatened by their fellow prisoners of war for their friendliness to Germany and their willingness to serve.

Representatives of the main SS office engaged in recruiting prisoners of war for the Waffen SS in the prisoner of war camps are to be reminded by the camp commandants that the security of these prisoners of war requires that steps be taken to have them speedily removed.

Should the enlisted prisoners of war not be able to take their physical examination at the SS, the representatives of the main SS Bureau must, when taking the prisoners away, report those turned back to the original camp in order that they may be assigned to another camp....

876. Re: *Treatment of Jewish prisoners of war.*
Ref 1. Compilation of Orders No. 1 of 16 June 1941, sec. 7.
    2. Compilation of Orders No. 11 of 11 March 1942, sec. 5.
The combined above reference orders provide as follows:

1. The bringing together of Jewish prisoners of war in separate camps is not intended; on the other hand, all Jewish prisoners of war are to be kept separated from the other prisoners of war in stalags and officers' camps, and—in the case of enlisted personnel—to be grouped in closed units for work outside the camp. Contact with the German population is to be avoided.

   Special marking of the clothing of Jewish prisoners of war is not necessary.

2. In all other respects Jewish prisoners of war are to be treated like the other prisoners of war belonging to the respective armed forces (with respect to work duty, protected personnel, etc.).

3. Jewish prisoners of war who had lost their citizenship by Regulation 11 of the Reich Citizenship Law of 25 Nov 1941 (R.G.B.I. 1941 I p. 722), are to be buried—in case they die in captivity—without the usual military honors....

894. Re: *Reports on escapes of prisoners of war.*

Mass escapes, escapes of small groups, or single officers—from colonel upward—as well as of prominent personalities represent such a menace to security as to render the disciplinary handling of the matter in accordance with paragraph 16a K St Vo entirely inadequate, in view of the possible consequences of such escapes. Detailed reports must under all circumstances be submitted concerning the activity of the custodial agencies which made such serious flights possible—whether through dereliction of duty or through mere carelessness.

895. Re: *Strict house arrest and preliminary (investigation) arrest of prisoners of war, including prisoner of war officers.*

A concrete case makes it appropriate to point out the following regulations:

1. An increase in rations through delivery of food and other articles of consumption by all outsiders, including the International Red Cross, is absolutely forbidden.

2. Additional food and other articles of consumption may be obtained by prisoner-of-war officers only through purchase, contingent upon good behavior, and in moderate quantities. In each individual case the approval of the camp commandant is necessary.

3. Tobacco may be obtained in quantity within the general limits provided in the smoker's card, but only when the danger of fire or disturbance of discipline is absent.

Note to 1–3: Prisoners of war under preliminary arrest, in order to obtain additional items of food and of general consumption, must also secure the consent of the investigation officer (leader) or the state attorney....

897. Re: *Escapes during transport.*

There is reason to point out that prisoners of war during transport sometimes try to use the toilet for escape. The guards must therefore, as a rule, accompany the prisoner of war to the toilet on transports and must keep their eyes on him with the door open. Should the prisoner of war close the toilet door with the intention to escape, the guard must fire on him through the door without warning.

Index